Contemporary Quee
by Russian Playwi

Tatiana Klepikova studied Slavic Literature and Culture in Passau (Germany) and Language Pedagogy, Linguistics, and Translation in Yaroslavl (Russia). She is a postdoctoral fellow at the University of Toronto, where she is working on a monograph about contemporary Russian queer theater and drama.

Contemporary Queer Plays by Russian Playwrights

Satellites and Comets

Summer Lightning

A Little Hero

A Child for Olya

The Pillow's Soul

Every Shade of Blue

A City Flower

Edited and translated by
TATIANA KLEPIKOVA

methuen | drama
LONDON · NEW YORK · OXFORD · NEW DELHI · SYDNEY

METHUEN DRAMA
Bloomsbury Publishing Plc
50 Bedford Square, London, WC1B 3DP, UK
1385 Broadway, New York, NY 10018, USA
29 Earlsfort Terrace, Dublin 2, Ireland

BLOOMSBURY, METHUEN DRAMA and the Methuen Drama logo are trademarks of
Bloomsbury Publishing Plc

First published in Great Britain 2022

Foreword and translations copyright © Tatiana Klepikova, 2022
Satellites and Comets copyright © Roman Kozyrchikov, 2022
Summer Lightning copyright © Andrey Rodionov and Ekaterina Troepolskaya, 2022
A Little Hero copyright © Valery Pecheykin, 2022
A Child for Olya copyright © Natalya Milanteva, 2022
The Pillow's Soul copyright © Olzhas Zhanaydarov, 2022
Every Shade of Blue copyright © Vladimir Zaytsev, 2022
A City Flower copyright © Elizaveta Letter, 2022

Tatiana Klepikova has asserted her right under the Copyright, Designs and Patents Act, 1988,
to be identified as editor of this work.

For legal purposes the Acknowledgments on pp. viii–ix constitute an extension of this copyright page.

Cover design: Rebecca Heselton

A catalogue record for this book is available from the British Library.

A catalog record for this book is available from the Library of Congress.

ISBN: HB: 978-1-3502-0377-8
        PB: 978-1-3502-0376-1
        ePDF: 978-1-3502-0378-5
        eBook: 978-1-3502-0379-2

Typeset by RefineCatch Limited, Bungay, Suffolk
Printed and bound in Great Britain

To find out more about our authors and books visit www.bloomsbury.com
and sign up for our newsletters.

To artists, who create worlds no matter what

Contents

Acknowledgments

This collection of plays emerged out of my research for a book about queer theater and drama in contemporary Russia, which was funded by an Arts & Science Postdoctoral Fellowship at the University of Toronto in 2019–2021. I am grateful to U of T for offering me the time, freedom, and resources to pursue this postdoctoral project. I wish to specially thank my host department, the Women & Gender Studies Institute, for an additional SSHRC SIG Explore Grant awarded to me in 2020, which supported the translation work. This funding was instrumental in enabling me to bring to life the ideas I had nurtured for some time. However, even more meaningful for me during my time in Toronto was the support that I received from U of T as a community. Working two years alongside talented, passionate, kind, and welcoming family of the faculty and grad students of the Women and Gender Studies Institute as well as other colleagues on the tri-campus was a gift. Their energy, enthusiasm, curiosity, and commitment to research and teaching alongside advocacy for social justice keep inspiring me even though Toronto is not my home anymore.

Opening a text in a foreign language to hearts and minds of an audience that does not speak this language is a kind of work for which the translator gets all the credit. However, rarely is translation done by anyone completely alone. This book would have been impossible without my many friends and colleagues on both sides of the pond who responded to my requests of reviewing my drafts. Words will never be enough to express the overwhelming sense of gratitude that fills me when I think of the fantastic contribution each and every single one of them made to this anthology.

Two people deserve a very special thank you for their reviewing earliest translations of each play. I am deeply grateful to my long-time friend Sarah Lillibridge who received the first three translated plays when the project was just taking shape and devoted her evenings to offering spot-on suggestions to improve them. I am also blessed to have Anya Noble as an incredible friend who spent her pandemic days meticulously editing all texts in this book. Her critical eye, sense of humor, and dedication enriched the translations with many original findings and made them sharper.

Over the course of 2020, these plays reached more friends and colleagues whose shrewd critique, questions, and notes on language nuances guided and inspired me in revising the translations over and over again. I want to express my special appreciation to Kevin Moss, Vitaly Chernetsky, Rebecca Friedman, and Tiina Rosenberg who supported this project in many different ways on its path to becoming a book. My heartfelt thanks also go to all the amazing and generous readers of early drafts (sometimes even more than one!)—Denis Ferhatović, October Browne, Matthew Harshman, Deirdre Ruscitti Harshman, Katherine Zubovich, Justin Wilmes, Christopher Fort, Greer Gerni, Susanna Weygandt, Laurie Essig, Julie Cassiday, Shana Ye, Olga Andreevskikh, Dmitrii Dorogov, Richard Mole, Roman Utkin, Lewis Siegelbaum, Amy Randall, Maria Brock, Gleb Vinokurov, Pauliina Lukinmaa, Olia Kim, Alexandra Novitskaya, Evgenia Komandirova, Kārlis Vērdiņš, and Maria Power. I cannot begin to describe how big a step forwards the plays in this collection made after each round of comments—there is hardly a scene in them that would not owe its beautiful complexity or simplicity to the questions and comments of these engaged and observant readers.

On the days when yet another draft was finished after many weeks of work and my eyes refused to see any weak spots in the translation anymore, they were the ones who caught things, asked questions, drew connections that had escaped me, and beyond that, always found words of encouragement that kept me going.

For advice that helped me navigate some tough choices, I send my warm thanks to Miriam Frank, Kai Erik Trost, Evelyne Datl, Ekaterina Suverina, Tracy McDonald, and Geoffrey Noble. I also want to acknowledge that these pages would not have arrived in front of you, dear reader, had it not been for the Methuen Drama publishing team. From the moment I brought the book proposal to them until the time these texts came to life as a published anthology, my editors Dom O'Hanlon and Meredith Benson have been excited supporters of bringing the voices of queer Russia to Anglophone readers all over the globe, and for that I am grateful.

Finally, none of this would have been possible without the playwrights—Roman Kozyrchikov, Andrey Rodionov and Ekaterina Troepolskaya, Valery Pecheykin, Natalya Milanteva, Olzhas Zhanaydarov, Vladimir Zaytsev, and Elizaveta Letter. They penned the plays you will be reading, patiently responded to any questions I had, as well as checked the translations to make sure no word had been lost. They also accompanied their texts with an address to the readers of this book, which appears in my translation before each play. I am grateful to them for their flight of fantasy and the beauty of their writing which took me on a wonderful journey to queer Russia for over a year while I worked on this anthology. Now, it's your turn—I hope this destination brings you a lot of discoveries and inspires you to keep returning to queer texts from Russia and beyond.

Foreword: Landscapes of Russian Queer[1] Drama

Tatiana Klepikova

In 2016, three years after the infamous "gay propaganda" law was passed in Russia, the playwright Olga Malysheva submitted a documentary play called *Community* to the Russian drama competition Lubimovka. This major festival of playwrighting craft annually receives a few hundred submissions, and the Kazakhstan-based Malysheva had been shortlisted before, with another play. This time, she tried her luck with a text about two gay men from Kazakhstan seeking asylum in Sweden and discussing the challenges of this process on Facebook Messenger with their friend back home. Malysheva's play was rejected by the jury and did not make it into the program of the drama festival in Moscow, where all shortlisted plays were presented to the audience through staged readings, framed by readings of new plays from established playwrights and other events. This would seem an unsurprising outcome, given the silencing and repression of the queer community in Russia that has intensified over the past decade and too often led to violence, torture, murder, and forced migration. However, what makes this story so interesting is that even without Malysheva's play, the festival ended up featuring two queer plays (not to mention plays by queer playwrights exploring other themes). During an interview at the staging of *Community* in Almaty a few months after the results of the competition had been announced, Malysheva was asked if she could think of a reason why her play had been rejected. She recalled seeing a post on Facebook by one of the Lubimovka jurors who had been positively surprised by the overflow of queer-themed plays submitted for consideration. It turns out, her play was rejected not because it stood out too much, but because it failed to do so among queer plays that were too many!

The news of the booming interest in exploring queerness that contemporary Russian culture demonstrates might come as a surprise, since media reports often fail to cover this side of the story in Russia. This collection, which includes the two texts that were presented at Lubimovka-2016 as well as five other plays, opens a window onto the landscape of queer drama that is as vast and vibrant as Russia itself—all despite the efforts of Vladimir Putin's constantly toughening regime. It is the first anthology of queer-themed plays from Russia to be published in any language, including Russian. It showcases the diversity of queer experiences that have found their representation in Russian dramatic writing around or after 2013—the year when the law banning the "propaganda of non-traditional sexual relationships to minors" was passed. These texts outline a variety of problems that people who identify as LGBTQ may confront alongside joys they may share with others. They also make clear that a queer scenario of life need not lead to tragedy just because it was imagined and set in Russia. At the same time, the tragedies that are depicted in this collection are very real for a lot of people living in Russia and elsewhere in the world, because homo- and transphobia are not tied to national borders.

Written by authors who range from established playwrights contracted by leading Moscow theaters to writers who are just starting their literary careers, these plays have followed various paths to reach their audience. Some have been shortlisted for major Russian drama festivals (e.g., Lubimovka, Remark, or Eurasia) and staged successfully for a few years in a row. Some have faced backlash from the authorities or anti-LGBTQ groups. Before you meet the playwrights and their works, it is also crucial to understand that while the sexual identity of the authors of queer-themed plays often remains undisclosed in the current Russian political climate, the profound and touching stories of queerness that affect hearts and minds on paper and on stage are just as important as the writing of openly queer playwrights. While an anthology of drama by Russian queer playwrights is a hope we have to hold for the future, this anthology of queer drama by Russian playwrights is a collection of texts written by queer and straight authors alike that have been sparking much-needed conversation and changing Russian reality today.

The curtain opens with Roman Kozyrchikov's *Satellites and Comets* (*Sputniki i komety*, 2019)—a one-act play that follows the return of a young man to his hometown, which he left after the tragic death of the man he loved. During his visit, the protagonist runs into their common friends and acquaintances; these meetings trigger memories about the moments they shared and reveal an open wound that keeps bleeding grief, which will not let the protagonist forget, which—possibly—will not let him keep living. Longlisted for the 2019 competition of new drama Remark, this text by the Ekaterinburg-based author is as powerful in portraying the unfading trace of a comet of queer love as its protagonist is powerless in reversing time and regaining his happiness with his beloved.

The anthology proceeds with a Lubimovka-2016 text, Andrey Rodionov and Ekaterina Troepolskaya's *Summer Lightning* (*Zarnitsa*, 2016). This rare example of a queer play in verse is the second play in Rodionov and Troepolskaya's set of poetic dramas dedicated to marginalized individuals in contemporary Russia that begins with their *Project Swan* (*Svan*, 2015, available in English in *New Russian Drama: An Anthology*, edited by Susanna Weygandt and Maksim Hanukai). Both plays transfer the reader into a dystopian poetic Russia of the future, where the migrants' right to work and live in the country depends on acing an exam in speaking in verse (*Project Swan*) or where people learn from childhood to reject same-sex relationships (*Summer Lightning*). Named after the Russian military-style game for teenagers, *Summer Lightning* portrays the love between two girls sparked by the ancient magic of forest spirits. The girls work to reverse the spell and dissolve the bond forbidden in the Russia of the future but grow fond of each other in the process. This mistaken identity play that re-imagines William Shakespeare's *A Midsummer Night's Dream* situates a love story within a broader conversation about marginality, national belonging, and ideological wars. Performed at the Meyerhold Center in Moscow by the actors of Brusnikin Workshop under the direction of Yury Kvyatkovsky since January 2019, this play is a brilliant satire of a state overpowered by its own ideologies and a promise of a better future under a dystopian cover.

This play in verse is followed by a play "in exile"—Valery Pecheykin's *A Little Hero* (*Malen'kii geroi*, 2014). The acclaimed playwright, whose creative collaborations with the director Kirill Serebrennikov at the Moscow Gogol Center theater have repeatedly sold out and have even reached the Avignon Festival, wrote this text in 2014 upon the request of Alexander Kargaltsev—a Russian gay artist who had left the country a few years before for the United States. Originally conceived as part of Kargaltsev's art exhibition in New York, it was a direct response to the 2013 law. In a witty and satirical manner, it depicts the coming of age of a boy called Vovochka (a diminutive from Vladimir—*the* Vladimir, as the play hints quite clearly). From a local vigilante against his homosexual neighbors, he grows into the founder and leader of Crematorium—an ominous organization whose mission is to identify homosexuals across the country and torture and humiliate them in order to "save" Russian children from "pedophiles." While the play is focused on the catastrophic results that a project of political homophobia can yield, it also uses the politics of sexuality as a lens to delve into broader questions of morality, tradition, integrity, and citizenship. In 2014, a staged reading of *A Little Hero* was presented to the public at the Gogol Center as part of a drama festival, but the play never made its full stage debut in Russia. Instead, its English translation by Zhenya Pomerantsev and John Turiano became the backbone for a dystopian phantasy titled *Crematorium* that Kargaltsev directed in New York in the summer of 2014. In 2018, the full version of the play was brought to life on stage by the White Bear Theatre in London. With Pomerantsev and Turiano's translation never made accessible to the general public, this anthology offers a new translation of the Russian text, connecting it with English readers who were not able to see the productions in New York and London.

Natalya Milanteva's *A Child for Olya* (*Rebenok dlia Oli*, 2016)—the other queer text of Lubimovka-2016—delves into the life of a lesbian couple and explores the challenges of navigating the landscape of parenting that queer families confront, which are often not so different from those that straight families may have. Her text foregrounds the relationship between two women, Olya and Zhenya, which reveals its shaky foundation when Olya, who wants to have a child but cannot give birth, starts pushing her girlfriend Zhenya to do that in her stead. While Zhenya eventually gives in to Olya, the pregnancy does not bring much-needed peace into their life but instead exposes a whole array of incompatibilities between the two of them.

Olzhas Zhanaydarov's *The Pillow's Soul* (*Dusha podushki*, 2012) offers insight into Russian drama created for children. Easily the kindest play in this collection, it is set in a daycare and features pillows—the stars of naptime—as protagonists. Their everyday routine is disrupted by the arrival of a new pillow different from all the others. Zhanaydarov's text leads the readers from the discovery of one's difference to acceptance by others and, finally, to acceptance by oneself. This heartwarming story of an unlikely friendship sends a message of kindness, diversity, tolerance, and the importance of embracing difference. The reading of this play at the Moscow International Open Book Fair in 2014 was banned by the Ministry of Culture of the Russian Federation due to its "potential for promoting homosexual propaganda among minors," thereby making this text one of the first but by far not the last victims of the 2013 law.

The exploration of the Russian queer universe continues in one of the longest-running queer plays on the Russian stage—Vladimir Zaytsev's *Every Shade of Blue* (*Vse ottenki golubogo*, 2014). *Blue*—or, rather, "light blue" (*goluboi*)—is a Russian euphemism for "gay," and this play has been telling the coming-out story of a sixteen-year-old since its 2015 debut at the Satirikon theater in Moscow. The play has been running uninterrupted for five seasons just a few miles away from the Kremlin, despite several fake bomb threats the company received while on tour in Saint Petersburg. *Every Shade of Blue* examines the life of a boy who comes out to his parents with the hope of preventing their divorce. While the family mobilizes all forces to "cure" him back to "normality," he is left to deal with his coming out completely alone. This text, which received a special mention at the Lubimovka festival in 2014, moves from comedy to drama like a rollercoaster, taking the family on a ride to an inevitable wreck.

The collection bows off the stage with Elizaveta Letter's *A City Flower* (*Gorodskoi tsvetok*, 2017). This emotional, confession-style solo play is an exceptional example of a trans voice within Russian literature in general and drama in particular. In an intimate dialogue with the reader, a young woman called Erika finds her true self after a journey of questioning, suffering, and regaining hope. Deeply autobiographical, this play has been performed by Letter herself in Moscow and Saint Petersburg at small, independent venues as part of the repertoire of the theater of social drama Garcia that she pioneered.

The plays you will read in this book are just a fraction of a vibrant and highly diverse dramatic scene that has championed conversation about queerness in today's Russia. One of the texts I have not included in this anthology but strongly encourage everyone to explore is the verbatim play *Coming Out* (*Vyiti iz shkafa*, 2016) by Nana Grinshtein. This text about diverse coming-out experiences of gay men and the embracing of this process by their parents has been performed at the theater Teatr.doc in Moscow since 2016 (directed by Anastasia Patlay). A slightly abridged recording of this play's performance is available on YouTube (https://youtu.be/64KebAvZy9c), with English subtitles based on the translation by Molly Flynn.

Many more dramatic works telling stories of LGBTQ persons in Russia are out there, and even more of them are yet to come—they will keep growing in number and varying in form and content as authors engage in conversation with the readers and each other in the coming decades. If you are curious to continue exploring queer literature coming from Russia and the broader Eastern European region beyond this collection and beyond dramatic writing, take the pathbreaking predecessors of this book in your hands—*Out of the Blue: Russia's Hidden Gay Literature: An Anthology* (1997), *120 storinok sodomu: suchasna svitova lesbi/gei/bi literatura: kvir-antolohiia* (120 Pages of Sodom: Contemporary World Lesbi/Gay/Bi Literature: Queer Anthology; 2009), *El armario de acero: Amores clandestinos en la Rusia actual* (The Steel Closet: Clandestine Love in Today's Russia; 2016), *Pod odnoi oblozhkoi: Sbornik kvir-poezii* (Under One Cover: A Collection of Queer Poetry; 2018), and *Life Stories, Death Sentences*, a special June 2019 issue of *InTranslation* journal. Published around the globe over the past two decades, these collections of literary texts have repeatedly drawn attention to the imaginativeness and agency of queer authors in the region. In so doing, they have shown the limits that any repressive power confronts in the face of artists' inspiration to create stories that always manage to find their paths to readers.

Despite this variety of queer writing from Eastern Europe and Eurasia that has been made available to readers in several languages, drama has been a rare guest on the pages of these collections. In fact, it would have remained completely invisible to the reader outside Russia had it not been for the play *The Slingshot* (*Rogatka*) penned by Nikolay Kolyada in 1989, which appeared in the first English-language anthology of Russian gay literature *Out of the Blue: Russia's Hidden Gay Literature* in 1997. Kolyada's groundbreaking text was the first queer play authored by a Russian playwright to be staged in Russia (by the openly gay director Roman Viktuyk in Moscow in 1993). It explores a fleeting and tumultuous romance between two men which sparks in many ways against their will when the younger of them saves the other—an Afghan war veteran now in a wheelchair—from committing suicide.

It's been over two decades since *The Slingshot* was published in English and over three decades since it was written. All this time, queer Russian drama has been waiting in the wings to speak to the reader in languages other than Russian—the situation that is not at all reflective of either the landscape of queer playwriting or of the special place that drama has held within Russian culture. Names like Alexander Ostrovsky, Anton Chekhov, and Maxim Gorky are carved into the canon of Russian literature. Most recently, drama as a literary genre in Russia witnessed profound transformations when around 2000 it took a radical turn away from the relatively canonical language and play structure. It made a decisive step toward a more experimental form that focused on the search for a language that could bring theater closer to the real-life experience of post-Soviet Russia. This new form that came to be known as "New Drama" drew inspiration from the rich legacy of Russian literary postmodernism and demonstrated unprecedented directness and a desire to inhabit spaces of discomfort, anguish, and trauma. The publication of two anthologies in the past decade in the United States—*Real and Phantom Pains: An Anthology of New Russian Drama* (2014) and *New Russian Drama: An Anthology* (2019)—has made it possible for global Anglophone readers to meet many key texts of this new literary tradition. These collections shine light on this exciting and potent experimental genre of dramatic writing alongside other, research-focused, scholarly reflections on it, such as *Performing Violence: Literary and Theatrical Experiments of New Russian Drama* (co-written by Mark Lipovetsky and Birgit Beumers, 2009) and *New Drama in Russian: Performance, Politics and Protest in Russia, Ukraine, and Belarus* (edited by Julie Curtis, 2020).

Moreover, in a country where freedom of speech was heavily curtailed in the Soviet years and has been shrinking again the longer Vladimir Putin has stayed in power, theater has remained—as it was in the Soviet years—one of a few niches where people can come and witness a bold conversation on a controversial topic or see aesthetic experiments that reshape the borders of the political. Although theater is an art sphere funded predominantly by the state in Russia, it has maintained its ability to speak relatively freely due to physical limits to its audience size—unlike cinema, which has been exposed to severe censorship in the 2010s. As a result, while queer characters and themes have been infrequent guests on film screens over the past two decades—at least, rarely in the protagonist role, with exceptions like the films *Winter Journey* (dir. Sergey Taramaev and Lyubov Lvova, 2013) or *The Student* (dir. Kirill Serebrennikov, 2016)—they have often appeared on theater stages in Moscow, Saint Petersburg, and across Russia.

The confluence of these unique conditions of a thriving theater landscape and ardent debates around the passage of the 2013 law has resulted in a tidal wave of plays that examine queer lives. Dozens of texts were available to me when I started thinking of this book. As a straight ally of the Russian queer community, I felt great responsibility for creating a collection that would be balanced in terms of themes and voices, as well as representative of the literary and theatrical process in today's Russia. I therefore included two plays that focus on the same-sex romance of women (including one written by a lesbian playwright) and one dramatic text by a trans author to enrich the fabric of queer stories that is dominated by gay narratives in Russia (just as it happens in many other places around the globe). Authors of plays in this book also represent the geographical diversity that nourishes the Russian literary scene. Only one playwright in this collection was born in Moscow—all the other authors have their roots in the Urals, Siberia, Ukraine, Kazakhstan, and Uzbekistan, with some still living and working outside of Russia's capital.

The plays collected in this book unlock the potential for imagining the yet non-existent queer futurities in Russia and beyond, making them more tangible today than they were yesterday. They are universal stories of humanity that spread a message of kindness and love. They show that breathing, growing old, falling in love, falling out of love, and falling in love again (among many other things) are just as challenging and rewarding in Moscow as they can be in New York, Tokyo, Johannesburg, or Buenos Aires. Erika, the protagonist of Letter's *A City Flower*, says at the end of her story, "Every life is a challenge. Every story deserves a beautiful happy ending. An ending, which marks not the end of life, but the beginning of a new wonderful long-awaited life." Not all stories in this book bring their characters to a happily-ever-after destination; it is their very existence that is a sign of Russia's queer happy ending-in-the-making. The words we read, the words which, in rare cases, we hear from the stage, are footsteps of this future approaching that we can discern from afar. And with stories like these imagined, put into writing, and shared, it is not too long a wait until this future is something we actually live.

Note

1 Throughout this foreword, I use the term "queer" when talking about culture and "LGBTQ" when referring to a broad spectrum of sexual and gender identities and expressions. My choice is reflective of the use of these terms in Russia: "queer" (*kvir*) is increasingly used in the cultural sphere, whereas the abbreviation LGBTQ mostly appears within the activist discourse.

Note on Certain Idiosyncrasies of Russian that Repeat Throughout the Book

Russian Names

Many plays in this book feature at least two different ways in which one and the same character is addressed by other characters of the play: Vladimir—Vova—Vovochka, Sergey—Seryozha—Seryozhenka, Alexander—Sasha etc. Such variants of first names are typical for the Russian language and reflect either formal or colloquial/affectionate way of calling someone by their name. Almost every first name in Russian has a few colloquial versions (used among friends, family, etc.), which might be shorter or longer than the formal variant of the name. The rule of the thumb with diminutives of Russian names could be phrased as: the longer they are, the more affectionate the use (for instance, Serezha is a neutral colloquial version of Sergey, whereas Seryozhenka is a variant of this name marked my deep affection).

Homosexualism/Homosexualist

In some plays, characters use the terms "homosexualism" and "homosexualist" referring to homosexuality and gay men, respectively. These terms date back to when male homosexuality was criminalized in Russia (until 1993) and are just as derogatory as "queer" can be to some English-speaking persons identifying as LGBTQ. The choice of endings "-ism" and "-ist" is intentional and presents sexual orientation as an ideology and gays as its practitioners (think of communism/communist or fascism/fascist). Currently, LGBTQ activists in Russia are pushing for the terms "homosexuality" (*gomoseksual'nost'*) and "homosexual" (*gomoseksual*) to replace these derogatory and inflammatory variants in the public discourse.

Parent Hierarchies

Another word pair that may strike the readers of this book as unusual is "Dad and Mom," which you will encounter in a few texts in this collection. If you have never given a thought to the order of parents fixed in the language, that's alright, neither had I—until readers of first drafts corrected my translation. While I immediately recalled many English-language films and TV shows that prove their point, I decided to keep the Russian hierarchy of parents the way it was in the original. More than just an order of parents, it is a signal of the dominant role of masculinity in Russian cultural and linguistic imagination, the ripple effect of which leads to many of the problems characters in this book face.

Satellites and Comets

A ONE-ACT PLAY

Roman Kozyrchikov

Roman Kozyrchikov was born in 1988 in a small town of Troitsky, in the Urals. He studied in Nikolay Kolyada's class at the Ekaterinburg Institute of Performing Arts. His plays to date include *River* (2014; published in the collection of plays *The First Bread*); *Je suis Justin* (2015; published in *The First Bread* and staged at the Center for Contemporary Drama in Ekaterinburg); *Satellites and Comets* (2018; published in *The First Bread*, in the journal *Ural*, and magazine *Happy*; staged at the HERE theater in Ekaterinburg and at the Centre for Topical Drama in Belgorod); and *A Quiet Light* (2019; published in the journal *Traditions and Avant-Garde* and staged at the Kolyada Theater in Ekaterinburg).

Author's address
In the night skies and on nocturnal Earth, I remember every satellite and every comet I encounter. In the remote depths of slumber and the sharp clarity of day, are they—my satellites and comets.

In October, when it drizzles, it seems that the rain doesn't fall on the ground so much as rise up from it, vertically touching your cheek, ear, and hand.

The train arrives; I step off. The familiar crossing by the school, and there, a bit farther, lives an old lady; in her front yard . . . Don't speak, memory.[1] As the rain licks me, I make my way home, to my mom. The wooden children's library (*Robinson Crusoe*), still as green as I remember it. The good old five-story apartment buildings, our "skyscrapers." The smell of the fresh, damp soil: vegetable gardens have just been harvested, and little patches of bare earth lie like graves at the cemetery—a picture so familiar to me, so dear.

My face grows wet, even though it isn't really raining, like when it's hot and sweaty. Further on, your house, but I won't go there. I'll take the turn and follow the road alongside the overground heating pipes.[2] The windows of your two-story apartment building—I can see them from my yard. Don't speak, memory.

—Oh wow, look who's here!
I turn around—It's Oleg.

Oleg   I haven't seen you for a year and a half.

Me   I haven't been here for a year and a half.

Oleg   Visiting your mom?

Me   Yep.

Oleg   Shall we sit down, talk a little?

I shrug; we go to the pipes, sit down. At first, we don't look at each other, but then, well, there's no choice, we have to.

Oleg   So, how are you?

Me   Been better. Work. What else . . .

Silence.

Oleg   You've grown up, so different somehow.

Oleg laughs; and then again, we're silent.

Oleg   My mom's fine now, and I got married.

Silence.

Oleg   Will you ask who I married?

I look at Oleg but don't ask.

Oleg   Do you think it was our fault?

Me   No.

Oleg   He was my brother, you know.

Me   No. No.

Oleg   You do think we're guilty, don't you?

Me   You aren't.

Oleg   Then say something. Talk to me.

I look at Oleg.

Me   In the morning, wasps came to me. One sat here.

I put a finger under his right earlobe.

—And then it moved over here.

I draw my finger from his earlobe to the corner of his lips; the lingering rain leaves a crooked line.

—The second one was here.

I touch the artery on his neck.

—And the third one was here.

I touch his shoulder.

It's so scary: each sting can bring you death. Are you afraid?

He is afraid.

Oleg   No.

Me   Well, I am, I'm afraid of everything.

Oleg pushes my hand away. Silence.

Oleg (*laughs*)   Remember that time, when a wasp flew into Seryozhka's curls and he was running around, his eyes all bulging out, nobody could get what was going on.

Me   Right. Right. Right.

I close my eyes. Memory, don't speak.

I want to open my eyes and be at home, to look out the kitchen window and see the roof of the small banya,[3] a bit of the garden, and to the right—the fence. Behind it, there's a short alley—a road for people, for cars, and for cows. The mud covering it has been distinctly sculptured by the October cold. And if I try to remember, it is now that is the easiest to walk this road. And of course, I do remember it.

Mom   The heating still isn't on, so I've lit the stove.

Me   It smells nice.

Silence. The stove takes up one third of the kitchen. It gives off this tasty aroma of the warmed brick from which it is made, or of cement; a smell so autumnal that you can even hear the rain in it. The sky is clear now, but the sun is still on the other side of the house, where the porch is; it is the morning sun, and the kitchen is lit with soft natural light. We are sitting by the window, each of us on either side, separated by a table with a blue plaid plastic tablecloth. It has red poppies in the corners, they are a little withered, as if they also already hear autumn approaching. I'm staring at them.

Mom   Well, tell me, how are you doing out there? You call so rarely.

Me   Everything seems fine.

Mom (*purses her lips, looks out the window*)   I can barely get a word out of you.

Silence.

Me   How are things going here?

Mom   The day before yesterday was Auntie Natasha's funeral, the one who lived down the street, you know. You've seen spruce twigs on the road, haven't you?[4] They're still there. She was such a good woman. They say it was her heart, probably. I saw her just this Wednesday, she was walking down the street, so lively, told me what was on sale. Sugar, at our corner store. And now here we are—her heart. But I didn't go to the funeral—too negative for me. And it rained that day. Just watched it from my window.

Me   I don't remember her.

Mom   Oh, come on! The house right by the river. We went over there all the time.

Me   Well, maybe I do.

Mom   Dark hair, not very tall. Has a lisp.

I shrug. Silence.

Mom   You must hardly remember my face, not to say hers.

Silence.

Mom   Not a visit in a year and half.

Silence. A cat cautiously pops his face into the door, stares at us. It's a new cat that I don't know. The cat I knew died that very October, two years ago; he's buried behind the woodshed, and the grass has already grown over that place; he came to me in a dream just once: he touched my neck with his nose and woke me for the train back home. This one, a white tomcat, with a few random spots (or maybe it's a female?) made a small circle around the room, paused next to my mom, said something. My mom waved her hand at him: go away. He thought a little and left the kitchen, the floorboards creaking twice under his paws.

Mom   You could say yes, sure, I remember yours, of course.

Me   I do.

Mom   Right, you do.

Silence.

Me   How's school?

Mom   Everyone's still hustling and bustling. Other teachers are trying to make Marina Arkadyevna retire, but she won't. They resent her for it, keep wondering whether she just plans to sit around and disgrace herself in front of the kids until she dies. She says, even after that, she'll rise from the dead and come back to teach.

Valentina Vasilyevna almost drowned in the snow last winter. She decided to make a path through the field behind the school. A faster way back home, she'd say, and others could use it, too. So, there she went, and fell under the snow. She said she barely made it out of that hole and had to crawl through the rest of the field. She walked into the teacher's room soaking wet, the snow falling off her skirt. Can you imagine, "others could use it," those were her exact words. Eighty-five years old, and still full of energy.

Me   I just ran into her on the train, on my way here.

Mom   I'd take a trip on a train, too, I like them. It's kind of romantic. One problem: where would I go? And the cats, too.

Years ago, in our old, other life, my mom and I would often take a train to go to the city. Most often, to the hospital; we'd get up around 3 a.m. to get there by the morning. I'd always wake up ahead of time and would lie for a while in darkness. Then, hearing my mom's alarm clock ring, I'd turn on the light. We'd quickly get dressed, in silence, take the bags we had prepared the day before, check if we had all the necessary (IDs, money), and leave the house. We would walk to the train station. Three blocks and two turns. I'd always run a little ahead of my mom—I was afraid of not catching the train, of not leaving, of missing out on something. My mom would also worry, but probably her worries were completely different from mine, unknown, unrelatable, which I'd only notice by her rare shouting to me: "Don't rush, there's still time!"

We'd always arrive at the station before the train. There was no one there at night, and we'd almost always stand alone on the platform, and I'd immediately hear the roar of the trains. And something enormous would rise and stir in my chest, and in the pitch-black darkness of the rural night I'd see a never-ending journey, a big city, its glistening streets. As if all of my future enormous life were pounding in my chest on the platform of the train station that belonged to me and my mom. The train would arrive slowly, its bright windows shining in the darkness, and we'd finally board. The warmth of the electric semi-darkness, the smell of the people who'd been sleeping there for hours, and upper berths—everything that I hate so much now—seemed the most genuine, the most spot-on signal of a life that was going in the right direction.

Mom   It looks like it'll rain again—the wind's picking up. This day used to be sunny, with no rain.

Silence. Well, the wind did bring a rain cloud. The light has sharply split the room from the threshold to the window: the area, where I am, is dark, and the other, where my mom's sitting, is still bright. My mom turns on the electric light. I remember this combination of natural and electric light before every thunderstorm: the rain clouds would cover the house, and the horizon would show the sky as a long strip of light.

Me   Your birthday, we almost forgot.

Mom   I'll make tea; we'll toast with teacups at least.

From her seat, she reaches for the kettle and turns it on. Silence.

Mom   Well, make a birthday speech or something.

Me   Maybe later? I'll make something up.

Mom   I'm all sober now. I don't even take a sip at school parties. Blood pressure, you know.

Silence.

Mom   Do you drink?

Me   No.

Mom   Why did you pause before answering?

Me   I don't drink, almost. Sometimes.

Mom   Tanya's sister's husband almost died of DT. Grabbed a knife, started to make a scene, and fell down on the floor. She called an ambulance, all tears, they barely saved him.

The kettle clicks, saving me. My mom takes out the cups. Oh my God. Our sweet old cups. Tall, with pinecones and lush spruce twigs (three pinecones and two twigs) printed unevenly over them; I close my eyes. Then I look at the window, scratch my lip with my teeth. My mom serves the tea. Silence.

Mom   We do need the wine though. Tanya will come.

Me   Why?

Mom   What do you mean, why? It's my birthday, we are good friends.

Me   I didn't know that.

Mom   We are really close now. I helped her a lot after Seryozhka . . .

Me   Right. Right.

Mom   It hit her hard. She was his mother, you know, and stuff . . .

Me   Right. Right. I got it. I'll go buy some.

Mom   She is a very good woman.

Me   I got it. I'll go now.

I walk on the grass along the side of the road to avoid messing up the sculpture of the mud. On the corner of the street, there's a convenience store, where a school friend of mine, Anya, works.

Anya   Oh, fuck, you finally came to visit.

She throws her arms around my neck; I'm silent.

Me   Did you get knocked up or what?

Anya   Huh, don't even get me started.

She goes behind the counter.

I can't wrap my head around it myself. Go figure, we were wasted. A real bender. I leave their place in the morning, and as I am walking, I feel a hair in my mouth; I fish it out—a pubic hair. Well, I thought, whatever, to hell with it. And now this! Turns out it was Slava, you remember him?

Me   You haven't changed at all, Anya.

Anya laughs and shows me the ring.

Me   Anya, I'll get three bottles of wine. Dry and cheap. And cheese, I guess.

Anya   It's also dry and cheap.

Me   Slava seems like a nice enough guy.

On a stuffy July afternoon that oozed a smell of honey, Anya and I hit Slava in the head with a stone. He started crying, and we ran into the forest. Anya took her braid in her mouth, so that it wouldn't get in her face, and her dress was wet in the armpits. We were hiding in the forest until the evening, but then they found us, and Slava pointed at me. Anya and I cried a bit to show our guilt and went back home. Me, sweaty Anya, and Slava, who was laughing, dried blood on his head. But I feel a hair in my mouth, and my memory stops speaking.

Anya puts the bottles in a plastic bag for me.

Anya   The best we have! I can down two of these in a night.

I count out my cash.

You haven't been here since the funeral, have you?

I'm silent.

It's fine. I get it.

Me   Anya, are you afraid of the dark?

Anya shrugs.

It sometimes gets scary at night.

Anya   Slava and I went to his grave not too long ago.

I'm sitting at the school playground. I'm drinking the best imitation wine; my eyes follow the raindrops on the bottle. I close my eyes.

On a tire half dug into the ground—Seryozha, hunched down, looking at me, smiling.

Seryozha   Tomorrow we start our last year at school. The last time. We'll bring flowers.

Me   I'll cut down our peonies.

Seryozha   Will you bring one for me?

Me   I will.

Seryozha   Just kidding. Bring it to my grave.

He smiles, stretches his legs, and rubs at the ground with his feet.

Me   I'll bring a peony, Seryozha, for you. Red, like your hair.

I put my hand into his curls, he looks at me.

Seryozha   I have money for some beer.

Me   There is a God, after all.

Seryozha   Shall we get a 40?

Me   Behind the monument to the revolutionaries.

We hit the road, swim by the kiosk. The 40 oz bottle is ours—the woman who works the counter loves Seryozha's eyes. Like everyone does. Like I do. Auntie Lyuba said: I love you, Seryozha, my bunny. We get behind the revolutionaries, the foam on our pants, in our pants, just like our desire. The beer is light, like our hearts. Warm, like our blood. We are silent, just smile, take turns drinking. I spot my mom. I give the bottle, the heart of mine, to Seryozha. I run to my mom without turning around. His silhouette will be getting smaller, but I don't want it to be smaller than it already is. When I do turn around, Seryozha with my heart is not there, his silhouette is gone. And a snowstorm began in the world. A blizzard began in the world, and a frost swept in. Snow covered the ground, and Seryozhenka, and my heart. And the planet now lies like a lump of ice in my chest. Because the snowstorm started, and the blizzard, and the frost. I close my eyes. Don't speak, memory, don't.

Mom   You got two bottles? Tanya may be the only one drinking. I'll just have a sip.

Me   I'll have some.

She purses her lips. Silence.

Remember the lullaby you used to sing to me?

Mom   Dili-dili-don.

Me   Right, dili-dili-don.

Silence.

Mom   The tea is cold. It's freezing in here.

Mom brings us slippers we leave by the stove to keep them warm: feet are always cold when it rains.

Mom   I can't stand the winter now at all. It used to be okay, but now I'm always cold. The stove is the only thing that saves me.

Me   It just used to be warm all the time. And sunny. I don't even remember any winters.

Mom   I remember pulling you once on the sled in the winter darkness. It was morning, but it was pitch dark.

Silence.

Are you warm enough there?

Me   Now it's also dark and cold.

Mom   Nina, who lives on our street, knits mittens and socks with dog hair. I'll order some for you.

Me   The sun seems to have gotten smaller.

Once when the sun was still steadily high in the sky, Mom and I went to see an eclipse. We had prepared pieces of glass. I had found mine by accident in May, dug it out in the garden behind the banya—deep in the darkness of the ground. Emerald, transparent, its edges rounded, it was a shard of somebody's vibrant alcoholic life. Who'd left it there? Was it a teen mom who had laughed there heartily with her girlfriends at night, at a party that their parents knew nothing about? Or did some half-naked relative dig up the planet and drink heavily, sweatily, from a bottle warmed by the sun? I'd been saving it secretly for two months under a rug, and here it was—today the sun would go dark; it would hide from us mortals so that we'd look at it and understand what we've lost. It would hide from all of Europe, and from us, too. My mom even said, "It's just like in Paris here! They'll have an eclipse, and we will, too!" We have a photo from that day. We don't even remember who took it anymore. Some neighbor whom we've erased from our memory took a picture of us and printed out copies for everyone in it. The sky is black, slightly lit with what's left of the sun, and here we are on the ground, with our contrast shadows. Our neighbor Nina is looking up to the sky with her mouth wide open, without a glass, she's got nothing to lose; it's as if she were ready to step on a path and start walking toward the place from which she'd been chased away long ago. Auntie Tanya has her left hand on her breast, as if she can't breathe, while her right hand firmly presses the glass against her eye. My mom is looking intensely at the star. And me—I'm not looking at it, I've buried my face in her skirt and am clenching it with my hands. This memory fades away, leaving Auntie Tanya in the room.

Tanya   I barely left my place during the summer. Would only go out into the garden and to visit you. I lay around like a seal, watched TV shows. I even got sick by the end of the summer—too much lying around doing nothing. Did no renovation, nothing. I signed up for Facebook though. I've friended all our girls there; we sometimes write to each other. One fellow messaged me there, not in Russian, a foreigner or something. I mean, it's clear from his photos that he's abroad, he might even be an American. Well, I called Lenka, and told her, come on, translate it for me, you're the English teacher here. She said it wasn't even English, she didn't understand a thing in that message, that it had to be some con. Told me to turn off my computer asap. And I'm like, what about the computer? Why? And she's like, well, you'll catch viruses from it, and will have to pay later. She knows nothing about the internet, only logs in on Classmates regularly.[5] Do you hang out there?

Mom   I do sometimes.

Tanya   Everyone is addicted to it already, of course. It used to be so nice: you're enjoying your vacation days, and you can forget about everyone. Now they write you all day long, post photos, like yours. If you don't like theirs—you're arrogant, Yelena Petrovna in particular is like that. She'll then act all hurt around you, and you'll keep guessing what it could be, and it turns out—a like. That's how she is now.

My mom replies something to her—I'm more interested in the roof I see out the window. All my thoughts are about how the glass windows that we used to have were better than the new plastic ones.

In summer, when all the windows in the house were wide open, and the curtains in them rose like sails in the wind, the house became suffused with indolence and a quiet laziness.

We'd wake up around noon, have tea, usually. Then we'd move to the shadow of the porch, eat some hackberry or sarvisberry, and after that—the pinnacle event of every day, the backbone of the free summer weeks—a TV show. We could barely breathe as we watched it; only rare gasps revealed our sympathy for the protagonists. I cared for the suntanned and beautiful Milagros and Diego just as much, and sometimes even more, than all the street gossip, games, and dramas. Noble Argentinians and Brazilians could beat Auntie Natasha and Yelena Petrovna (an ugly and gossipy woman), and all our teachers (nice people, but nothing special) on all counts. It seemed that the latter didn't have any eternal love, only potatoes to plant and students' homework to grade. After the heat of the screentime, the day would be coming to its end, the sun would penetrate almost all of our rooms and burn them with such hot beams that the windows were immediately curtained, and life in the house went quiet in anticipation of the cool of the night. When it finally arrived, we would move over to the porch, and women who lived nearby would come over, noticing the light of the table lamp, to have some adult, unimportant conversation: somebody was getting divorced, another one was getting buried, the cucumbers wouldn't grow, and somebody chased his family around with a knife. These were vague snippets of somebody else's big flow of life just next to us.

Of course, not every day was like this. We'd also have rainy, drab days, when your heart would be seized by such a melancholy, such a child's solitude, that a premonition of something bad would linger heavily over you from the moment you woke up. Once, on just such a day, when the rain had suddenly picked up and we could already hear long rumbles of thunder, and the wind started to rock the poplar outside the window in the living room, a phone ring pierced the room. My mom picked up and, after a moment of silence, gave a loud scream, covering her mouth with her hand in a flash. It terrified me so much I locked myself in a dark bathroom. It was some far-away death, some relative I didn't know. And neither the incredibly honest Milagros nor the good Diego could explain to me the fear that got so close to me for the first time, the terror caused by my mom's scream. I spent an hour or longer in the darkness, until the rain stopped, and my mom finished all her phone conversations.

Mom   Oh, somebody is pounding on the window on the porch!

My mom rushes out, leaving Auntie Tanya and me in the danger of each other's company. Silence.

Tanya   Well, let's catch up or something, I haven't seen you for ages!

Me   A year and a half.

Tanya   Oleg told me he saw you today.

I nod. Silence.

Tanya   Are you still single?

I smile.

Tanya   Well, let's talk before you leave!

Me   About what?

Tanya   About something important, what are the important things you think about?

Me   Well, the important . . . Alright, how about this. What do you think, there, in the army, did he cry or scream when they were throwing him out the window?

Silence.

Tanya puts her cup back on the table, freezes, looks out the window. Silence.

Tanya   It's getting dark too early.

Me   It's getting dark the same as always.

Tanya   What is it now? Which month?

Me   I think he screamed.

Tanya   I think, you know, I think I was wrong. I'm a coward.

Silence. My mom closes the door so that the cats don't get in. She's standing by the door.

Mom   It was your father. Didn't want to come in, he's ashamed, tipsy already. Left these socks for you though. Warm. Spent a few bucks on somebody else, never happens.

My mom smiles and sits back down at the table with us.

I'll drink just a bit with you, the wine seems good.

I take the socks—they're warm. I put them in my pocket so I don't forget them.

Tanya   You know, I often remember the day when we took them to school for the first time. Do you remember? They were so afraid; they were hiding their faces behind the flowers at the school assembly and crying. Because we weren't there with them. We made a home video of them later. I haven't gone back to that tape in a long while.

Mom   They had five peonies each, I remember it.

Tanya (*looks at me, smiling*)   Yes, he cried, he did, as if I don't know it.

I close my eyes. I'm looking at you through the peonies, I'm not afraid. I'm just looking at you and I'm smiling. Our moms are sitting there, talking to each other, and you and I are not afraid at all. There, where they are, is not interesting but important; here, where we are, is good. They are saying goodbye to each other—and we're saying goodbye, see you.

Mom   Will you finish the wine? Tanya left a little.

I nod, I drink.

Me   I saw Oleg this morning.

Mom   They're expecting a baby soon. This spring. I'm ready to retire. I'd play with my grandson. Or with my granddaughter. I had a dream that you'd have two daughters. (*Knocks on wood.*) I saw it very clearly. So, I'm waiting now.

Silence.

Me   People must love children because they miss themselves.

Silence. We sigh, we drink. My mom freezes, she looks out the window. The wind has picked up; it blows through the chimney.

Mom   When I was six, we moved into that two-story old wooden building that was almost falling apart. I always went out into our yard at night; and there were these raspberry bushes all around it, so scary. I'd lean my back against the house and stare at the sky, at the stars. I could stand there for an hour like that. And now I still go out on the porch in the evening and look out. I stand there for a while. And keep staring. And then I put my head back down, and my eyes look for those raspberry bushes. As if I'm six years old, and this life never happened.

Silence.

Mom   This world has seen so many things, but the sky doesn't change.

Silence. The wind breaks a twig, blows it into the window. We start. My mom whispers something.

Mom   Move away from the window, just in case.

We take the stools, move to the door.

Me   Mom, was I ever afraid of heights?

Mom   Oh, did you see the flash?

Me   Now I am. I'm afraid of everything now.

The wind blows right through the house, making it creak, as if it were breathing heavily. Something thuds on the roof, bangs, rolls down, bangs above us. I close my eyes.

Mom (*whispers*)   Walk the deadman off this place, go away and leave no trace . . .[6]

Me   Stop, don't say it, you're scaring me.

Outside the window, two wires shine with sparks at their tips, like two eyes, as the wind tears them from the house. The light in the room flickers, goes off. It's dark.

Me   Don't say anything for now. Easy, easy.

Don't say anything. Easy, easy, Mom, don't cry.

Mom   What's gotten into you? I'm not crying.

Me   Last night, I dreamt of an old woman, she pounded on the porch windows. Was it death?

Mom   Easy, easy.

All my old dreams suddenly flash in my memory. And our stove falls apart into bricks, and the high tower is swaying, and I'm on top of it, afraid to fall, and the forests nearby are burning. Scary visions that a child has after such a dream: I'd see something with eyes, hairy, laughing in a dark corner. And the light that saves me. No, there is no death. I'll just be lying in the grass, high grass that's taller than me, and will be looking through it at the black sun high in the sky, I'll be catching its beams and pieces of blue sky in between pointed grass blades. My crystal childhood is there, my life—eternal, inescapable. And there, I'm not afraid of heights or of death. Because it doesn't exist, because everything on earth and in heaven is eternal. And it's all just a dream, a hangover morning, the cigarette ash. The bulb flickers and comes back to life. Silence.

Mom   That must be it.

Me   I have to go, I'll be right back.

Mom   But it's raining?

Me   Yes, I know. I'll be right back, in no time.

I walk, I run. I get there quickly. I take a moment to regain my breath. I look at the slab of granite, touch the photo.[7]

— Remember that time when a wasp flew into Seryozhka's curls . . .
— Right. Right. Right.
— You haven't been here since the funeral . . .
— Right right right.
— Did he cry or scream?
— rightrightright, easyeasyeasy

when they told me seryozha that that's it when they came and told me well, that's it I seryozha didn't say anything in return. I seryozha walked out into the street I walked out into darkness I looked at your window. your window seryozha was quietly and humbly lit and I think I saw it all fill with red blood cells. I saw it fill with white blood cells and with grey matter. I closed my eyes then and that was it seryozha my dear boy. my bunny that was it.

and later when you came my boy, all still and zinky,[8] I chose not to open my eyes seryozha. I was standing there on the same spot in the yard on the yard and was listening in the twilight to the nails being pulled out of the wood in silence. in silence I felt your (my beloved) skull change shape seryozha. but I didn't open my eyes.

and maybe those black ravens those glistening ravens that I saw out the window were right. in the night, an old woman came to me she pounded on my window. was it your death or mine seryozha?

and you are lying now seryozha you are now seryozha lying with knees pulled up to your chest, and an ancient B.C. Greek island has perished; a six-month-old boy will not be born out of a thigh.[9] and nothing will grow nothing will flourish on this earth. the planet lies in my chest like a lump of ice. history will not begin my boy. my bunny photosynthesis will not start on the Earth, nobody will descend to say something from Mount Sinai.

your name in my mouth moves like liquid nitrogen: s-r-zh. And what do I do now seryozha do I bite through my lip or do I now keep pressing the laptop key until it cracks?

or are you lying now your knees pulled up to your chest seryozha not in a coffin but there you are lying your knees pulled up to your chest again a newborn baby in yet another garden. and I'll take you then seryozha into my hands and carry your my beloved body living body and you'll be my son seryozha my dear boy. my bunny reborn and the earth will flourish and the crops will grow then on this planet and everything will start all over again and they'll descend from the mountain and say something to us.

and I'll put you on my knees seryozha and keep my eyes closed. I'll wait for history to run its course again and you'll come up to me seryozha my dear boy my bunny and tell me

here I am again.

I get up, look at your face, stroke it. Dili-dili-don, Seryozha, dili-dili-don.

I want to go back to my mom. I walk home.

I stop, sit on a bench. I take off my wet socks and put on the warm socks, the ones my father left for me. I send a text: "Thanks, Dad, for the socks." I hurry back home.

My first memory of you is from my fifth birthday. We stood in matching shorts with a watermelon in our hands; we ran between strawberry patches in the garden; we ate sweet berries. We broke out in a rash and became friends. You gave us a camera, to take pictures—to keep memories, memories, memories. Well, that's what'll stay with me—the pictures, album pages that've turned yellow. This river will stop, and I'll look, I'll recognize us, recognize everything, and I'll save the memory of our cheerful sun and our happiness. And of the boys in shorts, let them eat the watermelon—red, ripe—and laugh. Let them have it. Let them.

I have to run now, you know, I have to say goodbye to my mom.

I enter the yard, I pause, I enter the house. My mom and I return to the table we abandoned earlier, but it seems so foreign, so cold.

Mom (*puts a cookie tin on the table*)   They always bring these cookies to the corner store. They're good. And more importantly, cheap, I always get them now. Try them. I like them so much.

I take a bite from a cookie, put it on the table.

Mom   You like it?

Me   Yes, Mom, it's good.

Mom   Absolutely.

Silence.

Mom   Why have you gone still?

Me   The tea tastes different.

Mom   Our water must taste different to you already.

Me   Maybe.

Silence.

I'll come here more often.

My mom smiles.

Me   I have to go.

Mom   Will you come for New Year's?

Me   Sure.

My mom nods, but she doesn't believe me. We go out on the porch, my mom turns on the light, the wet twilight glistens.

Mom   I don't like the night. Black windows freak me out.

Me   Well, put up curtains.

Mom   The cats mess with them.

Silence.

Me   Your birthday toast. I figured it out.

A brief moment of silence.

I think that there's a whole life ahead of you and I, Mom. We'll run on this earth, cry, laugh out loud. We'll hit someone, stroke the shoulders of a loved one. Then we'll send it all to hell and meet on a dusty road and walk forward together. We won't even get tired when we've already reached our porch, and the clear air will smell of a May cherry blossom; a sun beam will break through poplar leaves and will sit on the arm of the beloved. That's how it's gonna be.

We stand for a while silent, we look at the puddles, at the sky—small drops fall from it, shining in the streetlight, almost like stars.

Me   I have to go.

Mom   Don't rush, there's still time.

A warm hand rubs my back. Silence. I start laughing.

Mom   What's it with you?

I laugh.

Mom   What's with you?

Me   Mom, do you remember the Sunday when you ran to work at 6 a.m. and gave the guard hell for taking so long to open the gate for you?

My mom nods and starts laughing.

And Grandma ran after you in slippers and her coat, she thought you'd gone crazy, and gave you hell.

My mom laughs and wipes my tears away.

Mom   Of course, I remember.

I go down to the gate, I turn around.

Me   Mom . . .

Mom   Yes?

Me   Nothing, Mom. Bye, Mom.

My mom waves her hand at me, she's smiling. I'm standing in my bathroom, my bare feet on the ice-cold tiles. I turn around, but who do I wave at, dear God? I'm standing still and looking around, and I see no one. But the light curtain of time is moving, and I'm smiling, and waving at my mom. As if I'm six years old, and this life never happened.

2019

Notes

1   "Don't speak, memory" is a reference to the title of Vladimir Nabokov's English-language memoir *Speak, Memory* (1951).
2   In most places around Russia, heating is centralized. In many small towns and in some suburban areas of large cities, hot water that heats the pipes in apartments is delivered from

a boiler station to the homes through a system of overground pipes. Usually running at a height of under two feet, they are insulated and wrapped in tar paper, which makes it possible to sit on them. Gas heating is increasingly introduced in Russia, but these pipes of the pre-Gazprom era remain a distinctive landmark of many places.

3   Banya is traditional Russian sauna.

4   In rural Russia, when a funeral takes place, the body of the deceased is brought back into the house where they lived, for the family and friends to say their goodbyes. From there, the burial procession departs for the cemetery, and freshly cut spruce twigs are thrown on the road from the moment of departure until the procession reaches the cemetery. It is believed that they will help the soul of the deceased find its way back home.

5   Classmates (*Odnoklassniki*) is a Russian social network, like Myspace. It is mostly popular among middle-aged people from non-metropolitan areas.

6   "Walk the deadman off this place, go away and leave no trace" is part of an old incantation for banishing the spirit of a dead person from the house.

7   Headstones in Russia are often made of granite and usually have a photo of the deceased next to the name and dates of birth and death.

8   "Zinky" here refers to being dead. Zinc coffins became a marker of the Soviet army casualties during the war that the USSR waged in Afghanistan (1979–1989), which took many young male lives. Dead bodies were sent back home in coffins made of zinc. Svetlana Alexievich, a Nobel Prize in Literature, wrote a novel called *Zinky Boys* (1989), which explores the trauma of that war through the voices of the people who suffered from it: soldiers, their families, doctors, and nurses.

9   The author refers to the myth of the second birth of Dionysus.

Summer Lightning

Andrey Rodionov and Ekaterina Troepolskaya

Andrey Rodionov (b. 1971) has authored eight collections of poetry. His works have appeared in the almanacs *Babylon* and *Avtornik* and the journals *Novyi mir*, *Vozdukh*, *Homo Legens* and others. Since winning the Russian Poetry Slam in 2002, he has been organizing and moderating poetry slams around the country. He has worked together with the music band Elochnye Igrushki and the rock band Okraina. In 2002–2005 he was part of the artist collective Osumbez (Osumasshedshevshie Bezumtsy/Madmen Who Lost Their Minds). He curates literary festivals in Perm', Voronezh, Kansk, and Moscow. His publications include *Welcome to Moscow* (Saint Petersburg: Krasnyi matros, 2003); *Pierogi Mussels* (Saint Petersburg: Krasnyi matros, 2003); *Life Portrait* (Ekaterinburg: Ultra. Kul'tura, 2005); *Castle Maureau* (Moscow: Raketa, 2006); *Toys for Suburbs* (Moscow: Novoe literaturnoe obozrenie, 2007); *People of Obsolete Professions* (Moscow: Novoe literaturnoe obozrenie, 2008); *New Drama* (Moscow: Novoe literaturnoe obozrenie, 2010); *Animalistic Style* (Moscow: Novoe literaturnoe obozrenie, 2013); *Poetic Diary Started on the Day Yuri Mamleev Died (25 October 2015)* (Moscow: Novoe literaturnoe obozrenie, 2018); and the collection of plays in verse *Optimism*, co-authored with Ekaterina Troepolskaya (Moscow: Novoe literaturnoe obozrenie, 2017).

Ekaterina Troepolskaya (b. 1982) is a playwright, journalist, and producer. Born in Luhansk, Ukraine, she is artistic director of the Brusnikin Workshop theater in Moscow and has previously also been the managing director of the weekly *CINE FANTOM*. She curates the literary festival "A Nick" (*Zazubrina*) in Kansk, Russia along with the festival of video poetry "The Fifth Leg" (*Pyataya noga*). Together with Andrey Rodionov, she co-authored the plays in verse *Project Swan, Ice Hole, Happiness Is Close*, and *Summer Lightning*, which were published under one cover as the collection *Optimism* by Novoe Literaturnoe Obozrenie (Moscow, 2017). Together, they also curate Russian poetry slam competitions. Theater productions of their *Project Swan* and *Summer Lightning* have been staged by Yury Kvyatkovskiy with Brusnikin Workshop and have run at the Meyerhold Center in Moscow since 2017 and 2019 respectively.

Authors' address

We started writing plays together. It doesn't seem very modern to write them in verse. Their narrative often takes place in the future and has some magical element. Our plays could just collect dust on the shelf of out-of-place formalism were it not for their timely themes. Migrants and bureaucracy, teenagers and sexuality, political and social tensions in society. We do not search for these themes; we just try to talk about things that truly matter to us.

Summer Lightning emerged out of our work with teenagers, out of our poetry studio. Kids who come to us are fourteen years old—they try to figure themselves out and we try not to push them, not to manipulate, to be honest with them. *Summer Lightning* is about social manipulation. Sexual choice is left to forces of nature, whereas the reaction to it is left to society. If you remove the magical element, it is a play about teenagers who get pulled into the world of adults but manage to win in all the challenges they face because their hearts are open to the world and their future is wonderful.

Characters

Yaroslav (Yarik) *and* **Yaroslava (Yara)**—*teenagers, twins. Live separately because their parents are divorced*
Marusya—*thirteen years old, in love with Yaroslav*
Oleg—*thirteen years old, in love with Yaroslava*
Golden Angel—*Chief of Orthodox police*
Ripplina—*mermaid, woman of an indeterminate age*
Blowind—*sylphid, a young older man with wings*
Alex Moose—*spirit of the forest, an elegant man with antlers*[1]

Interlude

Four spirits enter.

Summer Lightning
   I am the Fire. I am Summer Lightning, the spirit of mighty rainclouds
   My revenge befalls you like a merciless blade

Ripplina
   My destiny is to steal human souls
   I'll tickle you to death, I am a mermaid!

Blowind
   Light like a feather
   I am the air, I am the breeze!

Alex Moose
   I am the forest master, the spirit of twigs
   The shepherd of trees!

Act One

Scene One

A clearing in the forest. **Yaroslav**, *alone, stares at something.*

Yaroslav
What a strange print
I wonder, whose could it be:
Neither human, nor animal. Or is it
A Humanimal—a yeti?
Nahh, that's just crazy, but on the other hand
These woods have always had bad fame
To tell you the truth, entry here is banned
But walking where allowed is just lame
Hey, sis, Yaroslava! (**Yara** *comes out.*)

Yara
Been here long?
You must have already wet your pants
Brother, you are so not hardcore

Yaroslav
Look at this print!

Yara
Listen up, nerd,
There's something I need you to do

Yaroslav
Isn't meeting in the forest a little absurd?

Yara
Well, sorry, I found this place last night
And sent you the GPS of this beauty—
Thanks for showing up

Yaroslav
I mean, we're family, so it's my duty
You're my sis, and I'm your brother
Be it dangerous or extreme
We should always help each other

Yara
Yeah . . . I need your help, as it seems

Yaroslav
Sure, it's all for the best, Yaroslava

Yara
Well, that's up for debate, but listen in:

Right behind those trees, there's a game—Summer Lightning[2]
Which I have to win

Yaroslav

What have I got to do with it?

Yara

Here's the thing: we look the same

Yaroslav

Duh, 'cause we're twins, you and I

Yara

That's why we have to switch:
I'll take your place and you will take mine

Yaroslav

Take your place? Why?

Yara

You'll pass their history test without a hitch

Yaroslav

It's a war game—attack, find the flag, crush the enemies!
Are you telling me they also have tests?

Yara

It's the nationals, man, not just about brawn, you gotta have brains
So, give me your clothes and put on my dress

Yaroslav

No way!
What if someone finds out I dressed like a girl?

Yara

Who're you calling girl here? And look, I cut my hair, okay?
Besides, you're kind of gentle and feminine,
You could easily pass for a chick

Yaroslav

Sacrifice my gender so that you get to win?
Not a chance, sis, I'm not doing this schtick

Yara

Come on, Yarik!

Yaroslav

They'll call me a same-sex fascist, they'll laugh!

Yara

Come on, Yarik!

Yaroslav

It'll be a stigma for my whole life! Whole life!

Yara
Come on, Yarik!
I'll take the PE exam for you! Since you're out of shape

Yaroslav
But I am a man, Yaroslava!
These things are not up for debate!

Yara (*menacing*)
Take off your clothes and put on my dress!

Yaroslav
Alright, but not 'cause she scares me . . .
I just want this trip from Moscow to make some sense
This dress better be clean!

Yara
It's brand new, man
What do you mean?!

They swap clothes.

Go! your tent's number eight
Speak to no one, not even a word
The captain's name is Katya, and I'm a big deal there
The test's early, I'll wait for you here. You got it, nerd?

Yaroslav
Tell me at least what the test is about!

Yara
It's right up your alley—
They saved heroic pioneers and stuff like that for the finale!

Scene Two

Marusya, *alone, in the clearing.*

Marusya
Oh, Yaroslav! What an odd place to go
Who's he meeting in these eerie woods
Where nettles and brambles grow
And the spider web is all over my route?
What if he's asked a girl on a date?
His GPS isn't far, I see it on my screen
Aha, I hear a female voice, I can't wait
To see with whom he has been!

Ripplina
When Father Fish on a journey departs

When Mother Earth wakes and the trembling starts
Then this world of ours to an end comes

Marusya *sees* **Ripplina** *sitting on a fallen tree by a stream. She has a jug in her hands and is drinking from it.*

Ripplina
Oh, divine Lake Ilmen, I greet you![3]
Your Sister Volga-River bows down to you

Marusya
Hi, I'm Marusya, and what's your name?

Ripplina
I am Ripplina, the spirit of water

Marusya
Not sure what you just said, but all the same
Are you hiking here, or are you a squatter?

Ripplina
I am sending tears off to the seas
Is your destination far away or near?

Marusya
I'm looking for a boy

Ripplina
There are only birch trees
Willows, rowans, and my stream here

Marusya
These woods are kinda frightening

Ripplina
Frightening, frightening (*Drinks from the jug.*)
At nightfall, the spirits of forest and water start their fight
And the woods crack like thunder and lightning
It's best to sleep under a hazel all night

Marusya
Is that water you have there? Can I have some?

Ripplina
Of course, drink up, dear

Marusya *drinks from a jug and starts getting sleepy.*

Ripplina
So, where are you heading, and why did you come?

Marusya
I'm looking for a boy that I like,
Yaroslav; I followed him from Moscow right here

Ripplina

Why did he secretly go on this hike?

Marusya

·The secret's all mine, I love him, and he's got no idea

Ripplina (*drinks from the jug*)

That's enough, my darling
This drink really makes you dream
The water is rippling,
And fish jump in the stream

Marusya (*falling asleep*)

I'll go and find him after I rest
Why did he come here? To meet whom?
When I see my baby, I'll confess . . . (*Sleeps.*)

Ripplina

Water lily opens in bloom (*Drinks from the jug.*)
Sleep, child
I must help this girl find her lad (*Drinks from the jug.*)

Deep, deep in the lake you grow
Drawing power from the riverflow
Out of the water you come, into the water I go!

Scene Three

Ripplina *and* **Blowind**. *Two girls,* **Marusya** *and* **Yara**, *are sleeping on opposite ends of the clearing.* **Yara** *is dressed in male clothes.*

Blowind

Oh, spirit of water that shines in the moonlight,
Majestic Ripplina,
Is that you I see?

Ripplina

That's right!

Blowind

Are you spending the night here?

Ripplina

I am

Blowind

I was putting fireflies on the leaves
And heard the rippling sound of your jug
The big sips you took made me believe
That you were longing for a man's hug

Ripplina

I was

Blowind

Whoa, wait! You are not alone?
I was an idiot, then, to bring you
This beautiful bouquet of mattiola

Ripplina

Cover yourself! Flying around not wearing a thing!
I have a girl here, just a young lass!

Blowind

Phew, she's asleep

Ripplina

On a pillow of bluebells, a bed of grass
Don't you freaking wake her, Blowind!

Blowind

Ripplina . . .

Ripplina

What?

Blowind

She's a human—in our realm
In our forbidden realm, right here!
Despite the guards under every elm
Oh wait, I think I see a tear!

Ripplina

She loves a lad who's also in our realm

Blowind

Another human? I'll soon have to move out here

Ripplina

He's there, in the clearing, deep in his dreams

Both study the sleeping **Yara**.

Blowind

Are you sure it's not a girl?

Ripplina

Marusya said it's a boy, and those are boy clothes, I think

Blowind

They're asleep in one clearing and haven't seen each other?

Ripplina

I admire them—into these frightening woods she came following this boy, her
heart

Blowind

So, Ripplina, tell me, does he feel the same?

Ripplina

No, he doesn't know it yet

Blowind

Oh, you're tearing me apart!
Night flowers release a heavenly smell
To promise their love for each other
Ripplina, I believe we must cast a spell
So these children will see one another
Let's rub magic powder on this boy's eyelids
So he'll fall in love with the first person he sees

Ripplina

What flowers have you sniffed today, you old fool?
We must stay away from human affairs!
Then again, if no one finds out . . . forget the rules!
We'll give Marusya the boy for whom she cares

They put the magic powder on **Yara**'s *eyelids.*

Ripplina

When you wake up, dear boy
You'll fall in love with this sweet girl

Blowind

This is such a joy!

Act Two

Scene One

Same clearing, morning, **Marusya** *wakes up.*

Marusya

Goodbye, darkness! Sunrise, hello!
I have dew in my hair
I had a nightmare, and now it's gone
But nightmare or not, I'm still scared
Where's the peace I thought the morning would bring?
Where's Yaroslav? Yaroslav, where are you?
The day barely started, and you're still missing
I keep looking, but I can't find a clue
Nature, help me in my enterprise
Tell me, where's my Yaroslav, is he fine?
Wild animals, wake up and rise—
Wait, who's sleeping there, where the path winds?
Yaroslav!

Yara

Ahhhhh . . . (*Wakes up.*)

Marusya

Hi! Here you are! It's me, Marusya!

Yara

Hi! Sorry, you're confusing me with my brother
I'm Yara, Yaroslav's sister

Marusya

What're you talking about?
Yaroslav, stop playing games, mister!

Yara

Oh, Marusya, come on, you're so cute
Come, pretty kitty, let me give you a hug!

Marusya

What is your problem? I came to see you!
To see him! Stop pretending and don't look so smug!

Yara

I came to see him, too! I'm his sister
My name is Yara, he's my blood brother
We're twins, I live with our dad
And Yaroslav lives with our mother

Marusya (*in distress*)
Yara!

Yara

Yep, you know what they say, blood is thicker than water
My bro is taking my history test
Behind those trees, where the war game is going
He's smart, so he took my place

Marusya

Are you for real?

Yara

Yeah, babe, he's doing the history part
World War II . . . Stalin, Donbass, you know
The youth resistance group, the Young Guard
Soviet young heroes, you follow?[4]

Marusya

Of course, I learned it all by heart

Yara

Marusya, babe, is it for him that you came all this way?
For that nerd? Chased him down here?
Oh, it's for sure my bro's lucky day
And you, Marusya, are so hardcore, you're my shero!

She puts her arm on **Marusya**'*s shoulders.*

Marusya

Whoa, what're you doing?!

Yara

Do you love him?

Marusya

Hold on! I had a dream
That the forest spirits, these magical folk
Were here, singing and dancing, and letting off steam
They plotted something bad against me under this oak!

Yara

Don't worry about anything when I'm around

Marusya

They had a big fight, and then left in haste
I can't remember

Yara

Marusya, calm down

Yaroslav *comes out in the clearing.*

Yaroslav
Yara, Yara, I aced it!

Yara (*puts her arm on* **Marusya**'s *waist*)
You did? Tell us everything!

Yaroslav (*notices* **Marusya**)
Marusya?
What are you doing here?

Yara
Well dummy, don't you understand?
Your girlfriend came from Moscow to see ya!

Marusya
Yaroslav, tell us something already, I can barely stand

Yaroslav
Well . . . if we follow the order of events—
Although, it was kinda a bit too much—
I went to spend the night in your tent
In this stupid dress

Yara
The dress is pure linen, just touch it!

Yaroslav
I got up, and, like, went to have breakfast
They gave us pancakes, tea, and honey

Yara
Did anybody suspect anything?

Yaroslav
That I'm not a real lady?

Yara
Come on, get to the point, your jokes aren't funny!

Yaroslav
So, there was a big clearing, one observer per mate
They passed out the test, no phones, just your mind
It opened with questions on every key date
But then . . . you'll never guess what I got assigned
The favorite poem of Ulyana Gromova
Symbol of the Young Guard's persistence
The one she recited before the fascists killed her

Yara
That's rad!

Yaroslav
The manifesto of the Donbass youth resistance

Yara

And did you know it?

Yaroslav

Of course, I knew it by heart, it's fantastic!

Yara

And what is it?

Marusya

Oh God,
You both gonna be so busted!

Yaroslav

But they haven't caught us! And the text goes like this:

"A Demon, soul of all the banished,
sadly above the sinful world
floated, and thoughts of days now vanished
Before him crowdingly unfurled;
days when, in glory's habitation,
He shone out a pure cherubim,
When comets flying on their station
rejoiced to exchange a salutation
Of welcome and of love with him."[5]
It's Mikhail Lermontov's poem "Demon."

Yara

Wait, a demon? Haha! Who authorized
A poem about a demon?

Marusya

I'm so confused, I don't get it at all!
A military poem has to be real!

Yaroslav

Actually, this text has a much wider scope:
It's about a fallen angel
Who seduces a Georgian princess

Yara

That's dope!

Yaroslav

Anyway, in the dark, moments before she died
Gromova read this poem to other Soviet fighters for freedom
After the fascists had tortured her all night—
Lermontov's poem "Demon"
I wonder why at the times when death is near
Girls think about love unrequited,
Why a child of revolution, this Soviet pioneer
Of all things this poem recited?

Yara

Well, philosophy is in your wheelhouse, not mine
The "Demon" stuff is cool, you're such a history whiz!
I knew that on a Soviet hero test you'd do just fine

Yaroslav

Interesting, right?

Marusya

It really is!
So, what happened to them? Were they tortured to death?

Yaroslav

Yep, their bodies were thrown into a mine

Marusya

And the demon? Why's he in the story?

Yaroslav

For beauty, I suppose?
Poetry gives history a better design:
Roses are better than no roses

Marusya (*pales and talks like she is daydreaming*)

A clearing, with grass soft like silk
Green arches of young hazel
And fog, thick as milk
Envelops the wild daisies

Yara

Marusya, what's up with you, dear? (*Hugs* **Marusya***, softly.*)

Marusya

It's gone! All gone! Stop hugging me, I'm okay!

Yaroslav

Oh, wow, sis, you got some kind of same-sex love affair here?
Hanging out with girls isn't really your game
By the way, I called our parents
Man, the news of Yara's girlfriend will be interesting

Marusya

I don't know about you guys, but I feel somebody's presence
Like someone's watching us, like someone's listening!

Oleg *enters.*

Oleg

I am watching you! I am shocked! My mind is blown!
I knew, Yara, that you have no brains—no offense—
And couldn't have passed a test on your own

Yara

Whoa Oleg, you sure know how to make an entrance!

Golden Angel *enters into the clearing.*

Marusya

Who's this? I told you, there are eyes all around

Golden Angel

True words, Marusya, so true

Marusya

Comrade Golden Angel, there's something crazy going down!

Golden Angel

That's why I'm here—to look into things, and you

Yara

This Oleg guy, he's been spying on me

Oleg

I was looking for you, Yara, that's why I came!
I worry about you, don't you see?

Golden Angel

And your worries aren't baseless, I have to say!

Marusya

Help us, Comrade Golden Angel! I'm really scared
These woods are filled with all kinds of voices

Yara

I had a feeling I'd fall in love; it was in the air
And it looks like I have, not that I had any choice

Golden Angel

Fallen in love in the wrong way
We'll deal with it! And we'll deal with the voices!

Yara

Fallen in love with Marusya. Come clean too, man! (*To* **Yaroslav**.)
He took my test today, although it was me who forced him (*Nods at* **Yaroslav**.)

Yaroslav

Instead of my sis I recited the poem "Demon"

Golden Angel

Demon, you say . . .

Yaroslav

It's a poem by Mikhail Lermontov

Golden Angel

Tell me more about those voices, Marusya

Marusya

Well, they talked about some magical things

Like, that they gave me the magic potion—
The demons, I mean
And put some crud on Yara's eyelids, to bring love into motion

Golden Angel

Who did?

Marusya

Some spirit jerks
And now she loves me, and you know it's a crime, it's not good!
Girls can't love girls!

Golden Angel

No they can't, they absolutely shouldn't . . .
Well, let's look into all of it closely
Have you had any food?

Yara

We've had some

Golden Angel

That's great! You are no adults and need to be watched
That's why I had to come
Kids, clearly you made a big mistake:
By cheating and running away from adults
You put your own lives at stake
And lives of those responsible for you. This all will have very sad results
Naturally, you will be punished
For all your acts, presumed and real
But your punishment could be reduced
If you repent and help me, dears

Yara

How?

Marusya

How?

Oleg

How can we help?

Golden Angel

Go to the woods for one night and one day
You have twenty-four hours
I need your help, this isn't a game
You must help me find these cowards
Find out who used whatever they used
And more importantly, why
As well as deal with this filth on the loose
This same-sex love—we'll wash it off just fine

Oleg
And what about me?

Golden Angel
Why are you even here?

Oleg
I'm worried about Yara

Golden Angel
You like her?

Oleg
A little

Golden Angel
Then, go with them

Oleg
And you?

Golden Angel
I'm too old and tired
You'll all depart in four directions
In these ancient woods, magical and wild
You'll find whoever started the infection
And collect evidence

Oleg
And what next?

Golden Angel
Next, there'll be a trial
So, go and clean up your mess
And remember, these woods folk, they're real
But it's to you, not to me that they showed themselves
And they might make another appearance
If you spot lightning up in the north
That's a signal to come back to this clearing
If in the south, then, for what it's worth
Run as fast as you can away from here
Oleg, I leave you in charge
See you later, dears

Disappears.

Scene Two

The same characters without **Golden Angel**.

Yara

Marusya, where are you going?

Marusya

I guess to the stream

Oleg

Shouldn't you ask my permission before and not later?

Yara

Get lost, you ratted out your team
Brought Golden Angel here, you traitor

Marusya

He kinda has to be watching us all,
That's literally in Golden Angel's job description

Yaroslav

Decent people don't bring them over
Avoiding these "angels" is the best decision

Marusya

Anyhow, I'm going to the stream

Oleg

I'll go with you. After all, the only person who knows anything here is you
And you're more at fault than I am, it seems—
You're the reason for this whole hullaballoo

Yara

Me too, Marusya, I'll go with you
Something inside me tells me I should

Yaroslav

I'd join you too if it weren't for this tool (*points at* **Oleg**)
How'd you even find us?

Yara

I'd kill this snake if I could

Oleg

I was looking for you (*looks at* **Yara**), and I used spyware
On your phone. Remember, I had it for a while?
You gave it to me to adjust and repair
So, I made some adjustments. Sorry, Yara

Yara

A dirty, hideous spy

Marusya

Oh, come on, he just has a crush on you
I bet you'll follow me just like this guy

Yara

Wait, Marusya, don't you want me to?

Marusya

I don't, but you stick to me anyway;
Yet, you hate him for turning up like a bad penny
I'm so sick of you all

Yaroslav

Am I the only one who just wants to get away?
The only one without love issues, like, not any?

Yara

Let's make a film about this trip!

Yaroslav

Marusya's Adventures in the Kingdom of Berendey[6]

Oleg

Don't you document anything—that's sick
Leaving paper trail is just insane!
On this mission, ours must be the only eyes
I'll go with you, 'cause you need a real man
But this brother of yours who hates my guts—
He can go alone, this fascist smartass with no plan

Yaroslav

I don't wanna go anywhere anyway, just leave me alone

Marusya

Yaroslav, come with me, let's leave them and be a team

Oleg

Did you listen to what Golden Angel said? So don't!
Don't disobey. Marusya, look for the stream

Yara

I'll go with Marusya

Marusya

Wait, but if she spots you
She might hide, you know, get scared

Oleg

She who?

Marusya

She has a dress, it's blue
Wet lips and green hair

Yara

Marusya, please, take me

Marusya

Alright, you can come, I'll figure it out

Yara

Come on, Marusya, don't be so mean

Oleg

Take me too, Marusya, I'll be useful, don't doubt!

They exit. **Yaroslav** *stays alone.*

Yaroslav

I'll stay in this clearing, be as it may
Won't go anywhere from here

Scene Three

Yaroslav, *alone in the clearing. He hears singing in the distance.*

Alex Moose (*sings*)

I'm Alex Moose, I'm Alex Moose
The spirit of woods, I travel on foot
I'm here now among oaks and spruce
'Cause today I pulled off something real good
I outsmarted and escaped the spirit chumps
Who are having a meeting about Summer Lightning
But I get to wander among trees and stumps
Seeing these relatives of mine is exciting!

Hello there, who're you?

Yaroslav

I'm Yaroslav, just a guy from Moscow

Alex Moose

Is it your friends out there, struggling through the thicket?
Who're they looking for?

Yaroslav

Folks like you, I guess, I don't know
Who are loud, and yelling, and creaking

Alex Moose

Not your thing to follow others?

Yaroslav

Nope, not something I'm after

Alex Moose

Not my thing either

That's why you and I found each other
Wanna hear my laughter? (*Laughs loudly.*)

Yaroslav

Listen, I'm not nuts, just a Moscow boy

Alex Moose

So what?

Yaroslav

So, I'm not into this stuff

Alex Moose

Well, I'm the forest spirit, so every owl
Loves to hear me laugh (*Laughs loudly.*)

Yaroslav

Right

Alex Moose

What's your story?

Yaroslav

It's too long to tell

Alex Moose

Harsh! But clearly you're here to help someone
Let me guess! It's a girl! Well . . .
Oh, I see . . . She's the daughter, and you're the son . . .
You were helping your sister . . .
And then something went wrong . . .

Yaroslav

Well, aren't you a psychic, mister?
Kudos, man, your telepathic game is strong

Alex Moose

So?

Yaroslav

So what?

Alex Moose

So what went wrong?

Yaroslav

Marusya thinks she saw something

Alex Moose

Who's Marusya? Your sister?

Yaroslav

This is the thing, she is not, but happened to tag along

Alex Moose
And your sister?

Yaroslav
My sister fell for her

Alex Moose
For Marusya?

Yaroslav
I don't wanna talk about it, drop it

Alex Moose
I wanna know more

Yaroslav
Tell me first about the witch who put a spell on Yara

Alex Moose
Which witch?

Yaroslav
How should I know? Maybe you did!
It's high time we found whoever did something so crass!
Whoever smeared potion on Yara's eyelids
They thought I was sleeping there, in the grass

Alex Moose
That's a setup, a major setup!
Well, who else was there? 'Cause there was someone else, right?

Yaroslav
Some Oleg guy, he fell for Yara

Alex Moose
No one else? You sure there was no one else in your sight?

Yaroslav
Golden Angel

Alex Moose
Who?

Yaroslav
Tell me first who you are

Alex Moose
I'm Alex Moose

Yaroslav
Is that 'cause you're so big and make people nervous?

Alex Moose
I'm the forest master, the shepherd of trees and bushes

Yaroslav

And Golden Angel is the shepherd of lightning; he's secret service

Alex Moose

Lightning?

Yaroslav

Well, you know, sparks, flashes, summer lightning
They are running a military game for teens in these woods
All the top brass of the Orthodox police
It's funny you're asking questions about Golden Angel, Mr. Moose
'Cause he's asking questions about you—that's an interesting coincidence

Alex Moose

So, lightning, you say?

Yaroslav

He talks just like you, the guy is no fun
(*Mimicking.*) "Demon, you say?"

Alex Moose

Demon?

Yaroslav

From the poem by Mikhail Lermontov
Soul of all the banished, you know, the famous one

Alex Moose

So, demon, you say . . .? Was he sad?

Yaroslav

He was

Alex Moose

Too bad (*Exits, laughing loudly.*)

Scene Four

Forest. **Yara**, **Oleg**, *and* **Marusya** *are looking for the stream and* **Ripplina**.

Marusya

So, tell me, Oleg, if you're a snitch
Then following us in the forest
And not in the city must be a nice switch?

Yara

Right? Singing with other birds, like a canary!
Give me your phone

Oleg

Why?

Yara
Just give it to me

Oleg
There, you can have it
The camera's on

Yara (*reads*)
"We are heading north; so far, good weather"
Did you write that? To whom? Man, come on!

Oleg
It's a journal

Yara
What the heck for?

Marusya
You're just like Mikhail Lermontov, the poet

Yara
Demon—an autobiographical novel
How does that sound?

Marusya
Sounds just perfect for the moment

Yara
North's in the other direction, guys

Oleg
Wait! Give it back to me! (*Grabs his phone.*) Told ya we were moving north
I have it all tagged

Yara
No, we aren't

Oleg (*to* **Marusya**)
Where were you heading? What's with my phone?

Marusya
I know where to go
I don't need GPS

Yara
Come on, city girl!
North's behind us, we got lost
In geography you'd get an F!

Marusya
I have an internal compass, my dad taught me from a young age
He's a professional traveler, an avid hiker

Oleg

Well, my dad is a minister, always on the public stage
Lots of people follow him and like him
I have to post everything, even boring errands

Marusya

So, you tattled where we're heading?

Oleg

I have to

Yara

You freakin' canary!

Oleg

Maybe. But I'm bound by an oath
And I love my parents

Marusya

I thought we had to go north, but now south, maybe

Yara

My GPS says west, as far as I can tell

Oleg

Mine say east, and wasn't our north before in that meadow?
Guys, do you notice that smell?
My GPS is off, so I say north is there

Marusya

I know where to go, I was heading north

Yara

Marusya, I'm on your side, I swear!
We all go where Marusya tells us—so, we keep heading forth!
We all go where Marusya tells us to go

Oleg

I go wherever I want. So far, I'll stick to this path, not another

Marusya

My dad's from Siberia. I'd find my way even under the snow

Oleg

Your dad is a jerk, and he cheats on your mother

Yara

My dad also cheats on my mom, what of it?
My dad is a handsome man, too
And my mom loves having a handsome lover
And Dad likes it when Mom finds it cool

Oleg

I'm cool, too, aren't I?

Yara

You're a canary!

Oleg

That's because I'm a real man, not a sissy
A real man is like a good referee,
If something's amiss, he'll blow the whistle!

Marusya

My mom is the best, she's the kindest of moms!
I want to go back to her! I'm no girl scout!

Oleg

I'm telling you, they wanted to name me Abraham,
But my mom said, he'll be Oleg! And everyone flipped out

Yara

And my mom is a beauty, she's a socialite
And she dated the French president

Oleg

And I know that your father was once indicted
I read about it in a secret document

Yara

I say the word, and you'll be expelled

Oleg

My dad could crush yours like an ant

Yara

A minister against a theater manager—that's a hard sell

Oleg

Everyone knows there are no real men in the arts!

Marusya *sneaks away.*

Oleg

Now I can't even see where we are on my phone
No coordinates, nothing. Wait, where's Marusya?

Yara

Well your mom looks like a Pokemon
And acts like an obedient Teletubby

Oleg

Where's Marusya, you see her?

Yara

Where's the love of my life?

Oleg

That's what I'm saying, Marusya is missing

And you're kinda almost her wife
Did you guys do it already? Okay . . . I get it, it's a secret . . .

Yara

Where is she?

Oleg

She didn't tell you?

Yara

My Marusya is missing . . .
My Marusya left 'cause of you

Oleg *looks at the bushes. The wind rustles. It howls ominously.* **Oleg** *and* **Yara** *are silent.*

Oleg

Do you hear the sound of the wind?

Yara

It's just wind. Or is it Marusya, maybe?

Oleg

The leaves are rustling, the twigs are creaking
I legit hear something that sounds kinda shady

Blowind *enters. He's singing.*

Blowind

Lalala-lala-lalala—an old classic
Rustling and blowing
It's Blowind doing magic
With his big silver wings
These kiddos are now
In the no signal zone
And I'm on search of this little crowd
Hey kids, where are you? Where have you gone?

Oleg

I think we got lucky. Hello

Blowind

Hello, dear younglings!

Yara

Hi! Are you the reason our phones don't work?

Blowind

Why do you need them? They are worldly, unnecessary things
We'll throw a party in the forest
Now that we have so many guests over
You look for Marusya? She's with the best—
Ripplina loves kids, though she's a little hungover

Looks at **Yara**.

Blowind

    Wait a second, are you a boy or a girl?
    Last time you were dressed like a guy, not a chick—
    Do you have a twig or a hollow?
    What is down there, a pocket or a stick?

Yara

    You dirty old . . .

Oleg

    I'm Oleg, and this is Yara—Yaroslava—here
    What is your name and why are you in this area?

Blowind

    I'm Blowind, a winged windy spirit
    So, you are that girl in love with another girl by gift of a fairy?

Oleg

    Where does this information come from?

Blowind

    Trust me, I know, I was there when it happened

Yara

    What do you mean, "it happened"? Nothing happened, come on!

Oleg

    We'll have to look into it, and look into you, Mr. Wing-Flapper

Blowind

    Look into it, sweetheart, look into it all
    In Blowind's thicket
    Plums, blackberries, and raspberries grow
    Sweetest in the world—you won't beat it

Opens his sack.

    Eat, my dears,
    Go on, don't be afraid!

Eats a fruit himself. **Yara** *and* **Oleg** *each enjoy a fruit too.*

Blowind

    You must be from the capital?
    Gosh, you're so healthy and so neat
    Now, I give everyone birds' names
    For example, you, Yara, are a jay

Yara

    Are you an ornithologist?

Blowind

You're such a mocking bird
Whereas you, Oleg, are a bird of prey
An owl, perhaps? Let me think . . . That's exciting!
No, not an owl. That is absurd
A falcon! You're here because of Summer Lightning?

Oleg

No, Yara's here for Summer Lightning
And I am here for Yara, to save her from danger

Blowind

Do you happen to know someone sparking?
You know, with lightning?

Yara

Oh, that's Golden Angel

Oleg

Is he a friend of yours? Why are you asking?

Blowind

More than a friend . . . You could almost say family

Oleg

Would you like to see him again? 'Cause that'd be an easy task

Blowind

I'm way too old to rejoice at seeing my peers. I'd rather see young people, mainly

Lightning flashes in the distance.

Yara

Was it north or south?

Oleg

My GPS isn't working. What do you think?

Blowind

South

Yara

South!

Blowind

Or maybe not! Looks like it was in the north!

Oleg

Here you are again, with your tricks
Let's have a look on what side of a tree moss grows
'Cause moss grows on the north side of trees!

Blowind

Sure, have a look, be my guest, please!

Oleg

Well, the flash was in the north. Sorry, we gotta go back, let's walk!
You're welcome to join our crew

Yara

Yeah, I think you and Golden Angel need to have a talk
He misses you a lot, asks about you

Blowind

And what does he ask?

Yara

He wanted us to bring you to him

Blowind

Did he now? Sure you aren't mistaken, sweetheart?
How would he even know I'm here?
Maybe I am in the sea, helping ships depart?
Or over the Urals, herding the clouds?
Or, in the desert, shaping dunes into forms?
Or, in the Siberian taiga, twisting turbulent blustery storms?

Disappears, laughing loudly.

Scene Five

Marusya, *alone, is sitting on a rock and crying.*

Marusya

Why, oh why? It's gross and not funny!
Where's this nasty old lady?
Why do some get fame and money?
But I got a girl in love with me . . .That's shady!
Oh, what will come of me? No idea!
Everyone will find out—I hate this spell

Ripplina

Why are you weeping and wailing here?
Where's your knight Yaroslav, do tell!

Marusya

Is that you? So it was all real?
Tell me, are you behind this whole plot?

Ripplina

What plot? Was my help not ideal?
Does your knight like you now, does he not?

Marusya

What knight? Yaroslav? What did you do to him?

Ripplina
Why do you need to know? Has he already confessed?

Marusya
Tell me exactly, what you did to him?

Ripplina
I just helped you a bit. I meant the best

Marusya
How? How did you help me?

Ripplina
Did some magic, that's all

Marusya
You did it to the wrong person, missus!

Ripplina
What do you mean? To Yaroslav, like you told me

Marusya
Only it was Yaroslava, a girl, his sister

Ripplina
I mean, he was where you said he'd be, and was dressed like a boy

Marusya
Well, now she's in love with me, you stupid witch!

Ripplina (*pulls a jug out of somewhere*)
She's in love with you?

Marusya
Yes, his sister, the twin

Ripplina
Wait, you're saying his sister's in love with you?

Marusya
Yes, a girl is in love with me!

Ripplina
Oh, I need a break from this whole ado (*Drinks from the jug.*)

Marusya
Missus witch, please hurry, this must be set straight

Ripplina
Why was she in that clearing?

Marusya
There was Summer Lightning there
What difference does it make?

Ripplina
Another girl?

Marusya
Summer Lightning is a game for youth, Yara took part in that thing
They met in the woods and traded clothes

Ripplina
I don't get it
Didn't you know she was his sister?

Marusya (*sobs*)
I didn't know she was in the woods somehow

Ripplina
So, there were two of them, but you saw only one—is that where the twist is?
And you think I can save her now?

Marusya
Same-sex love is forbidden in our state

Ripplina
How come?

Marusya
Don't you know? It's in our forest you're sitting

Ripplina
Your forest?

Marusya
This forest is ours!

Ripplina
Well, if love is forbidden, just keep it a secret

Marusya
Do you think this is some kind of a joke?

Ripplina
No, just life's full of turns, it's not a straight line
The hare's fur is white in winter, like a snow cloak
But it's grayish in summer, and he lives just fine (*Drinks from the jug.*)

Marusya
Missus Witch, Yara can't be in love with a girl
And don't try to sell me your childish spin
Such kinds of relationships are strictly forbidden

Ripplina
Why are they forbidden?

Marusya

Because of Pushkin

Ripplina

Because of Pushkin?

Marusya

He was shot by d'Anthès, and d'Anthès was gay
And Pushkin is our everything! You see how it works?

Ripplina

Pushkin, this forest . . . everything's yours, you say?
And what about d'Anthès?

Marusya

And d'Anthès was a jerk[7]
Oh, come on, stop this nonsense
They'll lock her in a nuthouse for "treatment"
And me too. There won't be any due process
Once we walk out this forest, we'll be revealed (*Sobs.*)
Golden Angel is already here!

Ripplina

Who? (*Drinks from the jug.*)

Marusya

He makes lightning

Ripplina (*chokes*)

Lightning? Like flashes? Like summer lightning? Oh, dear . . .

Marusya

He knows everything
He has information about all the things going on in the world
(*Lightning flashes over the trees.*) It's him! He's ordering us to hurry, he's near!
Please, give her something so that she can recover
And go talk to him, clear our names, show that you care!
Please, help us, Missus Ripplina, before we're discovered
Save us! We're just kids, and we're scared!

Ripplina

You're scared? Wait, is Yara scared, too?

Marusya

She isn't scared. She is not herself

Ripplina

So are you scared for her or for you?

Marusya

It makes no difference

Ripplina
Oh, but it does (*Drinks from the jug.*)
If it comes from the place of love and truth . . .
It means that you're also in love

Marusya
But I am not the one under a spell

Ripplina
You are afraid you might hurt your dove
Oh, there's truly something here . . . I can tell . . .

Marusya
I want everything to go back to normal!

Ripplina
Be honest, you fell in love with Yara too?

Marusya
Yikes, why would you say that? That's awful!

Ripplina
Well, I'm awfully sorry to ask you to go, will you?
I'm tired (*Drinks from the jug.*)

Marusya
What do you mean, you're tired? We need help! Or they'll put us in a nuthouse 'til the end of our lives!

Ripplina
So, sister
Sister instead of brother
Instead of a wife and a husband we get two wives . . .
Ah, too much knowledge—too much sorrow

Mumbles something indistinct and falls asleep.

Marusya
Where's north?

Ripplina *waves her hand to the side.* **Marusya** *exits in that direction, running.* **Blowind** *comes out from behind a tree. He leans over* **Ripplina** *and tenderly blows in her eyes.*

Ripplina (*opens her eyes*)
Blowind, hon, we've got a problem

Act Three

Scene One

Yaroslav *and* **Golden Angel** *are in the clearing; they are silent.*

Golden Angel

So, how was the swim? Did you run into anyone?
Although, as I see, you, Yaroslav, didn't even leave this place?

Yaroslav

I was about to. Per your order, I have twenty-four hours
Which you gave us to find those creatures' base

Golden Angel

So, you were what, getting ready? I can't say you hurried
To take off and locate them. It isn't that simple

Yaroslav

I was on it

Golden Angel

I did give you twenty-four hours, but I was worried
Because, as you noticed, we lost the signal

Yaroslav

I thought you were following us, not our devices

Golden Angel

I was, but the signal was also gone

Yara *and* **Oleg** *enter.*

Yara

Yaroslav, here you are! Whoa, this is priceless!
Whatcha telling him about us? That's just plain wrong!

Yaroslav

I'm not talking about you. I know nothing about you guys

Oleg

You could make something up; you're good at such games

Marusya *enters into the clearing.*

Yara

Marusya, breathe, you're blushing like a bride!

Marusya

Am I late? What happened? Is everything okay?

Golden Angel

I brought you some food—
Pasta, cutlets, zucchini caviar

It's all really good
Sit down, enjoy, will you?
And I'll explain to you
While you are eating
What you kids must do
After this meeting
But first, let's remember
What was before:
Facts that school taught you
About the days of yore
The time when brave Russians
Used no rhyme whatsoever:
When they led their discussions
In pathetic prose—not in poetry, never
Wars and crises raged
The country was in a recession
And some shady folks
Encouraged secession
There were rumors and protests
The society was divided
But magical spirits
Knew how to unite it
That's when to the president
With wise, solid advice
Golden Angel descended
To ask, wouldn't it be nice
Wouldn't it be sublime
If from now on the Russians
In poetry, with rhythm and rhyme
Lead their discussions?
So that first, politicians
Judges, and fighters of crime
Learned to be the magicians
Of the almighty rhyme
Then, it's up to the people
To pick up the rhyming
So that poetic talk
Helps their enlightenment
Poetry, as proven by Darwinians
Is the highest form of locution
It sends into oblivion
Riots and revolutions
So it's been, but now it would seem
Something lurks again in the dark
So, who'll be first to report what you've seen?
Marusya, why don't you start?

Marusya

Well, I was walking, and well, I mean

Yara

Stop saying "I mean"

Marusya

I stopped by a rock
And heard the stream's rippling
It broke the silence
The silence was broken by the stream's rippling water

Yara

And?

Golden Angel

Wait, Yara, wait, don't rush her

Marusya

So, I mean, that old lady was there, with a jug
She told me her name was Ripplina

Golden Angel

Did she ask you anything?

Marusya

She seemed drunk
I mean she was drinking from the jug to get wasted

Golden Angel

And did she not ask you anything at all?

Marusya

Not really
She asked about Summer Lightning though

Golden Angel

Summer Lightning?

Marusya

I said it was a game—military-patriotic stuff

Golden Angel

And the lady?

Marusya

She started to laugh!
Like this: (*Laughs out loud.*)
Ha-ha-ha
Oh-oh-oh

Yaroslav

Funny, I got asked about Summer Lightning too

Golden Angel
By whom? Did he come by this way?

Yaroslav
Some guy called Alex Moose

Golden Angel
And what did you say?

Yaroslav
I said Summer Lightning was a game
That my sister Yara took part in it

Golden Angel
And what did he say?

Yaroslav
He started to laugh (*Laughs out loud.*)
Then he left

Golden Angel
And you, Oleg and Yara, what did you see or hear?

Yara
Well, there was this old guy with wings, he dropped by

Yaroslav (*scornfully*)
With wings?

Golden Angel
Wait, Yaroslav! Go on, Yara, what about this guy?

Oleg
He asked about Summer Lightning

Yara
And then started to laugh, like this:
Hoi! Hai! Hoi! Hai!

All the kids start showing how each of the forest strangers they met laughed. **Golden Angel** *is thinking.*

Golden Angel
Quiet, kids, we need to talk
I must tell you something
Something that might bother you, that might even come as a shock
Are you ready to listen? Will you stop jumping?
So, all these forest friends of yours, that I tasked you with finding
They all asked about Summer Lightning, didn't they?

Everyone
They did! They did!

Golden Angel

Well, Summer Lightning is not just a game, it is also my name
And there's a reason they asked you about me
Will you help me? it's not as hard as it seems
To go and face those who messed with your heads
I must find out their plan! I must know what they scheme!
You have a big responsibility! Oleg, you must help!
Every day I talk to Viktor Ivanovich, your dad
I haven't been in touch with him today though
He'll like a story with a happy end
Where Oleg helps the Orthodox police lay down the law
Are you ready to help me?

Oleg

Aren't I already?

Golden Angel

I need a detailed report about this crime
I know you saw something! So, tell me!
Think, we don't have much time!

Oleg

He called me a falcon, and Yara a mockingjay

Golden Angel

A falcon?

Oleg

Yeah, a falcon. But first, an owl
Then he gave us some fruit. Fruit was local, tasted okay
Also, he blocked the signal—playing foul . . .

Yara

Blowind! Right, Blowind—that's his name!

Golden Angel

Go on, Yara. Oleg, that'll be all from you

Oleg

Will you tell my dad I did well?

Golden Angel

I'll tell him that in the end you came through
But it's up to you when he'll hear it:
With no signal, you're keeping everyone worried
Since you've drawn out Blowind, an evil spirit
You must make him talk, and you need to hurry!
Now you, Yara: you did a bad thing right off the bat
You created the problem that got this all started

Yara

I feel like the tomato from that ad,
That hid and hid but wound up in the stomach

Golden Angel

You broke the rules, do you recall?
You left the camp with criminal intent
And put your brother up to breaking the law
Causing a crime while at an unauthorized location
And this is a crime that really stinks
That tarnishes all your friends' names
You may be a victim, but you escaped in secret
You sneaked into the woods and broke the rules of the game

Yara

Will I be put on a trial?

Golden Angel

Moscow will decide this
But the case was only just opened
Sexual abuse of minors by use of witchcraft
Is an offense that is modern, sordid . . .

Yara

Political, kind of?

Golden Angel

Not kind of! Not kind of! It's really ugly
Both for you and your brother, trust me
By the way, Yaroslav, your behavior is striking:
You do know your sister is marked by the sin of sodomy?

Yara

But it's not my fault!

Yaroslav

If I may, I keep asking myself why we're still here?
Why won't you take us back to the city?
If everyone's looking for us. 'Cause it's quite clear
That all these tales about a trial are just silly

Golden Angel

Are you done?

Yaroslav

Yep, that's all I wanted to ask

Golden Angel

So, your question is why? Well, you're a smart guy, think
Why am I here, babysitting you suckers?

Instead of just sending you to pack your things?
You do know the answer, Yaroslav, right?
I'm giving you the chance to resolve this yourselves
So you can punish those who caused your plight
Vengeance is sweet, I can tell you myself!
Write a report, send it to Oleg, you'll be fine
Now Marusya . . . Your case is the hardest
A nice girl, wrong place, wrong time
You Marusya, caused witchcraft—your crime is the darkest
You drank from a jug? I need to have it
I need to learn more to stop this tumor
Remember, we aren't fighting women and men
We're fighting dangerous rumors

Golden Angel *vanishes.*

Scene Two

Same characters, without **Golden Angel***.*

Yaroslav

Do you hear the song of a nightbird
In the sky that is dark and strange?
Summer Lightning will soon be returning
That is, Comrade Golden Angel

Yara

If he comes, then he comes, whatever
When did he say he'll be back? At dawn?
I thought what you told him was really clever
Catch your criminals yourselves, we're kids, c'mon!

Oleg (*scornfully*)

Well done, Yaroslav, a real man!
Except everything you said is total bull crap

Yaroslav

Why are you piping up again?
You stupid cop-helping rat?
Go and look for your Blowloser

Oleg

Blowind! And take it easy, what if he hears us
We must also find this lady Medusa,
Whose charms made Yara fall in love and go totally nuts

Marusya

Yeah, it's gonna be epic, our coming home

Grabs **Yara***'s hand.*

Marusya

Hi Mom, hi Dad!

Yara

What do we do? We need to find a way out
We probably oughta try and lay low
We could just date in secret, you know, quietly

Marusya

No way! Are you crazy? What do you mean, quietly?
Yara, we really need to have a conversation
Why're you all laughing?

Yaroslav

Oh, this is wild!
I'd rather love no one and avoid these situations

Oleg

Let's just find these spirits and have a talk
Breaking the spell is worth the endeavor

Yaroslav

Or we can just sit here, under this rock

Oleg

Nah man, we can't just sit here forever
Let's go and see if there's a recipe they can give us

Yara

Oleg, what recipe? Sit down and relax!

Marusya

Sitting here is pointless, let's say no to obedience!

Yaroslav

We need a plan:
What will we tell them?

Yara

This sucks
Let's pin it all on this Golden Angel goof

Oleg

Or better yet, on these forest spirits!
But to pin it on them, we need some proof

Yaroslav

Right! Go ahead and look for evidence!

Marusya

I'm so scared, I feel like I'm drowning
Yaroslav, what will happen to us?

Yaroslav

It's all good
This place is anomalous, the police will surround it
Save the kids and take down the bad guys

Marusya

What about Golden Angel?

Yara

Is he Summer Lightning?

Marusya

And what do we do with Yara?

Oleg

Could a miracle help?
Maybe their witchcraft could be useful and not frightening

Marusya

Ripplina! it's Ripplina! Look, guys!
Off in the distance, Ripplina's walking over
And Alex Moose is by her side
And the old man's above them, kinda hovering

Oleg

Yep, I see them! That's our guy
Blowind—that's his name
The one who's just spun and flew up high
Hi, Blowind! What brings you? Nice that you came!

Yaroslav

Oh, Mr. Alex Moose, hello!
I guess we were right to stay here

Alex Moose

You wanted to see us, well here you go!

Oleg

Thank you for taking the time to appear

Yara

You guys got us into real trouble
First, we don't even know you at all
Second, I think it was rude and unsubtle
Of you to confuse me with my bro

Blowind

Oh, but that was just innocent fun!

Ripplina

Sometimes, we want to help people too

Alex Moose

Sometimes, you just feel sorry for them, kind of
So you help as you can, what can you do . . .

Yaroslav

Are you real spirits? Like actual, ancient?
How come you don't speak old Slavonic?

Alex Moose

Why, Yaroslav, why all these questions?
Are there other spirits you know? Why all this paranoia?

Yaroslav

I haven't met others

Marusya

Can you help us reverse spell effects?

Ripplina

I decided I would help you again
However, the new spell is rather complex
But it'll be dark soon—we can try then

Yara

Try? Try again? On me?

Blowind

Spells can't be removed. But we can redirect them, as a compromise
So that you fall in love with the first guy you see
We'll put a spell on you again when the new moon rises

Oleg

Oh, I want to be the first guy
I'm up for anything, and I mean it!

Yara

Ew, no; this decision should be mine
Definitely not him! Where's my phone? Just gimme a minute
I wanna show you a pic

Ripplina

No pictures, we need live action

Marusya

Oh you people! What're you doing? Stop it!

Ripplina

Well, there's your boyfriend! Ain't she perfection?

Yara

Oh God, I'm scared, what should I do?

Yaroslav

Well, Yara, they've got you in a bind

Boy, the choice they've given you. . .
But, sis, don't believe that your hands are tied!

Alex Moose

Think for yourself! Don't ask us!

Blowind

Think, think!

Ripplina

Think it through, this is no easy task!

Oleg

Think, Yara

Marusya

Think!

Yara

Marusya, you and I need to talk
We need to talk, just you and I
Oh, come on people! Take a walk!

All exit, except the girls.

Scene Three

Yara *and* **Marusya** *are silent.*

Yara

Let's talk about us and the fate that brought us together
I do wrestling, and I'm mostly friends with guys
Hanging out with girls wasn't really my thing ever
Meeting you though has opened my eyes
Marusya, I think you are a good influence
Tell me, why do you keep looking at your device?

Marusya

I'm looking at the world through a special filter
I always use the screen to look at life
Wanna try it? it's nice! (*Shows* **Yara**.)

Yara

You're right, that's a cute filter
It changes everything! Like a fairytale

Marusya

I try to use it often. I can't stand the real world
This filter adds some mystery, makes it less stale
This app has web links to everything:
Types of trees and works by cultural titans

Wanna know what Matsuo Bashō said about this tree?[8]
Or where we can find it on the paintings by Levitan?[9]
Or, a building—who built it and when?
By the way, that's how I met your brother—
In the school club for young architects

Yara

No way!

Marusya

Yep
But I can't afford it anymore, we don't have that money
What about you? Do you have hobbies?

Yara

Well, people around you seem pretty artsy
But I'm like my mom—practical, more into sports
Art and literature aren't my cup of tea
It's my dad who likes madness of this sort

Marusya

I must say I like you. You're strong and determined
Psychologically, Oleg might be a better fit for you
One could say I'm talented alternatively
Not popular among all, just a few

Yara

Oleg and I were part of the same club at school
Just like Yaroslav and you
You think looking at that virtual stuff is cool
And Oleg and I were part of an anti-virtual reality crew
I was against this virtual app—it was something to fight
I mean, the filter you just showed
But now I've seen these plants in a new light
Through your eyes. It's a feeling I didn't know
It must be boring for you with me
I'm sure you'd rather be with my bro if you could choose

Marusya

Yaroslav keeps to himself, you see
But he's well-loved. I'm not on his level, I'm just a loser

Yara

Tell me, what do you think,
How can girls get closer to each other?

Marusya

Well, we must have something in common
Maybe, there are books we can talk about?
Maybe, we could just dream together?

But you're so athletic and direct
Maybe dating Oleg for you would be better?
You must like active guys like Oleg
You need more traditional relationships

Yara

Do you know any couples who are in love?

Marusya

I live with my mom, Dad's always on trips
The romance between them has basically died
Anyway, married couples fight a ton

Yara

Oleg's parents are together—a real family
Marusya, be my friend, please, it'll be fun

Marusya

When they break the spell, you won't need me, let's be transparent

Yara

Yes I will. You've shown me a marvelous model of femininity
Compared to you, I'm like an unfeeling corpse
Let's be friends. We can go to the symphony

Marusya

And drive together to cool rock concerts

Yara

So, how did you love Yaroslav?

Marusya

How? Secretly!

Yara

Well, imagine I am Yaroslav

Marusya

No, Yara, no, that's a dangerous fantasy!

Enters **Ripplina**, *followed by everyone else.*

Ripplina

Hey, lovely girls, help me pick fireweed
If you drink it after sunset, at dusk
It'll help your body regulate your heartbeat
And improve your overall health status
Drinking fireweed tea normalizes blood pressure
It helps you sleep better at night
As it contributes to your relaxation
Which makes you more active during daytime

Everyone starts picking fireweed.

Marusya

There's no means of testing
Which decision is better. Because there is no
Basis for comparison with previous lives
We live everything without warning
We live everything as it comes

Ripplina

Fireweed stops you from growing old
It's a remedy that's almost universal

Yara

Like an actor going on cold
And playing their part in a production without a single rehearsal

Marusya

What can life be worth if the first
Rehearsal for life is life itself?

Ripplina

Do as I do; take the leaves in your hands and roll

Yara

One life hardly counts; it's more like a dream

Marusya

What happens but once, might as well not have happened at all

Ripplina

Now we let them ferment in a cool, quiet place by my stream[10]

Scene Four

Yaroslav *and* **Oleg** *are talking at the edge of the clearing where the others are picking fireweed.*

Yaroslav

Why don't we just leave this whole mess?

Oleg

Dude, what's your problem? Your sis has been charmed
Like she's some kind of fairytale princess
But you just keep joking; aren't you alarmed?

Yaroslav

Well, what are you doing here? Courting your future family?

Oleg

Yes, Yara is mentally and physically fit for a wife

Yaroslav

She's in love with Marusya, are you for real, man?

Oleg

Well, that's just a spell
The authorities will remove the charms

Yaroslav

Are these authorities of yours aware
That tonight, the crazies will cast a new bout
Of spells to conjure up another love affair?

Oleg

I doubt it

Yaroslav

And you? You'll make my sister fall for you— It's cool, I don't mind!
But what if you stop loving her? Leave her as a single mother?

Oleg

Oh no, we don't leave our people behind
Yara will be my significant other

Ripplina *comes up to them.*

Ripplina

Fireweed, fireweed

Oleg

Stay away from me, witch!

Ripplina

Winter's ahead, boys
We need supplies, so help us

Oleg

I am focusing, getting ready for the ritual
I can't waste my time on collecting biomass
Fireweed? Who are you kidding?
And you, Yara? Are you on their side?
Not on mine? The man to whom you should be fully committed?
Picking fireweed? You have no right!
You should be next to me, getting ready
To fall in love with me at first sight
Or is the fireweed drawing you to Marusya?
I can go and tell everything to Summer Lightning

Ripplina *(splashes* **Oleg** *from the jug)*

Water-water takes you high
River's daughter makes you fly!

Oleg *sits down on a stump.*

Oleg
Dad expects my report (*Falls asleep.*)

Scene Five

Evening. **Marusya** *walks in the woods, jug in her hands.* **Golden Angel** *walks toward her.*

Golden Angel
Hi, Marusya! How are things?
Where're you going?

Marusya
Looking for you. Look at this

Shows him the jug.

Golden Angel
What's that you're holding?

Marusya
Ripplina's jug. It's material evidence

Golden Angel
Give it to me. Well done! (*Drinks from the jug.*)

Marusya
What's going on? What are you doing?

Golden Angel (*drinks from the jug*)
Ahh, so good! Thank you so much, hon!

Marusya
You aren't supposed to drink though, are you?

Golden Angel
Emergency alert! Emergency alert! (*Drinks from the jug. Sits with his head down.*)

Marusya
There's something important I have to tell you
Since you said we should give you reports
They're planning to cast another spell soon!
Well, say something! Go and stop them!
They're going to use magic tonight
Yara will fall in love with Oleg then
And that's a crime, aren't I right?

Golden Angel (*drinks from the jug*)
Ah, Marusya, how long it's been . . .
I thought I'd never ever again . . .
Time, stop your course, like on the screen
Here, we need a freeze frame

Marusya

I spilled some of it, so it's almost empty

Golden Angel

And here is my jug, it is half full
Of emptiness, and solitude, and memories
And it reflects the midnight moon . . .
They left a while ago, those spirits
My friends of nature, from the woods
Like music that's no longer playing
Their voices left me, now for good

Marusya

They left because of you, you know

Golden Angel

Poetry was dying
The country was in pain, the people opposed it
So, we decided to create a poetic empire
And give the president special technologies

Marusya

Look, man, I don't care. They're ruining someone's life!
Who are these guys? Disgraced Golden Angels?

Golden Angel

There are no angels. Just Summer Lightning and my avatars
And those are old gods you found—those strangers
I got power thanks to poetry
Now this whole country speaks in verse
The spirits were late (*Drinks from the jug*), I beat them to it
But I paid for it with disgrace, that's my curse
I'm not an angel, I'm just like them, but I was pretending
So I could build a poetic empire with no worries
When in fact, I'm Summer Lightning, a spirit just as ancient
One of the lightning gods greedy for glory

Marusya

What about other lightnings? Do they obey you?

Golden Angel

They are me (*Drinks from the jug.*)
And me, I'm alone, an outcast
I am no Golden Angel, I'm telling you
I'm an ancient spirit from the distant past (*Drinks from the jug.*)
They are just old gods—forsaken, forgotten
Who make girls fall in love with each other
We have technologies to cure diseases like Yara's gotten
Let me show you some real power (*Struggles to get up in order to go.*)

Scene Six

The clearing. All are there, except for **Marusya** *and* **Golden Angel**. **Alex Moose**
is keeping an eye on **Oleg** *and singing a song. Everyone else is busy picking
fireweed.*

Alex Moose

Under the federal sky
There's angel made of gold
His piercing supervising eye
Keeps order and control
Away from all these duties
He's just a simple poet
Who makes the story beautiful
And stunning as he saw it
He gave to people poetry
The fire of his words
And branded prose boring—
Prometheus of sorts!
But if one day my friend
You get to be his guest
He'll welcome you with lightning
And also have you tasered
You'll see the company of Angel made of gold
And Alex Moose who all the woods patrols
With raging Blowind and sweet Ripplina
Whose majestic dream's so irresistible[11]

Ripplina
Where's my jug?

Alex Moose
There's not a sip left in it

Yaroslav
Or, I see you're having a Sorcery Night Live here

Oleg
Yara, will you please calm down this idiot?
Else I will, and he'll regret he's been near me

Yara
Man, you're really "laying on the charm"

Oleg
Where's Marusya?

Ripplina
Where's my jug? Ridiculous!

Yaroslav

Marusya went AWOL when Oleg tried to scram

Ripplina

And that's when my jug disappeared

Yaroslav

Pure coincidence

Ripplina

Slipped through my fingers . . . I'm a fool . . .

Oleg

Marusya and the jug vanished at the same time

Yaroslav

Youth doesn't care about the rules
Stealing alcohol is a very trendy crime

Blowind

This jug is so not for children, it's no juice!
Kids are underage, it's not their thing

Alex Moose

Maybe, she didn't steal it for personal use?
Must've done it for Summer Lightning

Blowind

Summer Lightning knows we're here anyway

Alex Moose

Maybe liquid courage is what he's after

Blowind

Oh, come on, Lyosha, don't get carried away
Shouting about things won't resolve them any faster

Yaroslav

First Oleg brought Golden Angel, this bossy sky guy
Now Marusya decided to ditch us
Steal the jug, and hang us out to dry
Both are in love with you, Yara, and both are snitches

Enter **Golden Angel** *and* **Marusya**.

Golden Angel

My lovely friends, let us embrace!

Starts chasing the others with arms outstretched.

Let me kiss you! Come here! Wait!

Yaroslav

This Angel ain't Golden, he's wasted

Yara
   Marusya, my angel, my babe!

Ripplina
   You thieves! Give me back my jug!

Marusya
   Yara, he promised to save you! To undo the spell
   He might prove useful to you after all

Golden Angel
   I'll save everyone! I am Golden Angel!

Alex Moose
   Your real name is Summer Lightning, as I recall

Ripplina
   Oh come on, not him! Marusya he's such a jerk

Rips the jug out of **Golden Angel***'s hands and starts drinking.*

He won't help, he'll just make things worse

Alex Moose
   So, how did people like your work?
   In your poetic empire everyone talks in weird stilted verse

All the spirits drink, passing the jug around. As they talk, a savage storm overtakes the woods: loud cackling can be heard, lightning flashes, rain pours down, trees creak, the wind howls. The sounds get louder toward the end of the scene.

Golden Angel
   Why are you all gathered here anyway?

Ripplina
   We're picking fireweed

Golden Angel
   Picking fireweed, you say?
   You old fox, it looks more like you're charming her to me!

Blowind (*drinks from the jug*)
   Fireweed is beautiful, the tea is tasty!
   I love looking at it when I fly overhead . . .

Oleg
   Oh, get to business, will ya? You're already wasted

Yara
   I'm in love with Marusya! I don't want Oleg!

Ripplina
   Well, here we go, the woods are getting darker . . .

Why is it always the same story?!
I swore not to meddle in people's problems
Your human affairs are too much for me, sorry!

Golden Angel

Well, aren't you snobs? Sitting around, smelling flowers
Pouting, I don't like this, I don't like that
Of course, our poetic superpower
For you is like pain in one place
All the time drinking or smoking (or both)
From Ripplina's apothecary by the creek
And then you just crawl around like sloths
Pretending you're like Ancient Greeks

Blowind

Fair enough, if we think about it,
You're right that we are uncultured, somewhat

Golden Angel

Uncultured, self-absorbed whiners,
You're afraid of politics, you're afraid of war
You don't love your country, you're vermin

Ripplina

Calm down, this new you is a surprise

Golden Angel

What did you come here for? I don't need your sermons!
I'm at home here! I'm fire fallen from the skies!

Ripplina

Lighty, just think of the storms of late May
Of a bubbly stream rippling through the woods
Of a grumpy bear hungry from hibernating

Alex Moose

Come on, stop it

Blowind

Drop it

Golden Angel

You're mean

Ripplina

But we came for you!

Yaroslav *wants to say something but* **Yara** *stops him.*

Blowind

There once was a wise man . . .

Golden Angel

>   Oh please, don't pontificate
>   Yes, we all lived well, but I left your palace
>   You don't like it—just pack and emigrate

Alex Moose

>   But listen, this is our house, too
>   These trees that I know by name
>   The fauna that looks like these kids
>   The flora, living and breathing in their own way
>   But I don't make badgers get an education
>   Or make frisky squirrels learn poetry
>   In order to build a squirrel or ape civilization
>   Making them study in my forest university

Golden Angel

>   Amateur. This is just forest-fool chatter
>   Don't equate humans with your animal scum!
>   I'm talking about things that really matter
>   I'm talking about service, not a hare with a drum!

Alex Moose

>   We came for you

Yaroslav *wants to say something, but the other kids restrain him.*

Blowind

>   A wise man once said, jug in his hands (*takes the jug*)
>   That one can drink and with his friends reunite
>   But another will drink and stay a lonely man
>   And this another is you, Summer Lightning

Yaroslav

>   We're no squirrels! Hey, Alex Moose
>   Watch out for the branches snapped by the wind!

Marusya

>   Missus Ripplina, it's pouring like the sky's broken loose!

Ripplina

>   This is all because of our talks here, kids

Oleg

>   That's it, you're drunk, enough of this hike
>   Thought it'd be nice to get out into nature
>   Yara, let's go!

Yara

>   I'll go with Marusya! It's her that I like!

Blowind

Goodbye, kids! Goodbye, youth!
Goodbye, Summer Lightning! Hello, Golden Angel!

Alex Moose

Goodbye, youth! You'll leave, you'll vanish
Turns out, we came for you in vain!

Ripplina

Oh, demon, soul of all the banished
Float sadly above the sinful world, alone again!

Yaroslav (*shouting over the wind*)

What's wrong with being alone?

Everyone laughs loudly in response.

Epilogue

Yaroslav
>And that's, in short, how our music band came to be
>When we made it through that hell of a night—
>Marusya, Yara, Oleg, and me—
>We decided to make music together; it just seemed right
>That night was frightful: the earth moaned and groaned
>The forest master argued mightily, like a hundred old oaks
>Meanwhile, Ripplina and a drunk mermaid horde
>Tickled Summer Lightning, but he was immune to their strokes
>Thousands of lightning bolts lit up the skies
>It was bright as day—we could see everything
>Blowind whipped up giant storm clouds
>Flapping the air with his big silver wings
>We had only Yara's sleeping bag, that's all
>So, to keep ourselves warm and dry
>The four of us sat on that bag under a rock
>Hiding from lightning, rain, and the storm all night
>They still managed to put us to sleep
>I woke up next morning to a calm sunny day
>I was worried we'd again been bewitched
>And was afraid to wake my friends
>Marusya woke up in Yara's arms
>Not far away Oleg slept under the Judas tree
>And the forest spirits and their scary charms
>Left us alone, were gone, as it seemed
>We went to the farewell bonfire of the military game
>And the next day got summoned to a federal building
>We expected to see a door with Summer Lightning's name
>But it had some other name printed on it
>The guy asked us not to talk about it, not to a soul
>Our story could get us sent to a psych ward
>All at once, we decided to make music our goal
>We just wanted to stick together going forward
>Golden Angel stepped out of our story;
>Though I glimpsed him once, passing by in a car, I guess
>But his invisible electrifying aura
>Has been the key to our band's success
>We feel his love—concealed, it keeps us well
>We recollect the trip—it was enlightening
>Music was the spirits' parting gift, their final spell
>That's why we called our band Summer Lightning
>Meet our crew: Oleg's on retro-drums, he keeps the beat sharp
>Karaoke-keyboard is Marusya's jam

Yaroslava found her calling with bass and harp
And I'm the songwriter and the band's front man
When Ulyana Gromova was reciting "Demon"
She needed compassion to carry on fighting
And sometimes, even Lermontov can inspire a hero—
We all just need something that can keep us united.

2016

*   *   *

Summer Lightning premiered in Moscow in January 2019. Specially for the staging, Rodionov and Troepolskaya wrote a song that is performed by the band Summer Lightning at the end of the show, after the epilogue.

You and I, we met up in the woods
You told me that I'd be saving you
You aren't meant my savior to be
Mighty Hedgehog will watch over me
In the woods a table set for two
We'll be entertained by the squirrel crew
Rabbit poet will make his debut
Mighty Hedgehog will watch over you

Refrain:
Only once, only once
Is like never, like a dream
It's what life is like for us
It'll vanish, leave no print

Fog is hanging over forest paths
A giant oak waves his branch at us
Here, in the woods, the place fate chose
You and I will hide in the hollow oak
You and will hide here from the crowds
We'll be downshifters, we'll live proud
We'll hide from the world that's ruled by lies
Mighty Hedgehog will watch over us

Refrain:
Only once, only once
Is like never, like a dream
It's what life is like for us
It'll vanish, leave no print

Wild berries, clear forest rain
You and I are saved to live again
He's the only one who has the soul
Mighty Hedgehog will help make us whole
You and I have hidden from all sorrows

We look out from the oak's hollow
You and I enjoy our blissful dreams
Next to all the animals and trees

Refrain:
Only once, only once
Is like never, like a dream
It's what life is like for us
It'll vanish, leave no print

Notes

1   Alex Moose's name is a colloquial variant of the Russian name Alexey. Another short
      variant of this name, which has an affectionate tone to it, is Lyosha—this is how Blowind
      addresses Alex Moose at the end of the play. Lyosha is phonetically similar to the Russian
      word "leshii," which means "forest spirit"—the master of the woods that Alex Moose is.
      The choice of the moose as the animal to represent the spirit of the forest takes its roots in
      the ancient lore of the Urals region (Perm'), which is dominated by the figure of a
      Mooseman or a Man-moose (this makes it clear that the print of a Humanimal that
      Yaroslav spots at the beginning of the play is the print of none other than Alex Moose).
      This forest spirit was part of the local pagan pantheon that found its wide representation in
      bronze casts produced in 7 BC–12 AD around the site where the contemporary city of
      Perm' stands. The combination of mythological creatures cast in bronze and the
      technology of producing the figurines is unique to this region and is known as Permian
      animal style.
2   Summer Lightning (*Zarnitsa*, in Russian) is a popular Soviet and Russian capture-the-flag
      game for teenagers with military and sports elements, which bears the name of the natural
      phenomenon. It is often organized in summer camps or in schools and involves two teams
      (= armies) that play against each other with the goal of capturing the "enemy's" flag
      located at their "base." Teen "soldiers" carry military distinctions lightly attached to their
      shoulders; one of the game's objectives includes stripping the enemy's soldiers of their
      distinctions, thereby injuring them (taking distinctions off one shoulder) or killing them
      (both shoulders). The game usually takes place in forests and includes orientation training
      in nature. One of the largest installments of this game is organized annually by the Russian
      Youth Union in cooperation with the military as part of the Russian national program in
      patriotic education of youth.
3   Lake Ilmen (pronounced as Il'men', with stress on the last syllable) is a lake in Russia's
      north-west, in the Saint Petersburg area. It is located near the city of Novgorod, which was
      the center of economic and political activity in this region in ancient times due to its
      situation at the crossroads of major waterways. As a result, lake Ilmen features in many
      old legends and folk tales of the Slavs, where it is represented with great veneration.
4   The Young Guard is an underground youth resistance group that was active during the
      Second World War in the Luhansk region of the USSR (contemporary Ukraine). It mostly
      included former high-schoolers not drafted to the war who ran a series of actions against
      the Nazi occupants of their city. Most of its members were executed by firing squad and
      their bodies were thrown into mine shafts at the outskirts of the city. Soon after the end of
      the war, their activities inspired the Soviet writer Alexander Fadeev to write the
      eponymous novel *The Young Guard* (1946/51) that closely reproduced the story of the

group, including the members' real names and fates. The novel gained wide popularity in the Soviet Union and was readily available in libraries across the country. Today, the Luhansk region, together with the Donetsk region, is the site of an ongoing war that began after the invasion of these Ukrainian territories by the Russian army in 2014. Both regions are part of Donbass—a coal-mining area located along the Donets river basin (hence Don-bass). Therefore, the reference Yara (and later Yaroslav) makes to Donbass is a double-entendre with both historical and contemporary interpretations.

5   "Demon" by Mikhail Lermontov, translated by Charles Johnston, in *Narrative Poems by Alexander Pushkin and by Mikhail Lermontov* (1983), New York: Random House. Mikhail Lermontov (1814–1841; pronounced as ˈLermontov, with stress on the first syllable) was Pushkin's younger contemporary who wrote Romantic poetry, often inspired by Russia's Oriental Other of the time—the Caucasus. He is considered the second most important poet of the nineteenth century in Russian cultural history.

6   Kingdom of Berendey (pronounced as Berenˈdey, with stress on the last syllable) refers to a mythical character from Slavic lore, a ruler of territories in Russia's north-west.

7   Alexander Pushkin (1799–1837; pronounced as ˈPushkin, with stress on the first syllable) is the most famous and venerated poet in Russia, often referred to as "our [Russian] everything." His vision of poetry (that relied on the use of lighter grammatical and lexical structures in comparison to the verse of the eighteenth century characterized by convoluted sentences and vocabulary) was revolutionary and is widely regarded as a springboard for the development of contemporary Russian literary language. Pushkin died from a fatal wound he received in a duel with Georges d'Anthès who had allegedly courted Pushkin's wife. The reference to d'Anthès's homosexuality in the play is not a widely known fact in Russia. Rodinov and Troepolskaya's reinvention of the public knowledge about the sexuality of d'Anthès—the culprit of Pushkin's death—binds queerness and villainy as qualities that go hand-in-hand and clearly portrays homosexuality as a crime against Russian culture, in an allusion to the infamous 2013 law on gay propaganda, which also presents homosexuals (and other individuals who "make propaganda" of so called "non-traditional" sexual relations) as ultimate villains who endanger the lives of the young generation of Russians and Russia's "traditional values."

8   Matsuo Bashō (1644–1694) is a famous Japanese poet, a master of the haiku genre.

9   Isaak Levitan (1860–1900; pronounced as Leviˈtan, with stress on the last syllable) is a Russian landscape painter.

10 In this scene, Yara and Marusya's lines that compare life with theater are a slightly adapted quote taken from Chapter 3 of the novel *The Unbearable Lightness of Being* (1984) by the famous Czech author Milan Kundera. Quoted here after Milan Kundera, *The Unbearable Lightness of Being*, trans. by Michael Henry Heim (New York: HarperPerennial, 1985).

11 "Under the Federal Sky" is a take on the famous song "City of Gold" (*Gorod zolotoi*) by the Russian rock band Akvarium. It was part of the soundtrack to *Assa* (1987), a popular film of the perestroika era, directed by Sergey Solovyev. The original song is available at: https://bit.ly/3oc6AmZ.

A Little Hero

Valery Pecheykin

Valery Pecheykin is an award-winning playwright, journalist, and screenwriter. He was born in Tashkent (Uzbekistan) and worked at the famous Ilkhom Theater with Mark Vail' before moving to Moscow in the early 2000s. Currently a chief playwright and curator at the Gogol Center theater in Moscow, he penned the scripts for Kirill Serebrennikov's productions of *Metamorphoses*, *A Midsummer Night's Dream*, and *Kafka*. His play *The Idiots*, based on Lars von Trier's eponymous film, was staged by Serebrennikov and selected for the 2015 Avignon Festival. Pecheykin co-wrote screenplays for Pavel Lungin's films *The Conductor* (2012) and *The Queen of Spades* (2016). He also single-authored the screenplay for the film *Acid* (dir. Alexander Gorchilin, 2018), which won the Debut award at the 2018 Russian film festival Kinotavr, was the winner of the 2019 goEast film festival in Berlin, and was featured in the international selection of the 2019 Berlinale. His literary works include the plays *Falcons* (2008), *My Moscow* (2011), *A Little Hero* (2014), *Philosophers* (2017), and *A Scary Word* (2020), the collection of essays *A Mean Boy* (2020) and others. They have been published in multiple journals and drama collections and have been translated into Chinese, English, German, and Spanish.

Author's address

Dear readers, the first staged reading of this play was in Russia. It took place at the Moscow Gogol Center theater as part of the festival A Dream Play in 2014. At the time, Ilya Shagalov directed the staged reading of this text. It was performed not on the main stage of the theater but literally under it—in the "hold." This is a space where the audience set foot for the first and last time in the history of the Gogol Center. The play was performed in-between the mechanisms of the revolving stage, which created a wonderfully accurate atmosphere for taking in this text. The audience seemed to be transported inside an actual Kafkaesque torture apparatus. A year before that, the law on "gay propaganda" had been passed, which forbids to provide positive information about homosexual relationships to minors. That's how this play came to be. It tells a story of a "little hero"—a boy who decided to exterminate people who love other, even adult, boys. I don't know if I can wish you to enjoy the reading. This is a text that brings both fear and laughter. Laughter arrives in the place where fear once was. And love arrives in places where people remained true to themselves despite fear and laughter.

With love,

Valery Pecheykin.

Characters[1]

Vovochka
Vanya
Lyubochka
Old Woman
Alexander Morozov
Sergey
Male Neighbor
Female Neighbor
Man
Voice
Children
Vovochka's Grandmother
The two who live together
Their neighbors
Vovochka's neighbor

Part One

Crematorium

Voice   Alexander Morozov, please stand and identify yourself.

Morozov *stands up.*

Voice   State your name for the record.

Morozov   Alexander Morozov.

Voice   State your patronymic.

Morozov   I wasn't raised by my father.

Voice (*to the side*)   Typical case . . . (*To the microphone.*) You must state your father's name.

Morozov   I saw him once in my whole life. He was standing in the doorway, with a melon, I think, and I don't like melons . . .

Voice   That's irrelevant. Answer the question clearly and concisely.

Morozov   Alexander . . .

Voice   I know your name; I'm asking for your father's name.

Morozov   I'm telling you, it's Alexander.

Voice   Alexander, the son of Alexander . . . Alexander Alexandrovich . . . Do you know that the name Alexander originates from the word "man"?

Morozov   Yes, I . . . think I've heard that before. But what does it matter?

Voice   Your name is Alexander Alexandrovich . . .

Morozov   So . . .?

Voice   It means that the same word comes up twice in your name: "man" and "man." Isn't that strange? Don't you find it mystical?

Morozov   I don't know. That's a very weird thing to ask.

Voice   What is your date of birth?

Morozov   Twenty-second of June, nineteen eighty-four.

Voice   Really?

Morozov   What do you mean, "really"?

Voice   I'll ask the secretary to check if this date actually exists. Where were you born?

Morozov   Saint Petersburg.

Voice   And what are you doing in Moscow?

Morozov   I work here.

Voice   Have you ever heard the saying "Bloom where you're planted"?

Morozov   Yes, I have.

Voice   And?

Morozov   And what?

Voice   What are you doing in Moscow?

Morozov   I work here.

Voice   Oh, drop the act, you're here because Moscow has more . . . more of your kind!

Morozov   What is this interrogation?

Voice   What was the name of your first pet?

Morozov   What? I don't get it, is this a court trial or am I resetting my email password?

Voice   Have you ever had a pet?

Morozov   I had a cat. What does it . . .

Voice   A cat. Well, of course it was a cat. If you'd had a dog . . . What was the cat's name?

Morozov   Murzik, and later Krzysztof.

Voice   Why?

Morozov   I thought it sounded better, more noble. As he grew old, he lost his teeth. I felt that it would be easier for him to pronounce a name with lots of "sh" sounds in it. Also, it is the name of the great Polish composer Penderecki.[2]

Voice   You had a cat, and you renamed it. Do you see the connection to your sexual orientation?

Morozov   No, I don't.

Voice   I think it's obvious. You believe that you can do whatever you want to a living thing: a name change is just a stone's throw away from sex change. Isn't that right?

Morozov   That's nonsense.

Voice (*gets out a copy of the* Big City *magazine*)[3]   Have you undergone the therapy assigned to you by the court?

Morozov   I have.

Voice   Any results?

Morozov   No, no results.

Voice   So, you mean, the result was negative?

Morozov   The device keeps registering sexual arousal . . .

Voice   Did you try the John Marquis masturbation method?

Morozov   I did. The result was negative.

Voice   Aversion therapy?

Morozov   I did. The result was negative.

Voice   Coitus with a woman?

Morozov   Oh, the result was categorically negative. With vomit.

Voice   Hormonal treatment?

Morozov   Still negative.

Voice   Therapy sessions?

Morozov   I fell in love with the therapist . . . So, it was negative, definitely negative.

Voice   What about riding a bicycle?

Morozov   Didn't work.

Voice   Riding a bicycle didn't work?

Morozov   No, it didn't.

Voice   Are we correct in understanding that, having tried all known treatments, you acknowledge your inefficacy in curing homosexualism and voluntarily agree to be treated with the apparatus known as "135"?

Pause.

Voice   What is your answer?

Morozov   Yes, I do.

Voice   Do you understand that Apparatus 135 is an experimental treatment, and its effectiveness cannot be guaranteed?

Pause.

Voice   You have to say "Yes, I do."

Pause.

Voice   Alexander Morozov!

Vovochka

Vovochka   Hi, everyone, I'm Vova. My mother raised me alone, no father in the picture, so I kind of had everything laid out for me to become a homosexualist. Moreover, at some point, my mom left me, too, so my grandmother had to step in. It's only thanks to my grandmother—with her harsh personality and will power, her shouting and beating—that I haven't turned into a pervert as a child.

My grandmother often pulled my ears really hard and told me that if I didn't listen to her, I wouldn't grow up to be a man, but a sissy wearing pants. If I cried, my grandmother would pull out her lipstick, put me in front of a mirror, and paint my lips red: "Look, you're a whiny little girl, just look at yourself right now."

Thank you, kind Grandma, for saving me! No wonder I started pondering at a very early age what would have become of me if it hadn't been for my grandmother's support. By now I'd have probably turned into a drug addict and would be prancing around in a miniskirt. Or I'd be grabbing kids on the street and kissing them on the mouth, just like perverts all over the world do these days.

Not everyone has the ability to distinguish gays from normal people. I must have been given this gift from Lord God Himself. For example, once I saw two guys on the trolleybus. They seemed off to me. You know, when you can't really put a finger on it; it's just something intangible: the turn of the head, the flick of the wrist, the pose, the voice.

They were talking about a meeting, that one of them hadn't felt well and then had felt okay again; they mentioned a café, an earring.

But it all pales in comparison to what one of them said to the other right after that. Before he did it, he looked around to check if anyone could hear them.

His eyes glanced over me—he must have thought, oh, he's just a kid, no worries. And then he stepped closer to the other guy and told him, "I love you."

I knew it! As soon as I saw them, I felt that there was something abnormal, something gross about them! But what really pissed me off was that they just dismissed me! Well, get that, you damn faggots, you should never dismiss children, I'll make sure you remember that! I'll show you that the state and society protect me! And so does my grandmother!

I decided to follow them. It turned out that they lived just a block away from my home. Sodom, in my backyard! They parted by the entrance to the building, and I overheard them arrange another meeting and a trip to the store to buy a big air mattress. Damn you, idiots! It's one thing to fondle each other secretly, in a dark alley, but it's a completely different level to go and buy a big bed together. I also picked up from their conversation that one of them was an artist or something, whereas the other was in the military. The military? Did I hear that right? Can there be fags in the army? My mother used to tell me that my father had been in the military, that he had beaten her, and would have probably beaten me if he'd stuck around any longer.

Oh, then my grandmother would have been spared this burden! If you don't beat boys, they grow up fags, just like these two. No wonder the first is a homosexualist. The art world is full of this poison. The bummer about it is that it's really hard to destroy the life of people in the arts. Their friends are usually homosexualists, too, or they sympathize with them and even protect them. I think the only right thing to do when you meet a homosexualist is to run, if you are unarmed, or to shoot or stab them, if you are armed.

It's hard to disgrace such a person in front of his dear friends who are all just like him. But we all have neighbors; most of them are normal people. Disgrace can mess with anyone's life.

You know, they say we repress homosexualists. But if we really repressed them, they would be living in a ghetto, but look, there they are, living freely among us. Which means that the neighbors of a homosexualist may and should know about him, don't you agree?

Oh, you don't? Well, let me explain! It all comes down to children. It doesn't matter much to an adult, but kids . . . If you share the hallway with a homosexualist, you know that your child is in danger the moment he steps outside the door. Even just a door ajar to a homosexualist's apartment can pose danger. A child might see something bright or colorful inside, just by accident, and get curious about it— eventually, get perverted by it. That's why . . . the neighbors have a right to know.

Pause.

But how do I find out where exactly these two air mattress guys live? I've been following them for two weeks, and it seems that they've started to notice me. Once, they saw me and shouted, "Hi." I sprinted away so fast I almost got run over by a truck. What do I do now that I can't get close to them anymore? As I looked for a solution, I realized that I needed help—a child who could carry out simple orders.

Come here, Vanya.

Vanya *enters.*

Vovochka   Look at him. That's exactly who I need.

Vanya   I'm Vanya!

Vovochka   Not now. Tell them where and how we met.

Vanya *won't speak.*

Vovochka   We met . . .

Vanya   In a cafeteria! In a cafeteria!

Vovochka   Yes, but now I'm telling the story. Vanya and I go to the same school. Once, my grandmother came back from a parent–teacher conference and told me that Vanya has also grown up without a dad. I thought then, oh God, this boy is also under the threat of homosexualism. Once, in the cafeteria, I sat next to him, looked him straight in the eyes and asked . . .

Vanya   If I knew what homosexualism was!

Vovochka   Jesus! Will you ever learn not to interrupt?

Vanya   I told him I knew! It's when it's like Pyotr Ilyich Tchaikovsky.

Vovochka   What about Tchaikovsky?

Vanya   He was . . .

Vovochka   What was he?

Vanya   That's what our teacher told us when . . . when we went to see *The Nutcracker*. It's not my fault! She said that, and everybody laughed.

Vovochka   She said what?! In front of children?!

Vanya   Yes . . .

Vovochka   Dirty bitch! We'll deal with her later. Tell them, now, Vanya, how you helped me with the mission.

Vanya   I . . .

Vovochka   You know what, it's better if I do it. So, I followed the fag couple back to their house, to the building entrance, but I couldn't follow them up the stairs. This is where Vanya came in. He agreed to follow the homosexualists to their apartment door. You have to agree, if you're being followed by an adult, it's dangerous and scary, but when you're followed by a kid, especially a sweet boy like Vanya, it's even kind of flattering. Vanya sneaked through the door when the two entered the building and took the elevator with them. I asked Vanya to go to their floor and see which apartment they entered and then come back, all without attracting their attention.

Vanya   When I stepped into the elevator, they asked me which floor I needed, but obviously, I didn't know which floor it was. So, I asked them where they were going. They told me they were going to the eighth floor, and I said, I am also going to the eighth floor. So, we came to the eighth floor, they got out of the elevator, and I also stepped out to see where they would go.

Vovochka   You did what?! They weren't supposed to see you! They could have killed you!

Vanya   They asked me, do you want something, kid? And I . . .

Vovochka   Oh God!

Vanya   And I asked them, are you homosexualists?

Vovochka   Jesus!

Vanya   They smiled and told me, you're too small to know these things, and they kept walking. "Yeah, keep walking—I told them—only, I'm not small. I've already seen Tchaikovsky with my school." One of them, the guy with big ears, laughed and told me to wait.

Vovochka   You should have run! He could have grabbed a rope inside to tie you up!

Vanya   They entered the apartment, and then the guy with ears came back and gave me a little ballerina—just like I saw in Tchaikovsky, only made of porcelain.

Vovochka   Alright, wrap it up, this is all rubbish. What's the apartment number?

Vanya   Sixty-four.

Vovochka   Thanks, you can go now.

Vanya   Just give me back the ballerina.

Vovochka   Go, I told you.

Vanya   Give it back to me!

Vovochka   Go! I destroyed it; it could have been infected. The things they could've done with it . . . (*Strokes* **Vanya**'s *hair.*) You could've caught homosexualism from it . . .

Vanya *pushes him and runs away.*

Vovochka   Now that I knew in which apartment they lived, I could act. (*He takes out a piece of paper and starts reading it out loud.*)

Dear neighbors! Good morning, afternoon, or evening, depending on the time of the day this letter finds you. It was written by a child who matured early and found himself in a terrible world that the adults had left for him. In this world, dangers are plenty, dear neighbors. One of them is homosexualism.

You may object by saying that there are many other dangers—pollution, pesticides, terrorism. You may even ask me where I have seen homosexualism. "In apartment 64," is my answer.

Have you ever paid attention to your neighbors? Alas, we have become too indifferent to each other. But sometimes you have to open your eyes and ask, who are these two guys who always come and leave together. They walk out the same door and both walk back in. And of course, behind this door, they can do whatever they want. But any door, even one that is properly closed, has a crack for the air to pass. And there is a crack just like this between the door and the wall of apartment 64. And the air coming through of it reeks. It reeks of sodomy, same-sex games, and same-sex caresses! This air can reach you, by chance, but more importantly—it can reach your children.

Oh, you say you don't care? You don't care who your son is going to become? You don't care if a boy starts putting on lipstick, wearing dresses, and cooking borscht? You don't care that you won't grow old surrounded by grandchildren, but in a sad state of loneliness? Sodomites always abandon their parents; they prefer to live with their own kind.

But if you do care, then we can seal up this crack together! We can plug the black hole of homosexualism!

Yours, LH.

He tucks the paper away.

LH means "Little Hero." I would like people to call me that. But I couldn't be the one to start calling myself that, obviously, so I would usually tell others that it meant "liquidator of homosexualists."

Pause.

Vovochka   The letter was ready, we made just enough copies to distribute to every apartment in the building. I printed the letter and tasked Vanya with putting it into every mailbox.

Vanya, come here, tell them how you followed my instructions.

Vanya (*voice*)   I won't . . .

Vovochka   Why not, Vanya?

Vanya   You'll yell at me again.

Vovochka   Damn right I will! Because you made the brilliant decision to put the letter in *every* mailbox, even the one that belongs to the homosexualists! What were you thinking!

Vanya   You didn't tell me anything about that!

Vovochka   Is it so hard to use your brain? God, you're such an idiot. Alright, come here, I forgive you . . .

Vanya   I won't, you'll start groping me and stroking my head again.

Vovochka   What?! Don't listen to him, he's just a stupid kid. So, we put the letters into all of the mailboxes and the waiting began. For three days, I watched the building, the windows, what was going on. Four days, five days went by, nothing happened. Damn neighbors! I decided to be more active. And as soon as both homosexualists left their home . . .

He changes into overalls, puts on a fake mustache. He approaches apartment 63 and rings the doorbell.

Female Neighbor (*opens the door*)   Hello, sweetie, is there something I can help you with?

Vovochka   Not really, I'm just here to deliver this package. And, by the way, I am not a sweetie, I'm a grown man, don't you see the mustache?

Female Neighbor   My mistake. I thought you were a kid who'd glued on a mustache.

Vovochka   I have a very young face, so many people think I'm a kid and propose a lot of indecent things to me. (*Hands her the box.*) Sign here to accept.

Female Neighbor   What is it? I didn't order anything . . .

Vovochka   You didn't? Oh, that's weird . . . I have the address right here: Bolshaya Dudukinskaya Street, house 42, apartment 63. Maybe somebody made a mistake, and it should go to that apartment, number 64? By the way, who lives there?

Female Neighbor   Oh, two nice young men. Alexander and Sergey.

Vovochka (*to the side*)   Alexander and Sergey . . . These are the sodomites' names.

(*To the* **Female Neighbor.**) I wonder what this Alexander and Sergey of yours could have ordered off a gay website.

Female Neighbor   Alexander works in publishing and Sergey is in the military. They're really, really nice.

Vovochka   Right, 'cause "nice" is just the right description of people who buy stuff off a gay website.

Female Neighbor   I don't think they're home right now.

Vovochka   Do you hear me, I'm saying gay website . . .

Female Neighbor   I'm not quite sure if I can accept the delivery on their behalf. I don't know whether it will be alright or convenient for them.

Vovochka   If I were you, I wouldn't be accepting a delivery that homosexualists secretly ordered at a store for homosexualists!

Female Neighbor   Maybe, it's a pump? They've got an air mattress, you know.

Vovochka   That must be it! A pump for sodomites!

Female Neighbor   Wait a moment, I think I actually have Alexander's phone number written down somewhere. I'll give him a quick call . . .

She leaves.

Vovochka   Damn old fool! How many times do I have to keep telling her that her neighbors are homosexualists who buy awful toys. It's as if she didn't hear me at all there, and now look, she's calling them. No way, I'm not sticking around to talk to these two. I'd better go . . .

Runs away.

Female Neighbor (*comes back*)   Yes, just a second, I'll pass him the phone. Oh, he's left . . . No . . . Alexander, listen, the boy with the fake mustache is gone. But I swear, he was here just a minute ago . . .

Vovochka, *alone.*

Vovochka   What can you expect from such neighbors? What decisive action against homosexualists? A homosexual den will flourish in their backyard, and they don't care! They don't care about the children who could accidentally end up in this den. "I need to act more decisively," I said to myself.

He rings the bell of apartment 65.

Male Neighbor (*opens the door*)   Hello, kiddo. I hope you're using a hypoallergic glue that won't make your skin hurt?

Vovochka   Excuse me? What glue are you talking about?

Male Neighbor   Well, the one that holds your mustache.

Vovochka (*fixes the mustache*)   Damn it. (*To the neighbor.*) I deliver packages for a sex shop. A gay sex shop. I have a delivery for this apartment—(*reads*) "Soft Silicone Huge Realistic Male Artificial Penis Motorized Sex Product 00069." Please, sign here to accept.

Vovochka *hands him the box and the papers.*

Male Neighbor (*signs*)   Thank you.

He takes the box and closes the door.

Vovochka   Hey, wait . . . (*Knocks on the door.*) Hey! (*Bangs.*) Hey!

Male Neighbor (*opens the door*)   What is it?

Vovochka   This package is not for you, it's for your neighbors. I made a mistake.

Male Neighbor   You have to pay for your mistakes.

He is about to close the door.

Vovochka   Wait! Have a heart! (*Tears the mustache off.*) I'm just a kid!

Male Neighbor   Why does a kid work as a courier for a sex shop?

Vovochka   Because our country has been overrun by the likes of your neighbors!

Male Neighbor   Well, don't worry. They'll be back home in the evening, I'll give them the box.

Vovochka (*hysterically*)   Do you understand what I'm saying? Don't you see that two guys live together and order an artificial penis from a sex shop?

Male Neighbor   Delivered by a little boy with fake moustache . . .

Vovochka   That part doesn't matter! What matters in this story is . . .

Male Neighbor   Listen, boy, why don't you go along now before I call the police.

Shuts the door.

Pause.

Vovochka   I was devastated, I almost lost faith . . . Put yourselves in my position: I know where two homosexuals live, I warn their neighbors like a city is warned about shelling in wartime, and . . . You think anything happens? No, nobody cares!

Stomps his feet.

I know why this is happening! It's all Vanya's fault, this little idiot!

Vanya (*voice*)   And here we go again . . .

Vovochka   You stuck a letter in their mailbox and gave them time to get ready! Those devils made friends with their neighbors—something we hadn't foreseen. What do we do now? What do we do? (*Sobs loudly.*)

Wait . . . I think . . . I might have a solution! Neighbors aren't just the people who live in the same building, they also live in the building nearby or just down the street from you. There's more of them. Some of them may be more open to what I have to say . . .

I printed more, way more letters and distributed them in the buildings nearby—all around the block, and on the bus stops next to the house. Imagine my happiness when the following day, I came to check on my same-sex bastards and saw that one of their windows was broken. But this wasn't the only joy—their door was smeared with paint, spelling out the words that I refuse to say out loud but that inevitably come to my mind whenever I think about these degenerates . . .

I was standing there, looking at the door with the words painted all over it with something sticky and stinky, and I realized that we so often underestimate our great people, the simple guy next door. Give people the right tools to express their opinion, and they will absolutely do so! Give them the right tools, and they will rise and punish those who make their lives unbearable! Give them the right tools, and they . . .

I watched the windows and the door of the homosexualists' apartment for a couple more days. They had taped the window glass, but it took them two days to wash the writing off the door. I contributed by writing "faggots" over it with a marker, but they managed to get that off, too. And when it seemed that my job was done and their punishment served, my next visit to their door revealed that somebody had used spray foam to seal it shut!

Laughs.

Just think of it! Somebody had the balls, the wit, to literally do what I had called for in my letter: "But if you do care, then we can seal up this crack together! We can plug the black hole of homosexualism!"

That's when I realized I had really underestimated our great people. Give people the right tools to rape . . . to represent their opinion, the things they can do! Give them spray paint and spray foam, and they'll be quick to identify those who bother them in their lives.

I just couldn't take my eyes off that door; my gaze was literally glued to it. What a beauty! I felt I could hear them scratching at it from inside . . . (*Puts his ear against the door.*)

Fags . . . Still breathing . . .

Apartment 64

Sergey   It started with this awful letter to our neighbors . . .

Morozov   We thought that was it.

Sergey   It was the end of the road for our life in that apartment. But Sasha said . . .

Morozov   I said, why don't we write a letter of our own?

Sergey   So, we did.

Morozov   Dear neighbors! A couple of days ago you received a strange letter in your mailbox alongside your bills and supermarket flyers. A sort of warning. A warning about us. About two guys who live together. We will neither confirm nor deny what that letter says about us. Why? Because smart people like you most probably don't care. You must be thinking, what difference does it make what these two guys do to each other as long as they don't break the elevator. If this is what you've been thinking, then we were not mistaken in our judgement about you as smart, educated people. It is a pleasure to have neighbors like you.

Respectfully.

Sergey   I tried to talk him out of writing this letter. I thought it was very dangerous, that we would just draw even more attention to ourselves . . .

Enters the **Female Neighbor**, *cake in her hands.*

Female Neighbor   Hello boys, may I take a few minutes of your day?

She walks into the living room and puts the cake on the table.

Female Neighbor   Is it true that you . . .? Is it?

Sergey   What?

Morozov   What?

Female Neighbor   Well . . . Is it true that . . . Well, I see that it is! I am so happy!

Morozov   You are?

Female Neighbor   Well, of course! It's so much better than having neighbors from the Caucasus or those things from Central Asia. Or if you loved girls and had loud parties with them. You are so nice and sweet, and you have a door mat. And some evenings you listen to music . . .

Morozov   Does it bother you?

Female Neighbor   Oh, not at all, I mean, after all, it's Saint-Saëns, Monteverdi, or Purcell. (*She takes out a photo.*) Tell me, boys, can you identify *this* from a photo?

Sergey   What "*this*"?

Female Neighbor   My grandson, I think he is . . . (*Gives them the photo.*) Have a look, please.

Morozov   Well, it's hard to tell anything from a photo . . .

Sergey (*looks at the photo*)   Yes, he is. I am almost sure.

Female Neighbor   Oh, that's just wonderful! I was so worried that the boy wouldn't achieve anything in life!

Sergey   How do you mean?

Female Neighbor   Well, you know, gays, they . . . well, they look after each other. Being gay is already halfway to success. Gays are rich, they're handsome, they eat yoghurt.

Sergey   Sorry to disappoint but I'm afraid your grandson will still have to do some things on his own.

Female Neighbor   Oh, but he does! He buys clothes, books, goes to the cinema.

Sergey   I am afraid . . .

Morozov (*jumps in*)   We'd be delighted to meet your grandson.

Female Neighbor   Oh, it will be such a joy to introduce him to you! Have a good day!

Leaves.

Sergey   What just happened?

Morozov   Well, I guess some people think that if you're gay, your life is easy.

Enters the **Male Neighbor**.

Male Neighbor   Not everyone thinks so. I think that people like you need treatment.

Sergey   What kind of treatment?

Morozov   Why?

Male Neighbor   Because you rape children.

Sergey   But that's pedophiles you're talking about!

Male Neighbor   Right, isn't that what you are?

Morozov   No, we're gays.

Male Neighbor   Well, but you break the elevator and write on the walls in the hallway.

Sergey   But that's punks you're talking about!

Male Neighbor   Right, isn't that what you are?

Morozov   No, we're gays.

Male Neighbor   Well, alright, but you embezzle public funds and you've destroyed our country.

Sergey   But that's politicians you're talking about!

Male Neighbor   Right, isn't that what you are?

Morozov   No, we're gays.

Male Neighbor   Alright, but . . . what do you do then?

Sergey   We live together.

Male Neighbor   Why?

Morozov   I guess because we love each other.

Male Neighbor   But how? . . . How can you love each other? How do you do that?

Sergey   You know . . .

Sergey *comes close to the* **Male Neighbor** *and whispers something into his ear.*

Male Neighbor   But that's impossible!

Sergey *shrugs.*

Male Neighbor   Have you ever wanted to hit on me? To wink at me? To ride the elevator with me so that you can . . .

Sergey   No!

Male Neighbor   And what about the elevator? Do you fancy breaking it? Smashing the lights in it, messing with the buttons?

Morozov   Never, why would we?

Male Neighbor   Then I don't care, do whatever you want as long as you don't mess with the elevator.

He leaves.

Morozov   See, Seryozha, one can always find common ground with neighbors.

Sergey   Maybe, maybe . . .

Morozov   Why are you acting like this? After all, it's different for you! Unlike me, you're a real man.

Sergey   All men are real men.

Morozov   It happened mid-autumn. You know, the time they call Indian summer. When it's still warm, the sun is still shining, you still feel like something good could happen. I was walking by a military base. I mean, I didn't know it was a military base. I was just walking along an ochre-colored wall.

Suddenly, I heard drums: rat-tat-tat-ratta-tat-tat. It was so unexpected that I was startled and I stopped, but I didn't shrink; instead, I straightened up, like a soldier. My heart was beating faster, stronger—as fast as it possibly could.

I heard young men's voices: they were shouting the count and the orders while marching. I couldn't see them, but I could hear each and every one of them. And each of them made my blood speed faster through my heart. Ten; no, more—fifty, a hundred, a hundred and fifty young throats were shouting there.

I stopped, leaned on my arm against the wall, my palm slid, and ochre paint got under my nails. The drumbeat, the voices, a year and a half without sex. I had an erection. Somebody walked through the door and stopped by the gate.

Sergey   I had already changed and was wearing my civilian clothes. I walked out the gate and paused to check if my earring was in the shirt pocket: I was afraid I'd forgotten it. Sometimes, when I got to the base, I would forget to take it out, sometimes I'd forget to put it on, and sometimes I simply had no idea where I'd left it. This time, I remembered it, when I saw a man. If he weren't so young, I would have thought he was having a heart attack: he was leaning on the wall and could barely stand.

Morozov   He came up to me and asked if I was OK.

Sergey   Are you OK?

Morozov   I told him I wasn't, I wasn't OK. Because if I'd told him I was, he would have left.

Sergey   I wouldn't have.

Morozov   He held me by the elbow and walked me down the street. I didn't need help walking but I liked it more that way.

Sergey   We grabbed a table at a street cafe.

Morozov   I told him I was a journalist and an editor.

Sergey   I told him I was a lance corporal.

Morozov   I ordered water.

Sergey   And I ordered vodka. I was really into him. And then I just got the earring out of my pocket and put it on. And he got it.

The air mattress fills with air.

Morozov   And I got it.

Sergey   You may wonder, what does it matter that a guy puts on an earring. Like, what's so special about it. But there are signs that only people who know will get, while others will miss them completely . . .

A stone breaks the window glass.

Because if others could understand them too . . .

Drumbeat.

You'd have to come up with new ones.

Morozov   New ones.

Sergey   And if you can't hide anymore . . .

The door of the room disappears.

Morozov   First, they broke our window, then they wrote on our front door, and then the door was just gone. I have no idea what they did, but it simply wouldn't open.

The lights go off.

Sergey   There was nothing but darkness in the peephole. They'd done something to the door. I just wanted to get out and beat the crap out of them. To keep fighting with them until I saw their blood. But the moment when I told myself, that's enough, it can't go on like this anymore, by that moment, I already couldn't get out . . .

Morozov   We didn't know what to do. We couldn't get out of the apartment to go to work: me—to the publishing office, him—to the military base. And then I called a friend. He came, called me back, and told us what they'd done to the door. We called the police, they came, walked back and forth in front of the door, gave it a couple of kicks for no apparent reason and left. That was it . . .

Sergey   That was it, do you get it? Nothing could be done, nobody could help. We had been imprisoned in our home, so that we wouldn't be able to get out; we had been put in a coffin like dead men.

Morozov   I told him that instead of worrying, we should see the humor in this situation.

Sergey   The humor? What fucking humor are you talking about? They won't let us get out of the apartment: I can't get out, you can't get out. At least we have a window so there's still air to breathe.

Morozov   I turned on the music to help the time pass while we were waiting for the police to come back.

Sergey   They won't come back!

Morozov   I turned on the music.

Sergey   Tomorrow our door will disappear, again. And then again, every single day!

Morozov   I turned on the music.

Sergey   It's all because of your music.

Morozov   That's not true!

Sergey   It made me do that thing.

Morozov   That's not true, I tried to talk you out of it. I told you that you shouldn't do it, that it was dangerous. Our apartment was on a top floor, but you told me that you'd done it in a training session, that climbing down the gutter was easy.

Sergey   There's no way I could have known this would happen . . .

The lights fade away.

Vovochka *fiddles with a porcelain ballerina.*

Vovochka (*drops the ballerina*)   Oops, it broke.

The air leaves the air mattress; it flattens down to the ground, ultimately disappearing from the view.

Crematorium

Morozov   I agree.

Voice   You have to state your consent three times for volunteer participation in testing an experimental treatment of homosexuality by Apparatus 135. State your consent now.

Morozov   I agree. Why would I live without him? And face loneliness, again?

Voice   State your consent.

Morozov   I agree. Why would I live alone in a society that hates me?

Voice   State your consent.

Morozov   Why would I live and suffer if even my death is going to be shameful?

Voice   Congratulations, you have confirmed your participation. You'll have to wait some time before . . .

Morozov   I want you to start right away.

Voice   The apparatus has not yet been set . . .

The lights fade away.

Morozov (*voice*)   Don't you dare lie to me! Turn it on! Turn your machine on now! I want you to do it right now! What else do I have to wait for? Here I am, and there is death. Bring us together, don't wait! You wanted me dead, so why wait? There's a limit to everything, even to death. It has already found me; I am dead from head to toe. Turn on the machine! I'm begging you! I can't, I just can't do it anymore! After all, I'm not the only one you can torture. It means nothing to you, nothing. Please . . . Just turn on the machine and pull the switch.

The lights fade away.

Part Two

Mom, Mom

Playground. **Lyubochka** *is sitting on a bench.* **Vanya** *enters and sits down next to her. He looks around, then gives* **Lyubochka** *a kiss. She blushes and immediately slaps him on the face.*

Vanya What are you doing?! Idiot!

Lyubochka I could say the same about you.

Vanya Lesbian.

Lyubochka I am not a lesbian.

Vanya If you aren't a lesbian, why did you slap me?

Lyubochka Because I don't want you to kiss me.

Vanya I knew it, that's how I know you're a lesbian!

Lyubochka Do you even know what a lesbian is?

Vanya Of course I do. They're women who don't want to kiss me.

Lyubochka So does that mean every girl who won't kiss you is a lesbian?

Vanya I'll tell everyone . . .

Lyubochka What will you tell everyone?

Vanya We have to tell everyone, so that people know that you lesbians are like this . . .

Lyubochka What are you talking about? Where are you getting all this?

Vanya That's what Vova says. Vova knows.

Lyubochka Oh, that clown.

Vanya He's not a clown, he's my best friend. Nobody wanted to be friends with me, but he did. Even if he's sleazy and always strokes my hair. But he's the only friend I've got. I told Vova that I've been in love with you for two weeks already, and he said, go and kiss her, if she pushes you away, she's a lesbian. He said we'll tell everyone about you.

Lyubochka It might have helped if you'd learned to kiss first and then tried it.

Vanya How can I learn? Vova offered me his help, but I don't want to do it anymore, his mouth is so slobbery . . .

Lyubochka Vova offered you his help?

Vanya (*gets scared*) Just don't tell anyone, or we'll tell everyone about you.

Lyubochka   Tell everyone whatever you want, I don't care. Then I'll just tell everyone that you two always hang out together, like two fruits.

Vanya   That's not true!

Lyubochka   Neither is your story about me.

Vanya   It's just that people who I like don't want to be friends with me. You, for example.

Lyubochka   Just don't start off with a kiss on the neck.

Vanya   I got the idea from Vova. He kissed me once like that, but it was my birthday.

Lyubochka   Stop hanging out with him. He's in high school and nobody likes him there because he's sleazy. You can be friends with me, just do something about your hair.

Vanya (*messes up his hair*)   For real? Do you love me back?

Lyubochka   That again? And so soon? Love is not something that happens immediately. Love is like Tolstoy's *War and Peace*. Very long. Sometimes you suffer for the person you love, maybe even die.

Vanya   Did Tolstoy say that?

Lyubochka   My mom says that.

Vanya (*sits closer to her*)   Wanna know what Vova says?

Lyubochka   I don't care.

Vanya   But it's really interesting, it's a secret I promised not to tell anyone.

Lyubochka   If you promised, then don't tell. He's your friend.

Vanya   He's sleazy . . .

Lyubochka   Even if he's sleazy, it's still a secret. What if I share a secret with you—will you tell it to everybody?

Vanya   I won't because you aren't sleazy.

Lyubochka   What if everybody tells you that I am, what then?

Vanya   My lips will be sealed. What's your secret?

Lyubochka   It's a secret.

Vanya   You must have already done it . . .

Lyubochka   Done what?

Vanya   Well, that . . . sex.

Lyubochka   No, of course not.

Vanya   Vova showed me a newspaper which says that all children our age have had sex already.

Lyubochka   As far as I'm concerned, Vova can go eat that newspaper.

Vanya   Alright, I thought that was your secret, that you've had sex, not that you have two moms . . .

Lyubochka   Wha-at?

Vanya   Oops.

Lyubochka   Wha-at?

Vanya *is silent; he stares at* **Lyubochka**.

Lyubochka   Did Vova tell you this?

Vanya (*nods*)   I won't tell . . .

Lyubochka   How does he know that, your sleazy Vova?

Vanya   So, it's true?

Lyubochka *is silent.*

Vanya   He followed you.

Lyubochka   Followed me?

Vanya   He is very observant. His grandma gave him a yellow phone, he makes notes of everything on it.

Lyubochka   Can you find out what he wrote there about me?

Vanya   I can . . . I think . . . I don't know . . . I will. For you.

Lyubochka   Please.

Tries to kiss him.

Vanya (*pushes her off*)   Not yet, I have to earn it.

Lyubochka   You're my little hero.

Vanya *winces.*

Lyubochka   What's wrong?

Vanya   He calls himself that.

The lights fade away.

The same playground but with **Vovochka** *in* **Lyubochka**'s *place.*

Vovochka   Go on, you were saying that I was your best friend . . .

Vanya   Yes . . . my best friend . . . There's no one like you . . . You're good, not like everyone else . . . You think about children . . .

Vovochka   Which children?

Vanya   Well, children like me, like others . . .

Vovochka   Oh, these children.

Vanya   You think how to make sure adults don't molest us.

Vovochka   That's true, sometimes I do think about children. Why?

Vanya   I'm so grateful to you. (*He takes* **Vovochka**'s *hand to mask his disgust.*)
Thank you.

Pause. **Vovochka** *leans over to kiss him, but then realizes something and moves away
from him.*

Vanya   What's wrong?

Vovochka   You're lying to me.

Vanya   Me? Why would you say that?

Vovochka   I don't know yet.

Vanya   But I . . .

Vovochka   Sexual arousal prevents you from thinking straight.

Vanya   What do you mean?

Vovochka   Do you masturbate?

Vanya   You mean, jerk off? What about you?

Vovochka   I asked first.

Vanya   But . . .

Vovochka   I asked first.

Vanya   Your questions are so . . .

Vovochka   See, you can't even tell me that and you swear I'm your best friend.

Vanya   I do sometimes.

Vovochka   How often? When was the last time you did it?

Vanya   Today . . .

Vovochka   Today? What were you thinking about when you were doing it?

Vanya   Well . . . parts of women . . .

Vovochka (*jumps off the bench*)   I knew it! I knew it! This idiot Lyubochka, she's
perverted you!

Vanya   That's not true!

Vovochka   Are you taking her side in this?!

Vanya   I have no one else but you, Vovochka!

Vovochka   She must have opened her legs for you already and has allowed you to touch her . . .

Vanya   No, she hasn't!

Vovochka   Oh, then it just means she's been perverted by her two so-called mothers! We have two child victims of perversion on our hands! I am sorry for both of you! I am so sorry for you, Vanechka!

He wants to kiss **Vanya**. **Vanya** *pushes* **Vovochka** *away; he falls.*

Vanya   I am sorry! I didn't mean it! I wanted . . .

Vovochka (*getting up*)   You didn't want . . . As always . . . And this girl of yours . . . Well, I knew it was going to end up like this . . . Be happy, the two of you, damn you!

He is about to leave. **Vanya** *catches up with him and hugs him from the back. They are standing together. Pause.* **Vanya**, *with a martyr's expression, kisses* **Vovochka** *on the nape of the neck.*

Vovochka   Nobody can find out what you just did.

Vanya   Uh-huh.

Vovochka   What you just did is horrible.

Vanya   Uh-huh.

Vovochka   I had my suspicions about these perversions in you. I saw them in the way you look at me, in the way you breathe . . .

Vanya   Uh-huh.

Vovochka   Are you in love with me?

Vanya (*looks like he's spitting something out*)   I am, very much.

Vovochka (*turns around*)   My poor boy, you've been perverted. But it's alright, I'll help you out of this nightmare. You and me. You and me. Say it.

Vanya   You and me.

Vovochka   Forever.

Vanya (*horrified*)   Forever?

Vovochka   Meanwhile, you can't tell anyone about . . . (*Looks him straight in the eyes.*) Did this girl ask you to do it to find out something about me?

Vanya (*nervous*)   What?

Vovochka   Why are you nervous?

Vanya   It's just . . . your arms, your eyes . . .

Vovochka   Oh, I see, it's just your perverse thoughts . . . So, did this girl put you up to finding out what I know?

Vanya   She didn't.

Vovochka   What if she had?

Vanya   I'd tell her to go fuck herself.

Vovochka (*laughs*)   Good boy. (*Pats him on the cheeks.*) Smart boy, that's how you handle these bitches who ripen too early.

They laugh.

Vanya   Vovochka . . .

Vovochka   Yes?

Vanya   I'd really like it if you could also trust me.

Vovochka   What are you talking about?

Vanya   Well, if you'd share some things that you find out with me. Of course, if you think that I might tell somebody else, then don't do it . . . But I'd really love it if you let me into your yellow phone.

Vovochka (*steps away from him*)   Why do you need to know all this? All this filth that people do . . .

Vanya   Because I am here to help you.

Vovochka   Well, if you betray me . . . I don't know what I'd do to you, but whatever I'd do, they won't put me in jail, 'cause I'm still a child, like you. It's adults that aren't allowed to do anything to us, but children to children—that's another story.

Pause.

Look, these two women, one of them is Lyubochka's biological so-called mother. The other one is her lover; she lives with them. I can't stand the thought that the first one works with children. Children with disabilities! She calls herself a special education teacher. Do you see how filthy this is?

Vanya   How filthy?

Vovochka   Well, these children are already out of luck because they have a disability, and now they have a lesbian working with them. As for the other one . . . She doesn't have kids of her own, so she must be tormented by that. That's why she got the crazy idea to adopt a child from foster care, not to feel flawed. What a monster!

Vanya   Why?

Vovochka   Why? Because she's a woman! She can give birth, she's healthy, but the thought of having to touch a man is disgusting to her. She can't even stand the idea of a man coming up to her, caressing her, holding her hand . . .

Old Woman

An **Old Woman** *pulls* **Vovochka** *by the ear.*

Old Woman   . . . hold your hand? . . . caress you? Do you want to be caressed by a man, you little bastard?

Vovochka   Ouch! I was talking about that lesbian!

Old Woman   Which lesbian?

Vovochka   The one who lives with the mother of a girl in my class.

Old woman   I can't hear anything, speak up!

Vovochka   I am saying . . . ouch . . . a lesbian!

Old Woman (*tries to grab him*)   Are you calling me a lesbian? Oh wait till I get to you!

Vovochka   No! Not you! In my class!

Old Woman   What? A classroom full of lesbians? How did you end up there? I knew this would happen . . .

She pushes her grandson; he falls.

What else do I have to do so that you grow up normal?

Vovochka (*rubs his ear*)   You've done . . . everything . . .

Old Woman   I don't have the strength anymore to beat you every day. Now the only thing I can do is pull you by the ear.

Vovochka   I am trying, very hard. I'm . . .

Old Woman   Oh, I'm so sick of you, so sick! Your father walked out on your mother the moment they showed him what she had given birth to. Even if you were lined up next to a bunch of monkeys, you'd be the ugliest. The face doesn't matter though—the man doesn't need a face. But even your mother left you because she knew what she had given birth to.

Vovochka   What?

Pause.

Vovochka (*louder*)   What? (*Loud.*) What? (*Shouts.*) What?

Old Woman   Why are you shouting?

Vovochka   What did she give birth to?!

Old Woman   You.

Pause.

Vovochka (*whispers*)   Why don't I just kill you?

Old Woman   Because you're a coward.

Vovochka   Oh, so you do hear me, you old witch.

Old Woman   I do . . . I hear every drop of saliva go down your throat . . . Why don't you kill me? Because they'll throw you in juvi with all the other little bastards just like you. People there will know what to do with your sweet little ass.

Vovochka   Do children get punished for crimes?

Old Woman   They do! And if I die on my own, then they'll shove you into foster care, where everyone loves sweet-ass boys like you just as much.

Vovochka   But I can just leave you here alone. Let you lie in your shit and not let you out of the apartment. I could even torture you. Aren't you afraid I'll do that?

Old Woman   Me, afraid of you, sucker? (*She beats him.*) I can beat you with my cane until your guts fall out, and your body gets cold at my feet. You don't even see what's right in front of you.

Vovochka   What are you talking about?

Old Woman   Our neighbor.

Vovochka   Which neighbor? Uncle Misha, from the upper floor?

Old Woman   No, I'm talking about our new neighbor next door.

Vovochka   Does somebody live there?

Old Woman   The owners rent the apartment out. I've written so many complaints about them! . . . They won't pay taxes. But that's just one thing. The other thing is who's renting the apartment.

Vovochka   And who is it?

Old Woman   Last week I was sitting by the window waiting for you to come back from school. I saw you walk down the street and enter the building. And all this time, a man was following you, staring at your back. And of course, from behind you aren't nearly as ugly . . .

Vovochka   Shut up!

Old Woman   If only you were just your ass! So, he was looking at you like, like . . . Like men don't look at boys . . .

Vovochka   Our neighbor? Are you telling me our neighbor is . . .?

Old Woman   I'm telling you, you don't even see things that are right in front of you.

Vovochka   So, our neighbor is . . .?

Part Three

A Powder Compact

Man   You don't need to know much about me. I'm a man, Russian, with a bit of Ukrainian blood. I'm thirty-three, never married, used to live with my mother in Arkhangelsk. That's pretty much it. Now, to the story.

It happened early winter, when I came to in Moscow. I didn't feel well: I had a toothache, my gums were bleeding, my lips were dry because of the cold air. Sometimes I felt a new crack appear on my skin, as if some tiny invisible insect were biting it.

Our company was in the logistics business, and over the past few years, I had often traveled to Moscow to meet with our business partners. This time, I went to a packaging fair. A colleague was supposed to travel with me, but the day before he had to pull out: his wife went into labor.

Already on the plane I was feeling strangely excited: my face was burning; I couldn't stop pinching my cheek in excitement. When we took off, the excitement took off with me.

I spent the flight staring at a young man sitting across the aisle from me. He was wearing headphones and his eyes were closed, so I could stare at him all I wanted. His neighbor was an old woman who woke up from time to time to blow her nose into a handkerchief. I was staring at the handsome guy and pinching my cheek. He looked a bit like the guy who was supposed to travel with me. My colleague. His wife went into labor earlier than expected. He stayed, and I went.

And so, here I was, first on the plane, staring at the handsome guy, and then in a hotel room, a double room, staring at the empty bed in front of me. He could have been sitting there.

I'm thirty-three and I've had sex five times in my whole life. First, when I was twenty-three, rather late, then when I was twenty-five, then twice when I was thirty, and then a year and a half ago, when I was thirty-one and a half.

It comes as no surprise though, because I always fall in love with guys who won't love me back, just like this one . . . Whose wife is in labor. We'd gone on trips to Moscow together before, and each time I spent a sleepless night next to him.

I would spend the first hour lying in the dark and waiting for him to fall asleep. Then I'd open my eyes and turn my head. I'd stare at him in the semi-darkness of the room, at his face in the dim light coming from the street through the window, at his uncovered shoulder.

Married, twenty-seven years old, well-built, at the last office party, we gave him a kalimba . . .

And now, looking at the empty bed, I cursed the world, cursed the man I was in love with, cursed his wife and their baby that was being born. Why do I have to go through all this? To what end? My body is getting old. What am I waiting for? For a twenty-seven-year-old athlete to fall in love with me? What am I waiting for?

I grabbed my laptop and went online. Opened a search engine . . . At first, I didn't even know what I was looking for. How do I put this into words? I know what I want, but how do I explain it to Google? I thought for a while. And then I typed . . .

Links popped up on the screen, lots of them. I clicked on them: one, another, one more. There were lots of ads, photos, words. I closed a couple of tabs that were really bad. Then I opened them again. Photos of younger guys, of men . . . Some not showing their face, some showing things that definitely weren't their face. Here's a phone number. So, do I just take my phone and call? Do I just do it, even though I've never done this before? Do I do the one thing that fills me with terror and panic? Do I really just call this number, the one with the triple one at the end? Do I call it? I did . . .

Hi, I . . . Yes . . . Yes, I'd like to . . . (*To the side.*) I'm so glad he said it for me so that I didn't have to. (*To the phone.*) Yes . . . I want . . . Yes, Maxim . . . I found him on the website . . . I don't know what individual means . . . I don't care . . . Are you healthy? . . . How can you prove that you don't have . . . Well, I understand that we'll use condoms but there are other skin infections . . . Right . . . Right . . . Yes, you can call me by my first name . . .

Now a Maxim will come and will call me by my first name. Well, not now, of course, but in an hour. He has a beautiful voice, I liked it . . . If the boy is as good as his photo . . . I have to meet him in the lobby and take him to my room. What if somebody checks his ID? What if they ask? . . . No, I shouldn't think about it. What's that, there, on my face?. .

I get closer to the mirror. There is a gigantic red spot on my right cheek next to my mouth. I touch it; it's burning, it hurts. What is this? A huge zit? A pimple? What is this? I can't meet him with a face like this. Maxim, my Maxim. Ow, it really hurts! . . .

I put on a scarf and leave the room. I look for the receptionist. She isn't in the lobby, or by the elevator. Finally, I find her in the ironing room. She is ironing a yellow shirt. Yellow.

Hi, thank God I found you. I have what may seem an unusual question for this time of night. Could you tell me where I find the nearest cosmetics store? You see, something happened to my face . . . on my face . . . You see . . .

She looks at me as if she had waited her whole life to stare daggers at somebody like that, and then tells me that all the cosmetics stores have closed at this hour—obviously—but there's a twenty-four-hour supermarket nearby, and they have a department where I might find something useful.

I write down the address and go back to my room to grab a coat. It has snowed, and the road is still virgin white, with no tracks on it. I must be one of the first customers after the snowfall, because there isn't a single track in front of the store either.

I go in; the checkouts are empty . . . I run into a sleepy guard . . . I must be the only customer in here now . . . I head to the cosmetics department and look for a powder compact. It's a round box with pinkish balls in it. I grab it and also some deodorant that I don't really need.

For some reason, I feel the urge to explain to the woman at the checkout that I'm buying the compact for my girlfriend and ask her opinion on whether it'll look good on her. She ignores my question and asks me if I need a bag. I don't know why but I take a bag, pay, and leave.

Once I'm outside, my phone rings: Maxim tells me that he's already exited the subway and is on his way to the hotel; he asks me to meet him at the entrance. I walk back fast, but I realize that I don't have enough time to go back to my room and apply the compact.

I find a dark alley and get the compact out. Damn it, there's no mirror! No mirror . . . I'm standing in the darkness and, for the first time in my life, put powder on my face.

When I think that I hear footsteps approaching, I hide the compact, and when the footsteps recede, I take it out again. I'm nervous, the powder balls fall into the snow. I'm anxious that there isn't enough powder, so I crush the balls with my fingers and rub them into my face until I can't feel my skin anymore.

Here I am, standing in the darkness, my face all covered with powder. Me, in the darkness. My face, in powder. I'm waiting for Maxim to call me, then I'll just walk back to the hotel. I can see the hotel entrance from where I am.

Maxim doesn't call, it's snowing, and the snowflakes are really light. Ten, fifteen minutes have passed, Maxim still hasn't called, even though it's only a five-minute walk from the subway to the hotel. He probably can't find the way there.

A man comes crawling to the hotel entrance, he must be drunk. He falls on the stairs, makes a few moves, and then lies still. Whatever, he'll lie for a while, and the security guard will send him packing, or he'll crawl away himself, or he may even die there, which is also fine. Maxim . . . I'm picturing his photo. His arms, shoulders, eyes, and his abs. The abs again. And below . . .

My phone rings, it's Maxim. His voice sounds funny, a few times he repeats the name I gave him: Arthur. Why does his voice sound funny? Is he kidding me or something? He's saying . . . I can't get what he's saying . . . What is he saying?

That he got jumped . . . That he managed to get away . . . That he's now lying in the cold and has just managed to turn on his phone . . . Something about it dying . . . Where are you? . . . At the entrance to the hotel . . . The man who I thought was a local drunk . . . At the hotel entrance . . . I'm running to the hotel, and while I'm running, a thought flashes through my mind: is there another entrance? What if I just use it and go back to my room, alone . . .?

'Cause I didn't give Maxim my room number. Who is he to me? Who am I to him? Yes, he got jumped, but I had nothing to do with it, right? Moreover, if they stop us at the lobby and start asking questions, what will I tell them? Who is he to me? Who am I to him?

But he has already spotted me and tries to stand up. The face is just like the photo, only covered in blood. The blood looks so red. Probably because of the snow. They can't have beaten him for long but they must have hit him hard. He clings on to me so tight that I know I won't be able to get rid of him. He keeps telling me that I shouldn't call anyone, shouldn't call for an ambulance or the police, that it is pointless, that he's been beaten up before, that it is alright. Yes, that's exactly how he says it, "alright."

Through the glass door, I see the receptionist and the guard helping the housekeeper carry a big rug through the door. I pull Maxim up, cover his face with a hood, and drag him inside.

As we enter the lobby, the guard gives us a glance. I smile into his fat mug, kind of like, hi, here I am, dragging my completely drunk buddy, happens all the time, right? The guard doesn't smile back and simply turns around to look at the carpet that still won't fit through the door.

In the elevator, Maxim faints. I have to carry him out of the elevator and drop him at the door, like a sack, before I drag him into the room. I put him on the other bed, walk back to the door to lock it, and turn on the light.

Fortunately, I always carry a medical kit with me, just in case, and this time, I can finally put it to good use. Now that the light is on, I can actually see Maxim: his face, which is really beautiful, the swollen cheek, the bruising, the chunk of hair that has been torn out over his right ear.

He opens his eyes and looks, not at me, just to the side. I call him by his name, but he doesn't react, I say "Maxim" again—no result. It isn't his name. I put my hands on his ears and turn his head toward me. What's your name? What is it? "Boy," he says and starts throwing up. I run to the table and bring him an empty pitcher. Boy—as I am calling him now—quickly fills it with greyish puke. I take the pitcher into the bathroom to empty it.

I come back, get out the bandages, hydrogen peroxide, painkillers. While I am attending to him, Boy doesn't say a word. Just sometimes a rare "ouch" or "bitch" crosses his lips. He will never tell me his name. I am touching his head, his neck, his shoulders, his arms. Then the abs. Then the abs again. Then, below the abs.

—I want you, and you need money, don't you? I like you, you're so nice. Somebody else might have left you down there, but I helped you. I'm not insisting on anything really, I'm just asking if we can do what we planned to do . . . What I planned . . . Of course, if you don't want to, you can sleep here for free until tomorrow, and then you can just leave. But if you can do more than just sleep, I mean, work, just a bit—and yes, I know, I did really say "work"—I would be really grateful. Can you do it, Boy? Can you? . . .

He doesn't say anything, just starts taking off his clothes. A couple of times, he misses the bottom of his shirt, which he wants to pull off, and when I want to help him, he pushes me away. He is standing naked, his clothes lying next to him.

"No, no, first you have to take a shower." In the shower, he almost falls, drops the shower head, drops the towel. When I am helping him to dry himself, he looks at me and asks, what happened to you?—What do you mean?—What happened to your face? I go up to the mirror . . . I totally forgot . . . The compact . . . The shower vapor made it flow down my face, turning it into a monstrous mask.

As I am staring at my face in the mirror, it appears to me that the skin is peeling off my face, with pink flesh revealing itself underneath it . . . I wash off the compact and look at my face again: the skin is inflamed and red—even more so than before.

I hear a noise behind me: Boy has fainted, again. I take him into the room, again, and put him into bed. He hasn't even fully come round when he starts to pull off my belt. I step aside to turn off the light and return to him. He quickly takes my clothes off.

"The condom, don't forget the con . . ."

He enters me, starts moving, moves faster, then faster still. I feel like part of the consciousness that Boy lost when he fainted transferred into me. I feel more lucid than ever.

I realize that I am being fucked by a guy who has just been beaten, he is fucking me on a bed in a double room, the bed where my colleague was supposed to sleep, who I'm in love with and who couldn't come because his wife was in labor; I can also feel the compact, the gigantic pustule on my face, the towel on the bathroom floor, the wardrobe in the room, the light coming in through the window, the curtains on the window through which the light penetrates the room.

I understand and feel everything except one thing—pleasure. I feel that first he is drenched with sweat, and he is sweating because he is aroused, and then the cut on his head starts to bleed, but he doesn't stop, and I don't stop, I'm breathing into a pillow; then I take his dick into my mouth and when I open my mouth for it, I feel the dry skin in the corners of my lips crack; before he comes, he throws up again, but he doesn't stop until he comes, comes a lot.

He takes two steps back and falls on the other bed. The towel on the bathroom floor, the towel with what was left of the powder on it, I somehow keep thinking of it, of its folds, and stains, and about the dirty water, dripping into the bathtub from it.

How much do I owe him? "You have to pay me," he says. "Well, of course, you don't forget about the money. Of course." I reach out for the envelope with the money I prepared for him in advance and throw it over to Boy.

He can't catch it, so, for a while, he's looking for it on the floor. Then Boy talks to me again, in a softer voice. He asks if he can stay the night. "That's not what we agreed. I agreed to pay for an hour. In the morning, you'll charge me more, and I don't have more money."

"I won't. Can I stay? I really feel bad."

"Okay, but then tomorrow we'll do it again."

"Do what?" "Don't play dumb. We'll do it again tomorrow."

He's silent, but then he says "okay" and turns away to the wall. He sleeps, and I am lying on the bed without bedsheets or anything—I took off the stained sheets and threw them in the corner of the room. In an hour, I get so aroused that I get up and mount him, and before he even realizes what's going on and moans, I've already come. And then I fall into the heavy darkness of sleep. In the morning, around half past six, I hear Boy wake up and crack his fingers. I watch him dress. He goes into the bathroom; I hear the running water. I have to blink really often, because I want to sleep so badly, so every few seconds I just doze off. The door shuts.

When I did finally fall asleep—I don't know for how long, maybe half a minute, he took off. I dreamt of the baby that my colleague's wife gave birth to. He was all yellow, like translucent yellow. And there was a long curvy umbilical cord reaching out from him to . . . I tried to see where it was going, but I couldn't . . .

And then it was day, an awful day. I left my phone in the room. But I guess, why do I need it in another city anyway? I was sitting at the conference, my head was heavy, and I was barely processing the lecture on how to facilitate, simplify, and speed up the delivery process. The goods packed in corrugated cardboard were driving, flying, sailing, driving again, walking, coming up to the door, ringing the bell . . .

All day long I couldn't get Boy's taste out of my mouth. Neither coffee, nor lunch, nor the water from the cooler, not even chewing gum helped me get rid of it, of the taste of his sperm in my mouth. I dreamt of coming back to the room, taking off my clothes, and throwing my body onto the bed where he had slept and coming just off the smell of his body left on the sheets.

But when I came back at night, the first thing I saw in the room was the money. The money he had forgotten to take. The other thing was my phone. There were like a hundred missed calls from Boy and a dozen texts. He had forgotten to take the money. I took my SIM out . . . You heard it right, I didn't call him back. I just left in the morning and . . . The next time I was sent to Moscow, it was a business trip that lasted a whole month. My boss told me he'd arranged with his relatives that I'd stay in a studio they were renting out. I stayed there four months, with short breaks. From early autumn to early spring. The spring when I noticed that there was a teenager living next door.

A Lonely Man

The **Man***, tied to a chair.*

Vovochka   God, it took us ages to catch you . . . Ages! It turns out it's so hard to trap your neighbor. Much harder than a pedophile from another city.

The **Man** *moves.*

Vovochka   When I turn on this camera again, it'll show your face . . . I don't know what it will look like.

Man   Why?

Vovochka   I can't predict what we'll do to you right now. Just being honest.

Man   When you say, "we," do you mean, Crematorium?

Vovochka   Yes, Crematorium.

Man   Why do you have such a horrifying name? There was once a rock band called that . . .

Vovochka   If you think that you can talk your way out of it . . .

Man   I don't.

Vovochka   Maybe we'll just shave your hair off and smear your face in paint . . .

Man   Just?

Vovochka   Well, yeah. You'll have to go back home with a blue face. You'll have to wait for night to come, hiding in a dark corner, shaking and sobbing, provided you'll have any tears left by the time we're done with you.

Then night will come, and you'll start heading toward your place, darting past the street lamps. Maybe you'll even wrap something around your head to cover it. And at your house, you'll have to wait for ages before you can go in to make sure none of your neighbors see you.

Then, you'll rush inside and spend hours over the sink trying to wash the paint off your face. But it'll stay on for days. You'll have to call in sick at work. Then, when your face goes back to normal, you'll go to the barbershop to have the rest of the hair that we've left on the sides shaved off. And you'll be struggling to come up with a story to tell your friends, family, colleagues. Well . . .

Man   Tell them about what?

Vovochka   Oh, they'll all know about your shame. Everybody will see your face, the piss streaming down your face, the lube you'll swallow.

Man   What are you talking about?

Vovochka   That's the best scenario of what can happen to you.

Man (*tries to free himself of the ropes*)   Let me go! Let me go! (*Breathes heavily.*) I'm having a heart . . . attack . . .

Vovochka   Don't you lie to me, I know everything about hearts. My grandma has a weak heart.

Man   But I really don't feel well.

Vovochka   Happens to everyone.

Man   Let me go, please . . .

Vovochka (*stands to the left of the* **Man**)   When you were walking over here, you were probably getting hard already, you were excited about a sweet pleasure waiting for you, you were picturing yourself deep in a little boy's ass? Weren't you? Weren't you? Weren't you?

Moves over to his right.

You were longing, burning with desire, craving me, checking if you had condoms, you were picturing yourself fucking my little naked body, how you'd put two fingers into my mouth, how I'd gently press my teeth around your engagement ring. Weren't you? Weren't you? Weren't you?

Stands on the left.

And, where are you now? Of course, we'll let you go, but what will become of you after we're done? Nobody will ever kiss these little cheeks because everybody will know we pissed all over them. Or, maybe, you'll have to switch over and explore the animal world? I can really recommend geese.

Man   Stop it!

Vovochka   Well, if you were just an ordinary fag, all enlightened humanity would be standing up for you. But you're a pedophile, and nobody will protect a pedophile, not even the Devil because he also has business to run on Earth. And God couldn't care less about you either, because God doesn't care about anyone, even about the kids you want to fuck.

Man   I don't fancy kids . . .

Vovochka   Then what are you doing here?

Pause.

What brought you here?

Pause.

Come on! Come on! Who did you come here for? Who?

Pause.

Man   I wanted you.

Vovochka   Come again?

Man   Do you realize what you look like?

Vovochka   What are you talking about? Of course, I know what I look like . . .

Man   When I saw you that spring . . . I didn't even realize it was you. I just saw a young man with the legs of a cyclist . . . The nape of your neck, your shoulders . . .

Vovochka (*moves away from him*)   Shut up!

Man   Your small hands . . .

Vovochka   Shut up. (*Points to the camera.*) I am recording everything, everything.

Man   You said it's off.

Vovochka It is . . .

Comes up to him.

I could destroy your face.

Pause.

How do you want to die?

Pause.

Man But you can't . . . It's a felony.

Pause.

If I have a wish to make, then mine is that you don't do anything to my body. Don't cut off my sex organs, don't . . .

Vovochka Come on, I was just kidding. Of course, we won't kill you. But after what happens today . . . you won't be able to live.

Man I understand that.

Vovochka It's good that you do.

Man They'll chase me, prey on me. And one day, they'll catch me. So, when it happens, I don't want them to mutilate my body. My mother is still alive, you know.

Vovochka Once she finds out about you . . .

Man She doesn't understand anything anymore. She is really old.

Vovochka So, what are you afraid of then?

Man Burn me. Why don't you just burn us? There must be some reason you call yourselves Crematorium.

Vovochka I thought about it. But it's all really hard. A proper legal base is required. The only thing we can do now is catch you and hand you over to the police. But of course, we won't stop at that. You know, I actually like your idea . . .

Man What idea?

Vovochka With burning . . . What if we put you on a metal spit and turned you again and again over a fire? Piss all over you and keep turning, with the hot coals beneath you . . . Do you believe in hell?

Man No . . . I don't . . . Do you?

Vovochka You don't? So, what do you call all this?

Man I am happy it happened . . . You look very much like him . . .

Vovochka What? Look like who?

Man You look like that boy. I'm really happy. I want you guys to kill me.

Vovochka   Well, we don't kill just anybody. You have to deserve it. If we kill you for no reason, you'll be a hero, and we'll be murderers, monsters. So . . . (*Pause.*)

Man   So, what?

Vovochka   So, you'll have to stay alive for some time until . . .

Pause.

Man   Until what?

Vovochka   Until . . . Well, you know . . .

Man   I don't.

Vovochka   What else is left for you?

Man   What else is left for me?

Pause.

Vovochka   Do you want me to let you go?

Man   What?

Pause.

Yes, of course, I want that.

Vovochka   Not through the door though.

Man   How should I get out then?

Vovochka   Well, how do you penetrate each other? Come on, think! Through a hole. If you can get out through this window, you are free to go. Do you want to?

Man   But . . . how? I'm not sure I can . . .

Vovochka   Well, if you don't want to, then fine.

Man   I do, I do! Just . . .

Vovochka *unties his hands.*

Vovochka   If you even as much as think about killing me, don't. Because then for sure your body will be mutilated, and your junk will be delivered to your mom in a cheap candy box. (*Looks at him.*) What? Alright, fine, we'll pick a nice, expensive candy box. (*Points at the window.*) Here's your window.

Man (*comes up to the window*)   This one?

Vovochka   Yes. Get to know each other.

The **Man** *opens the window and looks out.*

Man   But how do I get out here?

Vovochka   I don't know. Try it.

Man   I . . .

Vovochka   You, yes, you.

*The **Man** gets out the window with great caution and disappears. **Vovochka** waits a bit and then comes up to the window.*

Vovochka (*looks out the window*)   Well, just look at that . . .

Goes to the door, thrusts it wide open.

(*Shouts out loud.*) Help! The bastard has escaped! Help!

"Kill this Thing"

Lyubochka   First, my biological mom lost her job. Her boss invited her to her office and closed the door. She told her, "You know that I like you, that we all like you here. But it's not about us. We got a letter . . ." She paused and my mom understood what kind of letter she was talking about. "Of course, none of it would matter, but you work with kids. So, here's what I can do: I can transfer you to another job, at a different location. Of course, it's not as close to your home as this place, not as convenient to get to . . . But we'll reimburse all your expenses. Please, understand . . ."

My mom saw how hard, how awkward this whole thing was for her boss. And she felt awkward, too, because her boss was a good person who didn't want to be having this conversation. Which made it that much harder for my mom to tell her, "Sorry, but I can't agree to this offer."

That was my first mom. My other mom wanted to adopt a kid from foster care, a boy. His name was Bakht, which means "Good luck." He had a tiny crescent on his left pupil. The papers were ready, my other mom got toys and clothes for her child, but when she came to pick the boy up, they told her . . .

Vanya   That they'd got a letter.

Lyubochka   You see, we must look into the matter closely. A child's life is at stake here, after all. We must examine everything thoroughly. In the meantime . . .

Vanya   In the meantime, the toys and clothes will have to stay where they are.

Lyubochka   That's when I came to Vanya and told him, kill him.

Vanya   I didn't even have to ask who she was talking about.

Lyubochka   I told him, kill this thing.

Vanya   I didn't have to ask what he'd done. I knew it.

Lyubochka   Kill him as soon as possible, Vanya.

Vanya   I promised her I would.

Addressing the President

A TV studio.

Vovochka   Dear Mister President, hello. My name is Vladimir Pushkin. I share my last name with the great Russian poet, and my first name with you. Well, I won't be holding back—I would share all of myself with you! I've always known, I've always felt that there's some connection between us beyond the name.

Mister President, according to the laws of our country, I'm still a child, but by the law of conscience, I'm already an adult. My conscience told me, "Vovochka, you've learned a lot, go and share it with others."

I was scared, I tried to negotiate with my conscience, but it was firm, it kept telling me to go and share. So, I went, because I realized that children's lives are at stake, the life of every single child. Children like I once used to be.

Maybe you're not aware of this yet—although it is really hard not to be aware—but there are perverts in Russia. Well, of course, there are other people who live here, too, but it just turns out that these . . . well, you know who I mean . . . started to pop up among ordinary, normal people.

Since they are dispersed among ordinary citizens, it's very hard to fight them. You can't bomb them, because people will get hurt; you can't poison the water they drink, because some of them drink water while others may prefer juice. You can't even always tell them apart from others by how they look. As you see, their extermination is a hard and complex task that only the state can manage.

Maybe you've already heard about a group of brave kids who've united to catch these skunks. Despite our insignificant age, we've made significant progress in our cause.[4] It's true that not all of these idiots have been caught, but recently we've gotten much better at identifying them. And believe it or not, many even turn themselves in voluntarily. Because they understand that they can't hide from us.

We process all of them, get them into the system, rough them up a little, and let them go home. This type of person won't run away anymore. He'll just sit and wait until we come after him to . . . But here's where our rights are limited: we can't and don't have the right to kill them. Only the state can do this, only you, Mister President.

To show you that I'm not just fantasizing here, I've thought of what might follow your executive order. Of course, if we shot all pervs within a week, we'd have a mountain of dead bodies. They'd start rotting, and we'd end up with an epidemic on our hands. Not to mention, a pile of dead bodies isn't good for optics. The global media will spread pictures, and everybody will be saying that we're barbarians. They've certainly done this before!

So, Mister President, my proposal involves a simpler and smarter solution: burning them. We need a crematorium. I've even found a place for it already, it's in the town of Dolgoprudny. As you probably know, there's a landfill there. Piles of garbage.

One day, as I was driving past it, I realized that it would be the perfect location for our crematorium. The prevailing winds in that area will blow the ash toward Khimki, where political activists live. So, they'll fucking die, too! Now that we've identified the location for the crematorium, we have to get rid of the last doubts about whether these bastards should be burnt.

They should, I'm telling you. And this is why.

Like I said before, my last name is Pushkin. The great Russian poet Alexander Pushkin said in a poem: "Love knows no age . . ." These are well-known, beautiful lines. However, today, they have a new meaning, just like the rainbow now looks different. When Pushkin said, "Love knows no age," he didn't mean that an adult man has the right to love a child. Pushkin loved and protected children; you can trust me: I'm also a Pushkin, so I know.

They say that we have to distinguish between pedophiles and homosexualists, that some of them may actually be nice people. They say that they engage in perverse activities voluntarily, and they should be left alone. It's all nonsense, because they're all crazy. And I even know how they got that way.

Mister President, imagine that you're presiding over a really important meeting. Well, let's say, a dam breaks and floods everything in the area. So, there you are, leading the meeting, and suddenly, a mysterious voice tells you that you've got a small spinning top on the tip of your nose. Yes, you heard right, a small spinning top. You look closely, but you can't see anything, because the spinning top is on your nose, which is right between your eyes.

Thoughts about the top distract you, but you still have to run the meeting. People are reporting on the damage to the economy, the number of victims, but you can't focus, because you're trying to figure out where the voice comes from and whether you really have a spinning top on your nose.

Something really is bothering the tip of your nose, and you really want to scratch it. And you scratch it, and scratch it, and scratch it. Finally, the meeting is over, and you can get to a mirror. You look in the mirror and . . . Nothing! There's no spinning top!

But as soon as you stop looking in the mirror, you feel it again, the spinning top on the tip of your nose. It's just unbearable! And the voice comes back and tells you that terrible things will befall Russia if you let the spinning top fall and somebody notices it! And you start holding your head up to balance the invisible spinning top and keep it from falling. Every minute with other people turns into torture—what if the top falls? What if does fall?

You're visibly nervous, you lose weight and will soon turn cross-eyed because you're constantly trying to look at the end of your nose. Only alone or asleep, you are free from the constant pressure to keep this wretched, damn, devilish, tiny invisible spinning top on the tip of your nose. Oh, it's real torture!

It's literally driving you crazy, because you have to control yourself at all times. At all times! Day and night, the spinning top won't let you go . . . you're afraid that some observant person might notice your bizarre behavior and ask, "Why are you crossing your eyes? Have you gone crazy from imagining something on the tip of your nose?" "No, of course not," you'll say in a cold sticky sweat.

The moment you think the danger is over, a hand will grab you by the nose, and you'll hear the voice shouting: "Isn't there a spinning top on your nose, asshole?" And you'll respond in a pinched voice, "No, there isn't and there never has been! I can't even imagine something like that!"

And your heart will beat faster as you panic, and your nose will hurt and swell, turning into a gigantic blister that the spinning top has drilled into your face. They got you! And the person who catches you will show you the top in the palm of his hand, like a crashed fly. "Well, what about that, bastard?"

What a scary thing to imagine, Mister President. One day, you'll be crossing Cathedral Square in the Kremlin and you'll see a group of tourists and kids in front of you. The distance between you and them gets shorter by the second: twenty feet, fifteen, ten, two. They're all looking at you! Maybe, they see your spinning top? Kids are so much more observant than adults. Kids are actually angels. You meet the gaze of a boy and . . . your knees get weak. You go down on one knee . . . A little blond boy . . . a sweet little angel. He asks you . . .

Voice   What's your name?

Vovochka   Vovochka . . .

Voice   Why do you look so exhausted?

Vovochka   I have a terrible secret.

Voice   What's your secret, Vovochka?

Vovochka   I like boys, I like their hair, their eyes, their tiny lips . . .

Voice   What did you just say? Maybe you meant to say that you have a spinning top on your nose?

Vovochka   I have no top whatsoever. I'm looking at that boy over there, Nikita, and I want to kiss his belly.

Voice   Oh my God, oh my God, this spinning top has driven you crazy. Poor boy! . . . What are you doing?

Vovochka   Nikita . . . Nikita . . . When you whisper his name, it's sweet, like a candy. You pull his tank top up and kiss, kiss, and lick, you pull out your tongue and tickle the boy's belly with it, and then you press your teeth around a thin fold of his sweet skin . . . What a delight! That milky aroma of a child! You want the boy to be yours entirely, all of him, but . . . You're the President, you have to keep going. You get up and leave, keeping the memory of this child and the taste of his body forever. Nikita . . .[5]

Where was I? Right, I invented a machine. It's called "135," like the Article in the Code of Administrative Offenses that started this whole thing.[6] It's a simple name, don't you think? And the mechanism is very simple. It's a box with fireproof walls and a see-through lid. Why? To see whoever is inside. And who needs to see that? Well, anybody who wants and anybody who has to. Family, for example. You have to agree that the parents bear some responsibility for a child they brought up a degenerate.

The degenerate is put in the box, and the lid is closed. That's enough. We don't need belts or any other tricks. The important thing is that the box is solid, so when the burning gas goes inside, the degenerate will struggle in agony to get out. He'll obviously use all his muscle strength to try and destroy his own coffin. That's why it has to be really well-built.

Witnessing one cremation like this is enough to build stamina, further cremations will be less emotional. The heart gets kind of tempered by fire and becomes fireproof: it isn't scared anymore of the eyeballs bursting in the heat, of blisters blowing up on the skin, or of the exposed bones. And everything other than bones in the human body is just water. You'll see, there's no difference between people and puddles. That's it, so there's nothing to be sorry about. And the family will actually even learn from it. They'll start looking after their sons and daughters a lot better.

Within a short time, I've gotten a lot of followers and fans. Some of them have proposed putting a monument to me in front of the crematorium. But I think that this monument should be dedicated to you. They argue, however, that it's wrong to erect the first monument to the President in front of a crematorium. Alright . . . I agree to a monument, as long as it's modest! Not so much a monument but a sketch of a monument. Imagine a pedestal with my body on it, made of transparent plastic, or, even better, glass. It'll be hollow on the inside, so it can be used for our cause. I'm thinking . . .

. . . of my glass body to be used as a container for the ashes of those burnt in the crematorium. There could be a hole somewhere in the upper part of the body, for example, in the mouth, and it could connect to a pipe that will guide the ashes inside the body. Of course, this glass body would fill up really quickly because every burnt pervert leaves 70 to 85 oz of stuff behind. So, the statue needs to have another hole, to release the ashes. At first, I thought of putting it in the heel, but then I figured that I'm no Achilles, and came to what I believe is a cleverer solution—this hole will be in the ass.

Now picture this: a see-through figure, created as if out of thin air, and the ashes of the freshly burnt degenerates fall in through its mouth, ha ha ha, and then fall out through its asshole, ha ha ha. They fall into a pit that we'll have to dig out ahead of time. Of course, it'll require some work and labor, but we could actually use the faggots themselves to dig the pit.

We could tell them that we won't burn whoever digs the pit. But then we'll take and burn them anyway. Yep, we'll just play them like that!

I think you're up to the task, Mister President.

Mister President, let's be honest, you want the same thing I do—death. Death for the sake of life. Just like me, you don't want to wait. You want Russia to change now; not tomorrow—today! So, what are we waiting for? For a spinning top to show up on our noses? Or should we lay the foundation stone of the future crematorium right now?

Hero's Death

Vanya   When our grandfather died, he left us two guns: a TT 33, a Soviet pistol from the Second World War. And a Walther PP—a German Wehrmacht pistol. I thought a bit and chose the Walther. For some reason, it felt more fitting to kill Vovochka with the Walther.

Lyubochka   The day before was Vanya's birthday.

Vanya   I was born the day before him . . . that damn . . .

Lyubochka   I came over to wish Vanya a happy birthday. And as usual, instead of talking to each other, we turned on the TV.

Vanya   I wish we hadn't done it!

Lyubochka   A daytime talk show was on. Vovochka was the main guest. He was small, sitting on a huge red sofa and looking really scared. Everybody was shouting and not letting anyone else get a single word in, including the host. Then finally, the host made everybody shut up and passed the microphone to Vovochka. And he started talking . . . He was talking extremely fast. He said that he was doing it all for the kids, that kids around the world were in great danger, and that he wanted his own kids to live in a safe world. The host asked him the name of his organization.

Vanya   Crematorium.

Lyubochka   Crematorium.

Vanya   And then they showed a video of what they'd already done, what they were doing.

Video: men and women tied to metal spits revolve over a fire.

Lyubochka   And then they called on Vovochka's grandma.

Vanya   And she started yelling at him right there, in the studio.

Lyubochka   And he started crying.

Vovochka's *place.*

Vovochka   Thanks for coming.

Pause.

Yesterday was your birthday.

Vanya   Yep.

Vovochka   Sorry I didn't wish you a happy birthday.

Vanya   No problem, I saw your interview on TV.

Vovochka   Yeah, I was busy at the studio. Are you here to wish me a happy birthday?

Vanya   Of course, why else would I be here?

Vovochka   What a surprise. And what a nice one.

Pause.

Vanya   Why do you hate them so much?

Vovochka   I just do.

Vanya   You know what you are, Vova?

Vovochka   What?

Vanya   Satan. Like . . . Like Sauron from *The Hobbit*. You're pure evil.

Vovochka   I know.

Vanya   No, actually, you know what, you're not Sauron. Unlike you, Sauron had the decency . . . to attack the strong. Aren't you afraid you're going to get killed?

Vovochka   Nope.

Vanya   You're not afraid?

Vovochka   No one's going to kill me.

Vanya   How can you be so sure?

Vovochka   You know, I thought that there'd come a moment when they'd rise up and tell me, "Enough!" I was afraid one of them would get a gun, find me, and shoot me. I was waiting for it. Really, I did. I told myself that it wasn't cowardice, that there must be some other reason why it wasn't happening.

The animal world has laws, and I've always thought that their kind is no better than animals. They're cunning and devious; so they're going to strike, sooner or later. But they . . . I can't even laugh at it . . . they wrote letters and posted pictures online. I was shocked. Who are these people: are they angels or are they crazy? I thought, maybe I shouldn't have been so hard on them, if they're so . . . so . . . Or was it just a trick? But why didn't they strike? What about the laws of nature? . . . after all, everyone's afraid of dying.

And then I got it. I got it, Vanya. I am nature; I am its law. So, I waited . . . And then I stopped waiting, because nobody was rising up, nobody was coming for me. And then I got it . . . I realized that they don't protest, and those who do are a tiny minority . . . So, they don't protect the rest, they just want to get hurt a little and use it as a ground to emigrate.

They leave people like them behind; they leave them to me. And I tell those who've been left behind in the name of Mother Nature: it's time to die, you dirty assholes. I can take my mission all the way to its end. The end of every single one of you. If I were you, I'd quit my job, leave my car, even in the middle of a traffic jam if that's where I was, and just run, run to your friends who are just like you, if I couldn't escape anywhere else . . . I'd rip the clothes off my lovers and I'd . . . Well, I'd do everything you do.

You're living on borrowed time. And time is running out while you're sitting in a café, drinking coffee, and thinking that the table next you isn't listening to your conversation. You think that a famous director, a popular singer, or a great writer is going to stand up for you—that they'll let you hold hands, hold the hand of your child. Fools . . . hands really only turn you on when they're tied behind your back.

So go and drink your coffee. At the bottom of the cup you'll find death. (*Looks at* **Vanya**.)

They look at each other. **Vovochka** *gets up and walks to the window.*

Vanya (*takes the gun out*)   What if . . . what if somebody else decides to kill you?

Vovochka   Who?

Vanya   Somebody who sympathizes with them.

Vovochka   Nobody sympathizes with them.

Vanya   But what if somebody . . .

Vovochka   I can't imagine anybody take their side.

Vanya   But how . . . how can you be so evil?

Vovochka   I'm not evil. I'm still a child, just like you.

Vanya   We aren't children anymore.

Pause. He hides the gun.

Vovochka   Do you sympathize with them?

Vanya   I don't know.

Vovochka   Have you ever thought that you could . . .

Vanya   What?

Vovochka   Well . . . Do something like that.

Vanya   Once . . . Once I actually thought about it. I wondered how it would be to do it with someone like myself.

Vovochka   And who did you imagine?

Vanya   Not you.

Vovochka (*shifts his weight from one foot to the other*)   Not me?

Vanya   I've never pictured doing it with you.

Vovochka (*hurt*)   Why?

Vanya   Because . . .

Vovochka   Then who did you imagine? An athlete? Some kind of . . .

Vanya   You know what, I'm actually going to try it.

Vovochka   What? (*Comes closer to him.*) What did you just say?

Vanya   Why not? I turned eighteen yesterday. I'm an adult and can do whatever I want.

Vovochka   You know that there'll be no way back from that, it's a one-way street?

Vanya   Clearly you've never done it before. To get pleasure, you have to move in both directions.

Pause.

Vovochka   Why are you here, Vanya?

Vanya   What?

Vovochka   Why are you really here?

Vanya   To wish you a happy birthday. Oh, I almost forgot, your present! Right, your present . . . (*To the side.*) I put my hand in my left pocket, where the gun was, and almost took it out by mistake. I quickly dug into my right pocket and took out a small box. (*To* **Vovochka**.) This is for you.

Vovochka (*takes the gift*)   Thanks. I'll open it later.

Vanya   Open it now, please. (*To the side.*) I thought that while he was unwrapping the present, I'd have the chance to get closer to him, aim, and shoot. In Dostoyevsky's *Crime and Punishment*, Raskolnikov also wrapped his box really tight to kill the old woman.

Vovochka *unwraps the gift and cries.*

Vanya   Since his fingers were much more agile than the old woman's, he unwrapped the box a lot faster. And he cried.

Vovochka   Thank you.

He takes the porcelain ballerina out.

Vanya   He cried, he really did. I hadn't seen that coming, but I swear to you he was crying. He kept thanking me. I couldn't possibly kill him at that moment. Then he raised his eyes to me. He looked particularly ugly. He got up, came up to me, and fell down on his knees in front of me. He hugged my legs and buried his face in my knees. I had no idea what to do.

Vovochka *does what* **Vanya** *has just described.*

Vanya   He started saying something. I couldn't make out what he was saying, because I was scared. I had been just about to kill him, but now he was crying and saying . . . Saying that he loved me.

Vovochka   I love you.

Vanya   He also said that he was an adult now and could be thrown in jail or sent to the crematorium. He said that he'd seen such horrible things there that he couldn't be like them.

Vovochka   I caught the virus I'd worked so hard to eradicate.

Vanya   He said he had caught it, as if it were some disease. But if only I were to fall in love with him then he wouldn't do this to children, if only I were to love him . . . Because if I didn't, he'd kill himself. He wanted to kiss me.

Vovochka   Can I kiss you?

Vanya   No.

Vovochka   Please . . .

Vanya   No.

Vovochka   I'm begging yo . . .

Vanya   He put his hand on my chest, on the left side, where I had the gun. Did he feel it? Did he? . . .

Vovochka   Then I'll kill myself. I really will.

Pause.

Vanya   I took the gun out and gave it to him.

Vovochka   He took the gun, looked at it through the tears, then looked at Vanya.

Vanya   What if he kills me right now?

Vovochka   I asked him if the gun was loaded.

Vanya   I told him that before I'd come there, I'd shot it into a ravine, to check. I told him the gun was loaded.

Vovochka *leaves, gun in hand.*

Vanya   He went to the other room. I was waiting. A minute, two, three . . . Maybe, I should have let him kiss m . . .

A shot.

I jumped and ran toward the door into the other room. I paused for a second before shoving the door open . . . Vova!

Opens the door.

He was standing by the bed looking at the body of the old woman he had just killed.

Epilogue

Vanya   He was arrested and charged as an adult.

Lyubochka   This organization of his, Crematorium, fell apart soon after his arrest. There was an investigation. Members of his organization said that they were fighting against pedophilia, that they had never engaged in extortion, that they had never tortured people, only perverts . . . He died during the investigation. Yep, just like that, died.

Vanya   He had some underlying chronic condition.

Lyubochka   And everyone felt sorry for him.

Vanya   And journalists were sorry for the dead boy.

Lyubochka   Some fat patriotic-minded journalist even made a documentary about him, where he said that adults are powerless in Russia, and nobody can defend children's rights except children themselves. They even brought a boy in the studio who swore that as long as he lived, he'd carry on Vovochka's cause.

Vanya   At the end of the film they showed an unmarked grave in a cemetery. We couldn't figure out whether it was Vovochka's actual grave or not.

Lyubochka   We tried to find it. On an online forum, they posted information about where he might be buried; they even marked the spot on a cemetery map. On Saturday, Vanya and I went to a cemetery on the outskirts of Moscow. We looked for the grave for a while but couldn't find it. When we were leaving the cemetery, I saw a freshly dug mound that looked like the grave we saw on TV. I paused . . .

Vanya   Girls do that sometimes, I know. They say they sense something.

Lyubochka   Yeah, I sensed it was his grave. I don't know how, I just knew it. Freshly dug ground, no cross, just a piece of wood holding a plaque with dates, written in chalk, washed off by the rain.

Vanya   Who's stupid enough to write these things in chalk?

Lyubochka   We were standing by the grave.

Vanya   In silence.

Lyubochka   I know that he felt it too.

Vanya   It was cold.

Lyubochka   And then I saw, we both saw that the ground started moving. It looked like something had caved in, and the ground collapsed.

Vanya   Poor girl, she got scared and started screaming.

Lyubochka   It was really scary. Like . . . Like . . . I saw him fall into hell . . . Vovochka.

Vanya   She ran away, scared.

Lyubochka   I was running between the graves and felt that the ground under my feet was also about to collapse. I kept running until I realized that I was running alone. I didn't see Vanya next to me. I stopped to catch my breath and called his number. He didn't pick up. Then I pulled myself back together, I went back to the place where I'd left him. Vanya was standing by the grave and . . . I don't know if I should say it. Men don't cry, right?

Vanya   I was asking myself whether maybe, if I'd behaved differently around him, he might not have turned into this . . . And maybe then all those people wouldn't have been humiliated, victimized, put into misery? Crematorium would've never existed, nor there would have been any tortures or suicides. People wouldn't have jumped out of windows, wouldn't have crippled themselves and others. Kids would have stayed kids, and Vova, Vovochka, he would've also been different. Maybe, if that day when I noticed the way he was looking at me . . . What if I had kissed him then? Maybe, it's all my fault?

Lyubochka   Last night, I had a horrible nightmare . . . There was a grave. The ground was collapsing into it, and the hole was getting wider and wider. And the graves nearby started to cave in too, and the trees, and the roads, until there was a huge crater, like the ones left after an asteroid hits the earth. I couldn't see where the hole ended. It was very, very deep. But suddenly, deep down, maybe a billion kilometers down there, flames ignited.

Vanya   Maybe it's all my fault? . . .

Lyubochka   Flames ignited.

2014

Notes

1   Vovochka is a diminutive variant of the name Vladimir, used to address little children. It is also the name of a popular character in a series of Russian jokes about a mischievous boy. Lyubochka is a diminutive variant of the name Lyubov. In Russian, the word "liubov" also means "love."
2   Krzysztof is a Polish name, pronounced as 'Kshi-shtof (with stress on the first syllable).
3   The magazine *Big City* that the Voice quotes during Morozov's trial is, according to Pecheykin, "a hipster magazine that at a certain point [2013—T.K.] published a long article that offered an overview of attempts at curing homosexuality throughout history. I evoke it to demonstrate that the Voice of the trial is a young man who reads contemporary press." The Voice itself is Vovochka, which is hinted at by the question "Really?" with which the Voice reacts at Morozov's communication of his date of birth. In the Russian original, the question sounds like "Ne obmanyvaete?" [You are not lying to me, are you?], which is something children might say when they put the words of an adult in doubt (personal communication with the author).
4   Vovochka's organization, Crematorium, is reminiscent of the Russian radical organization Occupy Pedophilia (*Okkupai-pedofiliai*) that was active in the early 2010s. This vigilante organization and its followers used violence, blackmailing, and outing to fight against alleged pedophiles, which often resulted in violence against gay men.
5   The scene where the President kisses a boy's belly reproduces a real-life incident. In June

2006, as Vladimir Putin was walking through Cathedral Square in the Kremlin, which is open to tourists, he approached a group of them for a quick chat. Among them, there was a little boy, Nikita Konkin, who drew Putin's attention. When he crouched down to talk to the boy, he pulled the boy's shirt up and kissed him on his stomach. As the President was being on camera during the walk, the scene was subsequently televised globally and received a lot of attention from the media and the Russian public.

6   Apparatus 135, used by Crematorium in the play, is a direct reference to the infamous "gay propaganda law" adopted in Russia on June 29, 2013. It was officially registered as Federal Law 135-FZ and introduced an amendment into the Code of Administrative Offenses of the Russian Federation that foresees fines for "propaganda of non-traditional sexual relations to minors" by Russian citizens and business. Foreigners can face fines, detainment, and deportation.

A Child for Olya

Natalya Milanteva

Natalya Milanteva was born in Moscow in 1971. She is an alumna of Saint Tikhon's Orthodox University of Humanities. For eighteen years, Milanteva lived in a convent near Moscow. After that, she worked in construction. She started writing plays in 2013. Her texts have been shortlisted for multiple Russian drama competitions, including the major Russian drama festival Lubimovka (2013, 2014, 2016, and 2017) as well as Original Event—21st Century (Iskhodnoe sobytie—XXI vek; 2019), First Staged Reading (Pervaia chitka; 2020), and Remark (Remarka; 2020). Her play *Sawmill Plus* was published in the journal *Literature* and has been staged in three Russian theaters. *A Child for Olya*, included in this anthology, appeared in the journal *The Art of Cinema* and was staged at the Meyerhold Center in Moscow in September 2020.

Author's address
This play is about the love between two women, which ends in a separation. It does not focus on the marginalization of this theme or on the plight of LGBTQ persons in Russian society. *A Child for Olya* spreads the message that love is a precious gift that is rare to get and hard to keep. It is about challenges in a relationship that are unique to a female couple. I greatly cherish this text as a member of the LGBTQ community and as an author who invested personal struggles in the story. I hope the readers of this book will enjoy it.

Characters

Zhenya, *thirty-five years old*
Olya, *thirty years old*
Slavik, *forty years old*
Tatyana Vasilyevna, *Zhenya's mother*
Misha, *Zhenya's father*
Vita, *thirty-five years old*
Vlad, *Vita's husband*
Nanny
Kid
Women
Men
Girls
Slim Girl
Big Lady

Scene One

Office party. **Olya**, **Women**, **Men**.

Women

—We should cut the cake. Girls, come over here.
—We should wait for Alla Mikhaylovna, don't start without her.
—Wow, there's pastries here too!
—I got them in Bakhetle.[1]
—I'm going to Kalyaev tomorrow, to buy a fur coat. Anybody care to join me? If you wait too long, they'll sell out.
—We went there already, snagged one for Oksana, my daughter, it cost us only 70 grand. The place was packed, so don't wait, go tomorrow.
—Olya, do you have one already? Come with us.

Olya   I'm not into fur coats.

Women

—Well, just listen to that. Nobody is telling you to wear it every day on the transit.
—Totally, getting it all grody.
—A fur coat is a must-have, that's for sure. Like, I've got tickets for the theater early next month. Vovka and I will go together. I dressed him up for the occasion too, so he wouldn't look like such a bum.

Olya   Which theater are you going to?

—I don't remember, some place downtown. The tickets were only 700 rubles. Alla Mikhaylovna already saw this production, she said it's fine, nothing inappropriate.

Olya *walks out into the hallway.*

Olya   Max, can I have a smoke? Thanks. (*She walks outside;* **Men** *are smoking there.*) Hi.

Men

—Hi. So, I want to redo my living room, just like at Dan's place, you know, with extra lighting over the sofa, it looks cool.
—Right, everyone wants to do it like Dan did.
—Mine will be even better.
—Hey, Mikha, where did you score this briefcase?
—There's a website, I got my gloves there too.
—Send us the link, man.
—Come on, fucking google it. It took me forever to find it. (*Fiddles with his briefcase.*)

Olya *goes back inside.* **Men** *shout to her as she walks away:*

—Olya, will you dance with us?

Olya   No, I'm heading home soon.

—Why's that? Why are you so grumpy tonight?

Olya *walks up to a table and pours herself a whisky.*

Women

—Olya, stop wasting yourself on whisky. Look at all these cocktails! Sapunov's treat, specially for us girls. So many, all so fancy—come on!

Olya (*walks away, in a low voice*)   Drink the damn cocktails yourselves, fuckers.

Women *gossip; one of them shouts out loud:*

—Girls, when are we gonna dance at Olya's wedding? Olya, come, come over here. We're all tipsy, of course, but I'm telling you, you should take a closer look at (*points*) Orekhov. He's in research. They don't earn as much, but he's a decent guy, no kids—someone else might snatch him if you don't. Go, dance, you look so gorgeous tonight.

Olya   Svetlana Ivanovna, please stop, or I'll just leave.

—Geez, nobody is good enough for her.

Olya *walks out on the street, makes a call.*

Olya   Zhenya, I'm leaving, will you meet me at the subway exit? Yep, I've had enough of this party, I'm sick already. No, sick from something else. They're trying to set me up with some nerd. Ahahahah! Yep, why not, apparently, I just need to buy a fur coat tomorrow and I'm ready. Alright, see you soon, miss you, I'm on my way, bye.[2]

Scene Two

Zhenya *and* **Slavik**, *in a car.* **Zhenya** *is driving.*

Zhenya   Have they even started working? They've got only three days—after that, they've gotta be out of there.

Slavik   I told them all that.

Zhenya   You told them . . . they don't need to be told, they need to be handled.

Slavik   I'm on site every day this week, the place on Aviamotornaya Street, a Stalin-era apartment with a bathroom. I have Ukrainians working there, they need to be watched.

Zhenya   Slava, you can't control every cement bag, they'll take what they want anyway, no big deal. If they set their mind on it, they'll even do it at night. Don't you know Ukrainians? They're doing their job just fine, so for God's sake, let them have a few bags. What is that, 5 thousand rubles or something? At least they're doing the job.

Slavik   Well, it's a matter of principle, I guess, they've just gotten to me. Bunch of smartasses. I would have paid them more, but they fucking jabber and jabber, all day long, just like chicks.

Zhenya   But they do the job, and they do it well.

Slavik   That's true, they do it well, can't say anything about that.

Zhenya   So, whatever, leave them the fuck alone. Better check on the dumb ass Asians more.

They enter an apartment that is being renovated. In the living room, four **Uzbeks** *are sitting on the floor, drinking tea and eating bread.*

Zhenya   What is this party?

Uzbeks   Lunch.

Zhenya   Why haven't you even started to work?

Uzbeks   Hmmmm, we want an advance payment first.

Zhenya   What advance payment? It's a three-day job max. Come on, get up and work, or fuck off.

She goes to the bathroom. There's a worker there; he is standing in the mortar and leveling it around himself.

Zhenya   Is that how you do the slab? Where's your level, man?

Uzbek (*smiles*)   I don't usually do this kind of work, I'm a driver.

Zhenya   Who the fuck did you bring in here?! Damn it, Slava, I am talking to you!

Slavik   Well, where do you expect me to find good ones these days?! You know the story with this apartment—no money, no people. Kazbek sent me these guys from his fruit market—at least something.

Zhenya   How are they gonna pour the floors? Do you pour floors? Can you pour?

Uzbeks   We can do anything. Yes, we pour. And yes, we pour very well. Very well.

Slavik (*laughs out loud*)   Well, we also pour very well, vodka into glasses.

Zhenya   Alright, let's go, you'll be back here first thing in the morning. I'm giving you two days to finish it. If they have to work around the clock, you stay with them and watch them.

Slavik   Fuck, I asked him to give me normal ones. And this is what he gave me, fuck.

Zhenya   I'm fed up with all this. Let's get a drink. Do we have a place to crash?

Slavik   Let me check . . . Yep, let's go to Warsaw Avenue, there's no one there today, I've got the keys right here.

Scene Three

Zhenya *and her* **Mother**, *in* **Zhenya**'*s parents' apartment. They are drinking tea.* **Zhenya** *checks her phone.*

Mother   Can't you do something with your hair? Something normal? You've got nice hair, just let it grow, wait a bit, and you'll have a beautiful bob, like that French singer, Mireille Mathieu. It would really suit you, trust me. I don't understand why you're so set on looking ugly. What's with the GI Jane look? I'm not telling you to have braids, just why can't you have it a bit more feminine? Also, I see a lot of girls wearing leggings these days, well, you know the leggings, right, with booties . . . as for the colors, well, tan is very trendy now, khaki, all sorts of beige. You can't wear jeans all the time, you could put on a longer sweater and leggings, and . . .

Zhenya   Enough already! Don't you get tired of talking about all this?

Mother   Well, I wouldn't have to if you opened your eyes and saw what you look like. You should have a pair of heels, too—they don't have to be that high. Just a small heel, and that's already enough to keep you from swaggering so much when you walk. Nobody is telling you to strut like you're on a catwalk, just don't lumber around like a guy. Control yourself. Why does your mother still have to remind you about these things?

Zhenya   I have to go, got some work to do.

Mother   No need to get all pouty. When I die, who'll help you? Who'll give you advice? Honey, stay a bit longer, talk to me, we don't see each other that often. How's work? Do you have clients coming in? Is it alright? You're probably tired?

Zhenya   Everything's fine, work's good.

Mother   Are things going well with Slavik? He seems like a nice guy; you're spending so much time together. If you were just a bit savvier . . .

Zhenya   Stop it already, I'll deal with it myself!

Mother   Easy, easy, sure, deal with it yourself. Does that girl still live with you?

Zhenya   She is renting, ren-ting.

Mother   And how long is she gonna be renting? First, she said it was for three months, but it's been three years already, she's moved all her things in. Your father and I left you the two-bedroom place so that you could start a family, even if it's with a transplant—at least they work hard and don't need much. This girl is like a leech, look at her, so quiet. I know people like her, they tiptoe around at first, but before you know it, they've got you wrapped around their finger.

Zhenya   Mom.

Mother   Honey, listen, I know you, you're too kind and it'll be hard for you to throw her out some day, but she won't leave on her own. This is not a kind of friendship you need; you better stay away. What is she paying you for the room? You're making plenty of money anyway. If you feel like you need company, then just go out together, grab a coffee, walk in a park. There's no need to let God-knows-who live in your house.

Zhenya   Mom, shut up! Shut your mouth! It's my apartment! I'm fucking tired of these conversations!

The **Mother** *holds back tears.* **Zhenya** *leaves.*

Scene Four

Zhenya *and* **Olya** *at home, in the evening. A whisky bottle is on the table. TV is playing a soccer game.* **Zhenya** *is watching it closely.* **Olya** *is tipsy; she is scrolling through her iPhone with one hand, stroking* **Zhenya** *with the other.*

Olya   Do you even remember what day it is? Today's the thirty-first. (*Sighs.*) Well, I already figured that a restaurant was out of question . . .

Zhenya   Hmm?

Olya   Well, think, what happened three years ago?

Zhenya   What? Oh, right! (*Hugs her.*) Well, why didn't you remind me earlier, we could have gone out.

Olya   It's Champions League though.

Zhenya   Who cares about it! I'll pop over to the store, get something yummy for dinner.

Olya   It's fine, look, a yellow card.

Zhenya   What would you like, a cake? (*Gets up.*) Or should I get something fancy, like Japanese?

Olya (*holds her*)   Don't go, stay with me. It's so funny how I spent two weeks pacing up and down Arbat Street that month,[3] waiting for you to notice me, but you wouldn't.

Zhenya   Uh-huh. But when I did, I had to work to get you.

Olya   Yeah, picture that: you were staring right through me, your eyes full of sadness, and that stupid hat you were wearing.

Zhenya   That's when you decided to go all out and get your portrait done.

Olya   It was a matter of principle, I had to see it through.

Zhenya   Well, I had to hold down that spot, couldn't really pay attention to every client who'd sit down for a portrait, I was busy keeping an eye out for cops, so that they wouldn't notice my vodka bottle.

Olya   You were so focused. And I was sitting there, looking at you, chilled to the bones.

Zhenya   And I was like, are you cold?

Olya   Right, and meanwhile, your own fingers were red from the cold and black from the charcoal. I felt so sorry for you then.

Zhenya   And I felt sorry for you—it was windy, my ears burned from the cold, but here was this girl, sitting so still, so responsible.

They laugh.

Olya (*takes* **Zhenya**'s *hand, looks at it*)   I love this hand so much, so strong and warm, mmm . . . fuck.

They cuddle, kiss. The TV shouts: "Goooal!" **Zhenya** *turns around.*

Zhenya   I knew they wouldn't score enough goals. (*Turns the TV off.*)

They have sex.

After sex, they're lying together.

Zhenya   Has it really been three years already? Time flies. All those years, I'd been looking . . . for you.

Olya   Just imagine if there was a tiny baby lying right here, between us, and sniffling. Our sweet little baby. Kitty, don't be silent. You know how much it hurts me.

Zhenya   This is off the table.

Olya   For me, it is.

Zhenya   Well, for me even more so . . .

Olya   Zhenya, that's the only thing I'm asking you. I've never asked you for anything, you know that. You can't even imagine now how everything will change, all this routine—work, dinners, soccer, Facebook, those calls from your parents: How are you doing? We're fine! And it goes on and on and on, day after day . . . I've already got gray hair. Zhenya! The clock is ticking, and it's only months left now, or even days.

Zhenya   I don't count days, I just live. We aren't doing that bad.

Olya   I'm really happy with you, that's why . . . Silly, who'll tell you something like this ever again? Has any woman ever said that to you before? Some people would die to hear those words. Children are everything to a woman. And it will be ours, ALL OURS, our secret, our love.

Zhenya *sighs and turns away from her.*

Olya (*in a low voice*)   Bitch.

Scene Five

A week later. **Zhenya** *and* **Olya** *at home*

Olya   We're having a small party at the workshop tomorrow, you know, with the girls. I told them we'd come together.

Zhenya   I can't tomorrow, I'm going to Khimki, we have a derby.

Olya   Weren't you there last Saturday? Who are they playing against?

Zhenya   Loko.

Olya   Is it that important?

Zhenya   Of course, they're just a few points behind us.

Olya (*sighs*)   I barely get to see you. I'm tired of telling people about you without them ever meeting you. We should be seen together—we're a couple, after all.

Zhenya   What will I do there? Fucking gossip about all your sappy rubbish? Who got dumped, who's in love. Girl forum, so-o bo-o-ring.

Olya   Where did all this interest in soccer come from, anyway? Is this some kind of self-actualization thing?

Zhenya   Why does it need to be self-actualization? Not everything is done for a reason, maybe I just like it.

Olya   Sure. Slavik's into soccer, that's cool. You just have to do everything like him—walk like him, move like him, talk like him, you've even started to sniffle your nose like him. Girls at my work are into avant-garde, you should come sometime, listen to them talk; you have to develop interests beyond soccer.

Zhenya   No, I don't.

Olya   Fine, then go, I don't care.

Zhenya (*hugs her*)   Oh come on, kitty, sweetie, I'm also interested in you, but that's it.

Olya   You're an artist.

Zhenya   I draft apartment plans.

Olya   That's because you killed the artist inside you. It's like you're getting cruder and more primitive out of spite. Do you think it's cool or sexy? Maybe, you're doing all this for someone at your work, for some girl who paints walls?

Zhenya   I've always been like this.

Olya   That's not true, you're picking this up at all those construction sites.

Zhenya   Well, I haven't picked up enough yet. Or how about I go back to the streets to paint people's portraits and be a starving artist. There'll be no more vacations abroad, nothing . . .

Olya (*sighs*)   Alright, enough of it. I had a bad day at work. They were talking about their kids all day, and I had to sit there listening to how brilliant they all are.

Zhenya   Well, people have to brag about something.

Olya   Brag about their own progeny? Cats and cows also give birth, but they don't run around showing off their kids.

Zhenya (*imitates a cow*)   Moo! I'm Bessie, gave birth to Daisy. My Daisy is the most talented and beautiful cow, and whoever thinks otherwise is stu-u-pid!

Olya   If we don't have kids, I'll go crazy.

Zhenya   This again. I told you already, that's enough, Olya. It's absurd. (*She goes into another room.*)

Olya *walks out onto the balcony, nervously lights up a cigarette, looks over at a daycare center in front of their building. She can hear kids' voices in the distance.*

Olya   Wherever I go, fuck. (*She throws away the cigarette, slams the balcony door, flops down on the sofa, and turns on the TV—a commercial is playing.*)

Cheerful Female Voice   What's new today? Libero Comfort has a new and improved inner layer and softer leg cuffs. The diaper fits perfectly and stays in place while your baby explores the world!

Olya *turns off the TV, puts on a coat.*

Olya   I'm going to get some booze!

Zhenya   Now that's a good idea.

Scene Six

Zhenya, *in the clients' apartment. The owners,* **Vita** *and* **Vlad**, *are a married couple; they have a child and a nanny.*

Zhenya   This is a great space for a walk-in closet.

Vita   Oh, but where though? We wanted to have the living room here and put a wardrobe in the hallway.

Zhenya   Your hallway is too narrow. You'll also have to take out the partition between the kitchen and the smaller room.

Vlad   We were actually thinking of making that a nursery.

Zhenya   Well, you want to have an office, a nursery, and a dining room—you can't have them all, you have to choose.

Vita   Vlad, really, our kitchen is 130 sq. feet, that's your office right here.

Zhenya   You can take out the wall between the kitchen and the balcony, get heated floors, and there you go, you've got yourselves a nice office.

Vlad (*puts on a jacket; ready to leave*)   Alright, Vita, continue without me. If you say the balcony, then we'll use the balcony. Even the pantry is fine, I don't care anymore.

Zhenya   Vlad, everybody does it this way nowadays. You've got a beautiful big balcony—you can even fit a sofa in there, and the windows face the courtyard. It'll be paradise.

Vlad   Alright, I have to go. I'm fine with whatever my wife says, she decides everything in our family. (*Leaves.*)

A **Kid** *runs up to* **Zhenya** *and stares at her. She is unsure what to do, then takes a screw out of her pocket.*

Zhenya   Hi kiddo, here's something for you to play with.

The **Kid** *grabs the screw.*

Vita (*smiles, looks at* **Zhenya** *with surprise*)   Artyom, sweetie, this is not a toy, the lady actually meant to give it to your father. (*She takes the screw from the child; he starts crying.*)

Zhenya   How old is he?

Vita   Four years old. (*Pause.*) Do you have kids?

Zhenya   No, I don't.

Vita   You know, it wasn't easy to have Artem. We had to do IVF twice. My husband was against it at first; he insisted on doing it naturally. But natural wouldn't work. I kept miscarrying, had uterine hypertonus over and over again . . .

She gets a wine bottle out the bar and canapes from the fridge.

Vita   Would you like to have a drink?

Zhenya   Well, I'm not sure . . .

The **Nanny** *walks in from the hallway.*

Nanny   Hi, Vitalia Vladimirovna. Has Artyom eaten already?

Vita   Go for a walk with him first. I didn't have time to.

Zhenya   You know, I should go. I have two more apartments to visit.

Vita   I like you a lot, Zhenya. I think we could become friends, you know. Just have a glass with me, don't be shy.

Zhenya   I'm not shy.

Vita *pours the wine into glasses; they toast.*

Zhenya   You have an unusual name, Vitalia.

Vita   My mother gave me a male name after her first love, Vitaly. In fact, Vitalia is a Greek word, it means lively, full of life. I used to hate my name, it felt like life was playing a cruel joke on me, but now that I have Artyom, I think of it as my lucky charm. It made me believe in myself, in my connection to my ancestors. (*Pause. She stares at* **Zhenya**.) Men are so helpless these days, can't make decisions themselves.

Zhenya   Yeah, it's like that everywhere: the wife controls the renovation, and the husband just takes out the garbage.

Vita (*smiles*)   Right, but sometimes I just want to be weak.

Zhenya   I don't know, I've always wanted to be strong.

Vita   And it works. Are you married?

Zhenya   I'm not.

Vita   How long have you been in the renovation business?

Zhenya   A few years. I started this company with a friend.

Vita   You look too sophisticated for a person who works in construction.

Zhenya   I actually studied architecture. And what do you do?

Vita   Translations. Asian languages. Don't you like the wine? I think this one is great.

Zhenya   I'm not much of a wine drinker. I don't really get it.

Vita   Well, why didn't you say anything? Let me pour you some cognac.

Zhenya   That's fine, we'll toast when this place is ready.

Vita   Zhenya, relax, forget the renovation. We can just have a friendly chat, renovation or not. Let down your guard a bit, we're just chilling.

Zhenya *unzips her hoodie.*

Vita (*laughs*)   I meant metaphorically, you're so funny.

Zhenya *downs a glass of cognac.*

Vita   You're a very interesting personality type.

Zhenya   Like, a tomboy?

Vita   No. Although . . . well, you're afraid to let go, afraid of yourself, you're always on guard, ready to punch, ahahaha!

Zhenya *downs another glass of cognac.*

Zhenya   You know nothing about me. I'm like this just because life is like this.

Vita   Well, I think there's a gentle heart hiding under all this armor. (*Silence. She listens in.*) Well, they're back from the walk.

Zhenya *gets up, zips the hoodie.*

Zhenya   Thanks for the cognac, for the company. I'll email you the plans and the cost estimate, and we can discuss it all later.

Vita   Sure, sounds good. (*Walks her to the door.*) I'll give you a call, come over next week, we'll discuss the details. (*She takes* **Zhenya***'s hand;* **Zhenya** *grips hers hard.*)

Zhenya   I'll bring the cognac.

Vita   Oh God. (*Playfully pushes* **Zhenya** *out of the apartment.*) I'll give you a call.

Scene Seven

Zhenya *and* **Slavik** *are in an apartment that is being renovated. They're drinking cognac.*

Zhenya   How are things with Sveta?

Slavik   Shitty. Something's up with her, but I can't figure out what she wants from me.

Zhenya   She wants to shack up, not just have you coming and going.

Slavik   I don't know. It's gonna stay as it is for now. Also, her kid is so spoiled. She's still little, but already a brat. Shows me who's the fucking boss in the house. I come over, she starts slamming the doors, running around the apartment like a sardine—like she owns the fucking place.

Zhenya   Slava, she's a kid, what do you want? Svetka is sweet, she loves you, and this girl—she'll grow up and won't give a shit about the two of you. Just hold on a few years. Much better than being alone, anyway.

Slavik   Get your own first and raise them, then give advice. It's easy for you to say, you're hopping abroad all the time, and your girl is just like you, trips, shopping. I'm not saying that's bad, it's just you're fricking chicks, you have to have kids, it's in your DNA or something, right? (*Taps himself on the back of his head.*)

Zhenya   In our DNA, right, cemented in us, sure!

Slavik   Nature must have put it in you!

Zhenya (*shouts*)   Right, put it in us, put it in this one girl, turned her brain upside down, nature fucking calls her! She can't have a baby, God had a different plan for her, so accept that, move on, but no—she's decided that somebody has to do it instead of her; no, actually, not instead of her but for her. Bring her a present, a kitten in a box with a bow!

Slavik   Wait, do you mean this friend of yours wants to have a baby or something? What's wrong with that?

Zhenya   She wants a baby from me.

Slavik   Wait, I don't get it.

Zhenya   Of course, you don't. And that's not my thing at all. I don't have it in me. I hate kids and pets, birdies, goldfish, potted plants! That's how I am, dammit, deal with it! No, she keeps nagging me, go get IVF, we'll be happy, 'cause apparently now we aren't, and it will just magically appear out of nowhere, this happiness. (*Draws a big circle with her arms.*)

Pause. They are sitting and smoking in silence.

Zhenya   It's just, I can't live without her, Slava . . . If she leaves me, I'll fucking die.

Slavik *empties the bottle into their glasses, looks at* **Zhenya**.

Slavik   How are you gonna get home?

Zhenya   In style, as usual. (*Gets up, walks to the door.*)

Slavik   Have a baby, Zhenya, it'll be good.

Zhenya   Fuck off.

Scene Eight

Zhenya *and* **Vita**.

Zhenya   Hi, Vita, can I swing by now? Ehem, no, they aren't ready yet, but . . . We can figure it out without the plans, we can put marks on the walls, and I'll draft them up later. Are you there alone? OK, see you soon.

Zhenya *and* **Vita** *in* **Vita**'*s apartment.*

Zhenya (*opens a cognac bottle smiling*)   Where's the kiddo? Is he out for a walk?

Vita   He's sleeping. Zhenya, you said you wanted to mark up power sockets?

Zhenya   Yeah, I threw something together already, it's all pretty standard, I'll email it to you later. Oh, I knew you were into Asian stuff. (*She points at the walls decorated with Japanese landscapes.*)

Vita   We brought these from Japan, nothing special, just pretty. I wanted to discuss the walk-in closet with you. Honestly, I don't want to put a shed like that in the living room. It's a spacious room, lots of light. We could do something a lot more interesting with this space. Don't pour any for me, I won't be drinking, I'm driving soon.

Zhenya   Your call. I just suggested the most convenient option, but it doesn't have to be the final one.

Vita   As for the balcony, we'll definitely do heated floors, but we won't be combining it with the kitchen.

Zhenya   Whatever you want.

Vita   Just a minor renovation will be enough.

Zhenya   Just don't skimp on power sockets, you'll regret it.

Zhenya *comes up to* **Vita** *with a glass of cognac.*

Zhenya   It's good cognac, have some.

Vita   There'll be as many sockets as I decide, don't plan anything yourself.

Zhenya   As you wish. This dress looks very nice on you.

Vita   It's a negligee. Zhenya, I'm sorry, but I really have to get ready.

Zhenya *puts her hands on* **Vita**'*s waist.*

Zhenya   What's your deal? I've been thinking about . . . our last conversation all this time.

Vita   Well, Zhenya, you've found your place in life, you've figured out your style, you're like a lone wolf (*puts her hand on* **Zhenya**'s *shoulder*), but an experienced woman can see the mark on you.

Zhenya   What mark?

Vita   Of course, if you're doing well on your own, why would you need a man? But a woman who has no kids is . . . deficient. You need to change something about your life. (*She takes* **Zhenya**'s *hands off herself.*)

Zhenya   What the fuck.

Vita   You can't deceive nature. Sooner or later, it'll remind you of your calling.

Zhenya   I don't care what you see or don't see. I think I'll go now, bye.

Vita (*smiles*)   No need to be offended. Come by sometime, we'll talk. And take the cognac, it's quite expensive.

Zhenya (*walks out, in a low voice*)   Witch. And why do I even care again, stupid idiot.

Scene Nine

A while later. **Zhenya** *and* **Olya**.

Olya   Zhenya, you're so . . . (*Strokes her hair.*) I think it's cool that he'll look like you, I'll love him just as much as I love you. You're our daddy. (*She smiles, strokes* **Zhenya**'s *belly.*)

Zhenya (*slaps* **Olya**'s *hand, jumps off the bed*)   Maybe, I should get an abortion, before it's too late?

Olya   It's already too late, Daddy. And if you do that, then you might as well kill me too, you'll set yourself free from everyone at once.

Zhenya   Listen, when will it get big enough for everyone to notice? I mean, the belly?

Olya   Well, in your case, it's gonna be fast, 'cause you're so skinny. Why, you don't think you'll survive a few months? Do you think our neighbors will judge you? Zhenya, don't be a child, everybody will be happy for you, and anyone who won't—fuck 'em.

Zhenya   I just want to be done carrying this belly around; after that, I'm out.

Olya   Of course, of course, you'll be out. God, just please, don't turn into a pregnant cliché, I'm not gonna walk on eggshells for nine months. If I were you, I'd be so happy. Do you even understand how lucky you are? Idiot. Or are you just messing with me, I don't know . . . Or you've turned into such a dude that you just . . . no idea . . .

Zhenya (*lost in her thoughts*) Okay, when it comes to the guys at work, I don't really care how I look . . .

Olya Alright, kitty, pull yourself together, life goes on!

Zhenya My gym subscription is gonna be wasted for half a season . . . No champagne on New Year's Eve . . . And I'll be bumping people in the elevator with my belly . . .

Olya (*throws a pillow at her*) Stop it already! Look, I've been meaning to show you this (*brings over the laptop and points*), this woman knits all these cool things, so cute! Onesies, mittens, caps. We'll have to order a few.

Zhenya You can get all that in stores.

Olya Stores suck, kids all dressed the same, like orphans, but these are all natural, handmade, just wonderful.

Zhenya Who cares.

Olya You have to. We also have a lot of books to read before the baby comes.

Zhenya I am scared, Olya. Really scared. This is a lifetime commitment. How did I even . . . It's like I'd been hypnotized . . .

Olya Well, I'm with you. So, it's all good, isn't it?

Scene Ten

Zhenya *and her* **Mother** *talk over the phone.*

Zhenya I'm in the fifth month.

Mother And you haven't thought to mention it before?

Zhenya Surprise.

Mother Honey, I'm so happy for you. God, it's hard to even wrap my head around it. What about the father? Is he a nice man?

Zhenya Mom, let's not talk about it, who cares, I just told you so that you know, don't start all . . .

Mother Okay, okay. Are you going for checkups? You need vitamins, a good diet, is he taking care of you or did he just do his job and . . .

Zhenya (*yells*) Mom, I have people who can take care of me! I have everything, I know all these things, so stay out of it!

Mother Do you mean that girl who's leeching off you, is she still there? I thought my daughter had finally come to her senses, decided to start a normal family.

Zhenya   She doesn't leech off me, she has a job. Mom, stop it, or I'll hang up.

Mother   Sorry, honey, forgive me. God help you, do as you like, there's nothing I can do. The most important thing now is to carry the baby. Your dad is gonna be so happy to hear this! Thank God, we lived to have a grandson! We'll be helping you, call more often, tell me everything.

Zhenya   Mom, it's fine, it's alright, I have to go, bye.

Mother   I'm so happy we're talking again, honey, darling. (*Cries.*)

Zhenya   Bye, Mom.

Scene Eleven

Zhenya *and* **Olya** *at home. The bell rings; it's* **Zhenya***'s parents.*

Mother   Hello, honey! Oh, why are you so pale? Let me have a look at you, both of you, both of you, hehehe. (*Hugs her belly.*)

Father   Well done, Zhenya! Heh, really well done! Giving us grandkids!

They walk into the living room. **Olya** *is standing by the window, tense.*

Olya   Hello.

Mother (*doesn't look at her*)   How do you do. Zhenya, look, here are some berries for you, straight from the farmers' market, homemade cottage cheese, and cream. Have some right now, try it.

Zhenya   Mom, come on . . . (*Awkwardly takes the things they bought and carries them to the kitchen.*)

Mother   I guess the crib will go over here, right, Misha?

Father   It shouldn't be too close to the window. Maybe we'll just have to rearrange everything: move the bed up against the wall, it makes no sense that it's in the middle of the room.

Olya *goes into the kitchen.*

Mother   Oh, excuse me, so touchy.

Father   Tanya, come on, don't. Leave her alone.

Mother   A vampire.

Zhenya *and* **Olya** *come back into the room.*

Zhenya   This is Olya. You must remember her.

Mother   Sure we do. How are you, Olya, how's work?

Olya   Work is good, Tatyana Vasilyevna, it's all fine.

Mother   You don't have kids of your own, do you? Are you planning to have any?

Zhenya   Mom! Stop it!

Mother   What, it's just a question. Why are you yelling at me?

Olya   I can't have kids.

Father   Ahem, ladies, shall we have some tea? Who's better in the kitchen here? Olya, will you make some for us, hehe?

Zhenya   Dad, I have to go to work now, can you drop by some other day? Sorry, don't be mad.

Father   Sure, if you say so.

Mother   Let's go, Misha. We'll drop by during the week.

Father   Alright, stay strong, Zhenya, stay strong, hehe!

Mother (*opens the fridge*)   How do you expect her to stay strong? The fridge is empty. This girl has no food for Zhenya at all. She's skin and bones, just her belly sticking out. Do you want your baby to be retarded or something?

Zhenya (*slams the fridge door*)   I don't want any baby at all! I don't need all this, you understand?! It's an accident, just a stupid accident, that's it. Stop lurking around here.

Father   Don't yell at your mother.

Mother   Really, honey, you shouldn't be stressing yourself out, relax. Let's go, Misha.

Zhenya *opens the door and sees her parents off.*

Mother (*from the stairwell*)   Is he at least Russian?

Zhenya   Who?

Mother   Well . . . is the baby gonna be white, or did you sleep with a migrant? Were you sober at least? Just tell me, I'm your mother.

Zhenya   Are you out of your damn mind? (*Slams the door.*)

Scene Twelve

Olya *and* **Zhenya**, *on a walk.*

Olya   Damn accounting, I hate it. If I could, I'd just fucking quit. It's not too late to go and study something else. Everyone lives as they want, doing creative stuff, and I've been wasting my life on these village idiots. Should I just quit? What do you think, Zhenya? My English isn't bad. The money though . . . What would we do without the money?

Silence.

Olya   I just wanna go and live somewhere else, where I don't know a single damn face. Rent is cheaper in Saint Petersburg. Think about it Zhenya, I mean it. Why stay in Moscow? They won't leave us in peace here, anyway.

Zhenya   Who's not leaving you in peace here? My mother?

Olya   I don't think she'd come to Saint Petersburg every week. And all these miserable Slaviks of yours won't be there either.

Zhenya   There'll be new damn faces—new colleagues, new Alla Mikhaylovnas, new Slaviks. What's wrong with Slavik, anyway?

Olya   He hates me.

Zhenya   *You're* the one who hates everyone. How are you going to raise a kid?

Olya   Oh, now you're worried. (*Laughs.*) Don't you worry, my kid will have everything—the best education, best books, foreign languages, arts and sports, normal people around. Or do you want him to end up sitting around on his fat ass in front of the TV, with your old Soviet folks by his side?

Zhenya   My grandma raised me, and it was great.

Olya   Right, I can see that. Zhenya, it has to be our child, do you get it? Maybe, we'll even move abroad, get married? He doesn't need to get all this brainwashing from the moment he's born. We'd manage fine without any grandmas and grandpas, grow up already. Remember my friends Dasha and Mila, the ones I told you about? They had a child, they're LGBT activists, always on the front lines, taking part in exhibitions and roundtables, they even got sent to Europe a few times from their NGO, 'cause they're a couple, a family, you know, oppressed, marginalized, and yada yada. It's only a matter of time before they get refugee status, if not in Europe, then in Israel. People hustle, they don't just sit around and wait.

Zhenya   Olya, don't be stupid, I won't go anywhere. You wanted to have a child, didn't you? You don't even know what you want.

Olya (*takes her hand, leans over to her*)   I just want to be happy, like any other person, with you. Don't be angry, kitty, just listen to me sometimes, not just your mother.

Scene Thirteen

Olya *and* **Zhenya's Mother**.

Olya *is alone at home. The door opens;* **Zhenya's Mother** *comes in with lots of bags.*

Mother   I don't get this weather: one day it's winter, then it's not. (*Grunts, the bags are rustling.*) Zhenya, honey!

Olya *comes out in the hallway.*

Olya   Hello, Tatyana Vasilyevna. Zhenya's out, she'll be back in the evening.

Mother   Where is she?

Olya   She's on site with a friend, they're drafting a plan.

Mother   Do you mean with Slavik? Why? She shouldn't be drinking.

Olya   She isn't.

Mother   It's Sunday, why is she working? Are you hiding something from me? Is she in hospital?

Olya   Everything's fine.

Mother   There's a new bakery on General Molokov Street, lots of women, long line. I bought a few pies for 600 rubles. Zhenya loves them. I don't know, maybe they're shitty.

Olya   You could have called before coming over.

Mother   It's none of your business, is it? I'm not gonna ask for your permission to come here. Why don't you go back home on the weekends anyway? Doesn't your mother live near Moscow? It's not far. You should have your own place, stick with your own family.

Olya   Am I bothering you?

The **Mother** *sorts out the groceries in the kitchen, then walks through all the rooms and inspects the shelves and wardrobes.*

Mother   People have to have some decency. And if they don't, other people have to let them know. Your postcards are all over the place, and these horrible paintings—all this devilish stuff has to go.

Olya   It's esoterica, and Zhenya likes them.

Mother   Zhenya used to be a normal girl, willful, happy. Now she's turned into a softie, anxious all the time. I'm surprised she even decided to keep this baby, there must be a God after all. There'll be a baby here soon, you must actually understand that that room will be the nursery.

Olya   I'll be helping out, what's wrong with that?

Mother   I'll be helping out, you got that?! I am the grandmother. And grandpa will be helping too. Take your damn pictures away, I'll bring over some icons to put up instead.

Olya   How about we don't touch anything here until Zhenya comes? If Zhenya tells me to leave, I'll pack my stuff and go. Why are you so aggressive to someone who's friends with your daughter?

Mother   I don't mind friends, friends are fine, nobody cares, but why the fuck would you move in here?! Do you get me, Olya? No need to get offended, I'm just telling you how I see it. And rest assured, I'll talk to my daughter. That's all I have to say, bye. (*Leaves.*)

Scene Fourteen

Evening of the same day. **Olya** *is at home,* **Zhenya** *and* **Slavik** *come in.*

Zhenya   Olya, I'm so tired, can you give Slavik something to eat? I'm gonna go lie down.

Slavik (*smiles*)   Hi, Olya.

Olya   Hi. (*Talks to* **Zhenya**.) Your mother crammed the fridge with food for a month.

Zhenya   Oh, did she come over again?

Olya   Can you tell her not to come here and snoop around? Why should I be wasting my day off on your mother? And why have you both decided that you can shit all over me?

Zhenya   I'll handle it. (*She walks into another room and closes the door.*)

Olya   You'll handle it, right. When it comes to cooking, cleaning, and doing groceries, it's all Olya, naturally. Her mother convinced her that I'm a leech, and she's happy to believe that. Do you want soup?

Slavik   Sure.

Olya *angrily puts cutlery and a soup plate on the table.*

Olya   She'll handle it. She could handle it by telling her parents: that's my wife, got it? And she'll be living here with me! But of course, she doesn't have the balls to dó that.

Slavik (*grins*)   What're you talking about, wife, no way, you're fricking hilarious.

Olya   Of course, it's better for her like this: she gets it both ways, there's Olya, there's Mommy, and let them figure things out and fight each other, I'll just sit here, I'm pregnant, they have to take care of me, pity me. I thought when a girl gets pregnant, she gets smarter, grows up a bit. But no, she's always been like a teen . . . and now she's turned into a complete baby. And there's another baby coming soon. And let me tell you, I'm gonna have to take care of all of them—the baby, its mommy. And if I'm not around, she'll ship the kid off to her mother. She doesn't need any of that. She'll just turn on a soccer game, and it doesn't even matter who's playing, some Costa Rica or whoever, she just needs to escape reality. She used to do the same thing on Arbat, just staring into nowhere . . . I don't know (*sighs*) . . . When we started dating, she tried so hard, her courting was so awkward, so adorable. Why are you sitting over an empty plate? (*She grabs* **Slavik**'*s plate, and gives him the main course.*)

Slavik   Olya, you know, sitting here listening to you . . . Of course, I don't really understand all your, you know . . .

Olya   What's that smell? Slava, is it your sweater?

Slavik *sniffs his sweater.*

Olya   Can you take it off? It's hot in here, so you're just sweating in this thing.

Slavik *takes off his sweater, unbuttons the top of his shirt, and looks at* **Olya** *with lust.* **Olya** *opens the window to air the room and gingerly takes the sweater out into the hallway.*

Olya (*in a low voice*)   This male scent, I hate it.

Slavik   What I wanna say is, let her have this baby, her mom and dad will be happy to have it, there's zero chance she'll get married, so they'll live like a family, all together. I don't get what you see in her. Olya, you both are just wasting your time, you're such a beautiful girl, men check you out all the time, like I would take you with me right now, if you'd go.

Olya   I thought you had someone.

Slavik   Well, it wasn't really serious, and it's over anyway, and she had a daughter too. You on the other hand . . . I realized I don't want to have kids, not to mention to raise anybody else's. Why raise somebody else's kids? It's a cross you'll have to carry your whole life, a burden. And I've got my own place, and yes, it's only one bedroom, but there aren't any mommies and daddies, they're far away and won't get to us, he-he.

Olya   Slavik, get the hell out.

Slavik *waits for a moment, then he gets up and walks out of the apartment.*

Olya *walks into the room, sits down next to* **Zhenya**. **Zhenya** *is lying down.*

Olya   Should I also leave?

Zhenya   Why? What are you talking about?

Olya   You tell me. I'll be a nuisance here soon, apparently.

Zhenya   Olya, I told you already, I'll talk to my mom, don't start up again. The day's been bad enough already.

Olya *lies down next to* **Zhenya**, *hugs her.*

Olya   Tell me, please, that everything is fine, and nothing has changed, that you still love me. (*Hugs her, caresses her.*)

Zhenya (*moves away from her hand*)   I can't now, really, I'm sorry.

Olya   You're not into me anymore? You know, you're not off the hook for marital duties just because you're pregnant.

Zhenya   Olya . . . you . . . how do I put this . . . you have to have compassion, or something. I don't know if it's good or bad, or even ridiculous, maybe, but I'm a mother now.

Olya *gets up, laughs nervously.*

Olya   That's great. That's fricking awesome.

Scene Fifteen

Olya *is in a nightclub.* **Olya**, **Girls**, *then* **Zhenya**.

A queer nightclub. It's crowded, lots of cigarette smoke, electro house music blasting. **Olya** *is at the bar. A* **Girl** *comes up to her.*

Girl   Why are you alone? Where are your friends? Where's your girlfriend?

Olya   I like it better alone.

Girl (*leans over to her*)   What did you say? I'm here with friends. (*She nods at a table.*) Smile, cheer up. Come on, come on, you gonna do great, just go up to anyone and say, "I want you."

Olya   I don't want anybody. (*Turns away to the bar.*) Whisky, please.

Girl   Whoa, you're a piece of work.

Olya *goes to the smoking room; it's quieter there. There's a brightly made-up* **Big Lady** *over forty and a* **Couple** *of* **Girls**, *who are showily making out while checking out the room. A* **Slim Girl** *sits down next to* **Olya***; she has tattoos and her head is shaved. She is really drunk, and puts her arm around* **Olya**.

Slim Girl   Any plans for tonight? What's your name?

Olya   Does it matter?

Couple   Come on, don't be a party pooper. People come here to have fun.

Olya   I'm having fun my way. (*Finishes her whisky.*)

Slim Girl   Let's have some vodka. Do you like it rough?

Olya *moves away from her. The* **Girl** *leaves to cruise the room; she strikes up conversation with everyone she runs into and hugs them.*

Big Lady   Don't judge her by her height, she only looks like a pathetic cunt, but she's fucking amazing in bed.

Olya   How do you know that?

Big Lady   Everybody knows her in here. Take her home with you before she blacks out. You won't regret it.

*The **Girl** drapes herself on **Olya** again.*

Slim Girl   Have you ordered the vodka?

Olya *gives a sign to the waiter.*

Olya   Where do you study?

Slim Girl   I drive a troll.

Olya   You're a trolleybus driver?

*The **Girl** nods.*

Olya   Wow. Do you like it?

Slim Girl   Are you for real?

They're drinking vodka.

Slim Girl   You can find me on Vkontakte,[4] I'm Axel Cavaglieri. Got it?

Olya   Fuck you, you're no Axel, trashy bitch.

Slim Girl   What did you just say? (*Punches **Olya** in the face.*)

*There's a commotion; people pull the **Girl** away from **Olya**, bring **Olya** over onto a sofa, and wash the blood off her face. A few minutes later, **Zhenya** pushes through the crowd; she is looking for **Olya**. She is dressed in awkward maternity clothes.*

*She comes up to **Olya**, grabs her hand, and pulls her to the door.*

Voices
—Wow, here we go . . .
—Left her preggo wife at home and went clubbing.
—This is love.

Olya   Zhenya, what're you doing here, why did you come? You need to be sleeping.

They leave the club, get into a car.

Olya   Fuck, you're so clumsy with this belly.

Zhenya   Will you shut up, or I'll shine up your other eye too.

Olya   Kitty, honey, I'm sorry.

At home.

Zhenya   Let's go to bed.

Olya   What am I, a grandma? I don't want to sleep, I want to dance.

Zhenya   Knock yourself out, dance, I'll just stand here, cheer you on.

Olya   Awesome, a house party, cute. (*She turns on the music, dances.*)

Zhenya *is sitting and watching her.*

Zhenya   Cutting loose, damn it.

Olya (*dancing*)   Don't be like your precious mommy, one mother-in-law is more than enough for me, two would be too much. Do we have something to drink?

Zhenya   You're asking *me*?

Olya *looks in a cupboard, takes out a bottle, pours herself a glass, keeps dancing.*

This continues for a while. The whole time, **Zhenya** *is sitting in silence and watching* **Olya**.

Zhenya   Well, tell me, honestly, why did you start all this.

Olya   Can't I have fun once in six months?

Zhenya   That's not what I'm talking about. I mean this. (*Points at her belly.*)

Olya (*smiles*)   It was a test.

Zhenya   Come again? A test?

Olya   "You have been weighed on the scales and found wanting."[5]

Zhenya   Wanting? Wanting this? (*She gets up and shakes her belly.*)

Olya   Kitty, well, how do I put it . . . You aren't a mommy or a daddy, you aren't even a surrogate mother, you aren't a husband or a wife, you're just too . . . wanting.

Zhenya   What the fuck do you need? This is our baby, our baby! What for? What is this for?

Olya   Our? It's your baby, your family's baby, the blood of your mother. You've changed. You're lost somewhere, channeling your ancestors from the depths.

Zhenya   What depths, what the hell are you talking about? (*She sighs, a pause.*) And what did you expect? They're people too. Maybe I've finally . . . I don't know . . . gotten to know them.

Olya (*stops dancing, leans against the wall*)   I wanted to have a family. It was a stupid wish, of course.

Zhenya   And I wanted you. It was a stupid wish, of course.

Olya *looks through her, into nowhere.* **Zhenya** *stares at her for a while, at her face, neck, arms. Then she grabs her by the clothes, squeezes it in her fist, then lets go and drops her hand. The music keeps playing.*

Scene Sixteen

Two weeks later. **Zhenya** *is at home alone; she's lying on the bed, wrapped up in a quilt. The place is a mess, clothes are scattered all over the room; dirty dishes, pots, and food scraps pile up in the kitchen. An ashtray with cigarette butts, empty wine bottles. Doorbell rings a few times. Then the key turns in the hole, the door opens,* and **Zhenya**'s *parents walk in. Her* **Father** *is holding a crib, her* **Mother** *has shopping bags in her hands.*

Father   The guests have arrived!

Mother   I smell cigarettes. That girl must have smoked on the balcony. Is anybody home?! (*Walks to the kitchen.*) Good lord. Misha, look at this mess, and she's having a baby in two weeks. Go straighten her out, are you her father or what? As for this tramp, there's no way I'll let her back in here. Left a pig sty behind. "She'll help take care of the baby," my ass. Damn vampire will sap everything out of the baby too, no way, I'm not letting this happen.

Father (*walks to the room*)   Zhenya, is that you? Zhenya, why are you in bed? Are you not feeling well? Zhenya, talk to me.

Mother   Honey, what happened, tell us, should we call an ambulance?

Zhenya   No.

Mother   No what? Can you talk to your mother like a normal person? Why do I have to pull every word out of you? Turn around, we're talking to you. Zhenya, what's wrong with you? (*Tries to pull the quilt off her head to see her.*) Are you crying, honey? Dear lord.

She looks around, notices the absence of the esoteric pictures she hated so much. She gets up, walks into the other room; the shelves and the wardrobe are empty.

Mother (*in a low voice*)   Well, thank God. (*Sits down next to* **Zhenya**.) Honey, did Olya move out?

Zhenya   Can you just go? Please.

Mother   Then who's been smoking here? Honey, have you lost your mind?

Zhenya   Please, go.

The **Mother** *sits at the table. There's a crumpled letter on it; she takes it and reads it. Then she sits in silence for a while. The* **Father** *is cleaning the garbage out of the kitchen, grumbling.*

Father   She seemed like a nice and neat girl and left such a mess after herself. People these days . . .

The **Mother** *passes the paper to the father; he reads it.*

Father   Jesus Christ. (*Sits down.*) Hmm, Zhenya, don't you worry, your mother and I have also been like this our whole life—fighting, then making up.

The **Mother** *stares at him reproachfully; she twists her finger next to her head to indicate that he's insane to have said that.*

Father   What? It happens.

Mother   Misha, clean up all this garbage. Go, do it. Zhenya, I'll pack your things and you'll come with us to our place. You shouldn't be here alone right now, in this negative atmosphere. I made borscht yesterday. Your father will sleep in the kitchen; it won't be the first time. Come on, honey, happy days are coming, we have to stick together, come on, come on, keep your head up—when you cry, the baby cries with you. And we need a healthy and happy grandson.

Zhenya   You'll get one, don't worry.

Scene Seventeen

Six years later. **Zhenya** *is sitting in a sports bar, watching soccer.* **Slavik** *comes up to her.*

Slavik   Hey there. Zero–zero? Is the beer good? Fuck, why do you like it here, this place is packed with idiots. You used to watch games at home. Zhenya, you don't look terrific, are you sick or something?

Zhenya   Or something.

Slavik   You're drinking quite a lot.

Zhenya   Oh, you think so?

Slavik   I do. I haven't seen you for how long, six months? Listen, come back to work, don't be stupid, you can't manage alone, it'll be easier together. You look like hell.

Zhenya   Nope. It won't be easier.

Slavik   Whatever. How long did we bust our asses together and never had a single argument.

Zhenya   Slava, I can't hear anything, neither the game, nor you, I came to watch Barça play, if you're bored, just leave.

Slavik   Easy, easy. I'm into the French League now. They're having a really great season, surprised me actually.

Zhenya   I don't know. All the oldies went to China, who's even left to watch there?

Slavik   Check it out some time. Their outsiders put on quite a show there, it's fun to watch.

Zhenya   As long as money is out of the picture, it's always fun to watch. But then they place tenth, and goodbye dream team from the hood, then it's just business and showbiz. Look, look what he's doing, what a champ!

Slavik   Well, of course, it's Neymar.

Zhenya   My kiddo is also trying these tricks, just like him, ahahaha, with his little heel, totally cracks me up.

Slavik   How is he doing there anyway, does he like it?

Zhenya   He does, he's getting used to it.

Slavik   Doesn't he miss you?

Zhenya   He does, mostly his grandma and grandpa, though, they spoiled him. But it's fine, it'll help him man up. I mean, of course, when I drop him off on Mondays, my heart aches. But it's only like this as long as he's little, in five years, he won't even think of me.

Slavik   Zhenya, you're all alone, you've kicked everyone away, how are you, really?

Zhenya (*shouts*)   It's her son! (*Pause.*) The moment he was born, he started crying, and cried, and cried, and when he was three years old, he pursed his lips at me, just like she used to. I'm not going to wipe Olya's nose all my life. Talked me into making this fricking substitute for herself. Why are you staring at me like you've never heard of it, what do you know? I was about to give birth and instead of getting ready I was crawling around on the floor. I had thrown out all her shit, so that nothing would . . . And then suddenly, some random . . . (*Pause, holds back tears.*)

Slavik   Easy, easy.

Zhenya   Some random bead in the corner, all dusty but so familiar . . . (*Talks to the waiter.*) Another beer, please.

Slavik   Calm down, Zhenya.

Zhenya   But really, if it hadn't been for my mom and dad, I don't know what I'd do with all this. You know, it's all for the better, Alyosha is so different now, turning into a little man. When he stays at my place over the weekends, he won't shut up about his life there.

Slavik   Well, of course, it's all better than wasting his life in front of a computer here.

Zhenya   It was really hard for me to get him into that school. After all, it's not just any place—a legit soccer academy, TsSka, national champions, you know.

Slavik   We've missed all the goals.

Zhenya   Well, why did you start all this, what is it to you?

Slavik (*looks at* **Zhenya** *cautiously*)   Wow, you're a tough case. Maybe, what they say is true: that you people should get treatment?

Zhenya   Get treatment . . . but they refuse to give us proper treatment, fuckers.

Both laugh.

Slavik   Maybe, you and I should give it a try. You're single, I'm single.

Zhenya   That would work if we were rabbits . . .

Slavik   We know each other better than just about anyone. You'll have another baby. (*Winks at her.*)

Zhenya   Hmm, a child for Slavik? I guess, everything's possible, Slavik, but not in this life, not in this life.

Soccer commentator is shouting hoarsely; he can't keep up with the intricate lace Catalonians are masterfully weaving on the field:

—Neymar . . . moves past the midfield again. Suarez is open . . . He plays around the defender, passes to Messi . . . The goalie is helpless . . . Go-o-al! That's the way to do it! Another miracle from Lionel Messi! It's FC Barcelona. Rise, gentlemen, and give a big round of applause!

2016

Notes

1 Bakhetle is a chain of high-end city markets in Russia that specializes in pre-cooked dinners and Tatar cuisine—in particular, sweets and pastry.
2 Zhenya in Russian is both a male and a female name, which makes Olya's call to Zhenya in Scene One quite ambiguous, as it is unclear yet that she's calling her girlfriend.
3 Arbat Street is a pedestrian street in downtown Moscow, a famous tourist place with street artists, souvenir stands, patios, and cultural venues.
4 Vkontakte (or VK) is a Russian social network, modeled after Facebook.
5 "You have been weighed on the scales and found wanting" is a verse from the Bible (Daniel 5:27), which means that the person has not measured up to the expectations placed on them. As it is part of the larger prophecy "Mene, Mene, Tekel, Parsin," which appears as a writing on the wall of Belshazzar's palace and foretells an impending catastrophe for his kingdom, it can also be read as an omen for Olya and Zhenya's relationship.

The Pillow's Soul

A PLAY FOR CHILDREN

Olzhas Zhanaydarov

Olzhas Zhanaydarov is a playwright and drama teacher based in Moscow. He was born in 1980 in Kazakhstan and has lived in Russia since 1987. He started writing plays in 2009 and has since penned over a dozen texts. Zhanaydarov's work explores themes like the migrant experience in Russia (*Earplugs*, *The Store*, *Aldar*), children's and youth's problems (*The Pillow's Soul*, *Dances Plus*, *Friend Zone*), solitude and madness (*Mania*, *Falling Apart*), and collective memory (*Jute*, *A Plan*). His plays have won multiple drama competitions, including Lubimovka and Eurasia, and have earned Zhanaydarov a nomination for the Russian version of Olivier Award (or Tony)—the Golden Mask—in the category Best Work by a Playwright. Zhanaydarov is director of the Kazakh festival of contemporary drama Drama.KZ and artistic director of the Russian drama festival Lubimovka. He has taken part in international projects like "LARK + Lubimovka" (organized by the Lark theater laboratory in New York in 2015) and "Staging the Stans" (hosted by the Silk Road Rising company in Chicago in 2019). His plays have been translated into English, German, French, Polish, Czech, Turkish, and other languages. Personal website: olzhas.ru

Author's address
Greetings, dear readers, I am excited that *The Pillow's Soul* is now coming out in English. This play is very important to me. When I was a kid, I was often very anxious about being different from others. This play is my message that you have to embrace yourselves the way you are and not go against yourselves to be the way the society wants you to be. I think this is something that kids and teens really need to know, because their parents, friends, and others often try to tell them what to do and how to be. I hope reading this play brings you to a happy place and helps you get another perspective on yourselves and your lives.

Characters

Pillows:

Bucky
Fuzzy
Rose
Smarty
Emma
Cushy
Ivanovna[1]

Kostya, *a boy*
Chacha, *a rat*

Setting

Daycare, winter

A spacious nap room.

A row of beds.

Children's voices, which fade into the distance.

Naptime has just come to an end. **Kostya** *is the only child left in the room. He is sleeping, wearing pajamas.*

Seven pillows varying in size and shape are scattered around on the beds and floor. They start moving.

The rat **Chacha** *runs out of a dark corner of the room and sniffs the pillows on the floor, one after another.*

Chacha (*whispers*)   Emma, are you here? The concert is soon, soon's the concert!

Cushy   Huh? What? (*Looks around.*)

Chacha *discreetly runs to the far corner and sneaks into a hole in the baseboard.*

The pillows sit up, fluffing and patting themselves to smooth the wrinkles on their cases.

Fuzzy (*stretches*)   Ah, so good! And so fun!

Cushy   Good and fun. I agree.

Rose   Good, good! Got some sleep, and now stretched a little.

Fuzzy   I could get some more sleep.

Smarty   The allotted time is two hours. No more. That's the regimen!

Rose   Right, Smarty. Well, start sharing, start sharing! Fuzzy, you start.

Fuzzy   Mine tossed and turned a lot at first, you know. See these dents in my back? (*Points to the dents.*) Finally, he fell asleep. He dreamed about a train. It was moving, puffing out smoke, you know. And suddenly, a bear jumps right onto the rails. Gets up, you know, on its legs, and starts dancing.

Rose   And what happened next?

Fuzzy   Next mine woke up. Cushy landed on him.

Cushy   Yep. Mine wasn't sleeping. She was lying down, singing a song. Playing with a giraffe. (*He shows a toy giraffe.*) And then out of nowhere, she just throws me across the room! Boy, that's when it all started . . . A full-out battle.

Smarty (*reports*)   Attention please. My ward. Slept an hour forty, dreamt for thirty minutes. In his dream, there was a house, two stories, made of brick. On the roof of the house, there was a clown with a red nose. Next to the house, there was a coniferous tree. No accidents noted. The child did not participate in the pillow fight. That's all I have. Thank you for your attention.

Rose   And mine, mine had such a beautiful dream. The sky, so, so blue. The sun, so, so golden. Mom and Dad, holding hands.

Emma   Ugh. Rosy rubbish.

Rose   What's wrong with you, Emma?

Emma   I'm nauseated. Ugh.

Rose   Oh, fine, fine. What was in your dream?

Emma   The basement. And the rat Chacha, my friend. And cockroaches, too. Brown, with antennae. Rustling, skittering around. Hundreds, thousands of them! Their antennae were so thick, and their backs so smooth and moist.

Rose   Oh, stop it! This again?

Cushy   I agree with Rose. That's enough.

Smarty   You've gone too far, Emma! You know we don't talk about the Mentbase here!

Emma   The basement?

Everyone (*except* **Bucky**, *together*)   Emma!

Ivanovna (*sneezes*)   A-achoo!

Rose   Bless you, Ivanovna. What about you?

Ivanovna   Mine was driving a tank in his dream. Through the forest. Last time it was a plane. Now a tank. He'll surely join the military, the little rascal. A-achoo! As for pillow fights—I'm too old for that. (*Sighs.*) Soon they'll send me there . . . to the Mentbase.

Rose   Don't you worry, Ivanovna. You still look great. And what about the new pillow? Bucky, what did you dream about?

Everyone looks at **Bucky** *while he inspects himself with a surprised look on his face. His case is partially removed, slightly torn—there's a little pile of buckwheat on the floor next to him. The grain keeps falling out of the hole in* **Bucky**'s "body."

Bucky   Well, I have this . . .

Rose (*scared*)   Oh, what is it?

Fuzzy   Something black.

Ivanovna   Oh my, oh goodness!

Smarty (*comes closer*)   It's buckwheat. It's classified as grain.

Bucky   It was inside me . . . (*Tries to cover the hole, in vain.*) I've got a tear.

Cushy   Where's the goose down?

Rose   Where are the feathers?

Bucky   I don't know . . .

All the pillows except **Emma** *take a step away from* **Bucky**. *They start whispering.*

Rose   He is not like everyone else.

Fuzzy   Even though he looks like us, you know.

Smarty   They'll send him to the Mentbase. Sure thing!

Cushy   I kind of I like him.

Ivanovna   I feel sorry for the little fellow. His first day in the daycare. A-achoo!

Bucky *walks back and forth and observes—buckwheat keeps falling out of the hole.*

Rose   What if all, just all, all the buckwheat falls out of him, and nothing is left?

Smarty   That means certain death. A pillow cannot survive without filling.

Ivanovna   Oh dear! A-achoo!

Cushy   How can we help him?

Smarty   Pillows are of no help here.

Pause.

Fuzzy   By the way, we are getting fresh cases today! I want one with a doggie.

Rose   And I want a floral one. The floral ones are my favorite.

Smarty   I like neutral ones. Without print.

Cushy   And I don't need one. I am doing alright without a case.

Emma (*approaches* **Cushy**)   "Doing alright." Half-pint, not even that. You don't need a case; you need a sock. (*Laughs.*) Do you agree?

Bucky *approaches the other pillows.*

Bucky   It's still falling out . . . This buckwheat.

Fuzzy (*ignoring* **Bucky**)   So, what now? We need to rest.

Emma (*quietly*)   The chubster is tired.

Fuzzy   Huh?

Rose   Yes, we need to, we definitely need to. I'm tired.

Ivanovna   Me too . . . a-achoo! Too old. Me riding a tank—ridiculous! I need to get some rest.

Cushy   I agree. We need to get some rest.

Bucky   What do I do though? Tell me!

Smarty   One hour rest time. Noted.

Everybody gets back in their beds.

Fuzzy (*lying down*)   Cases . . . You know . . . Fresh . . .

Bucky (*looks at everyone*)   Why am I filled with buckwheat?

But nobody is listening to **Bucky** *anymore. He wanders between the beds.*

Stops next to **Ivanovna**.

Sits down on her bed.

Bucky   Ivanovna!

Ivanovna   Pardon?

Bucky   I don't get it. What's wrong with me?

Ivanovna   Everyone has down and feathers, and you have buckwheat. Where did you come from?

Bucky   From a store. There were many of us there.

Ivanovna   And did all of you have buckwheat?

Bucky   I don't know. We didn't check. And I didn't check. Until today. I thought I had down and feathers, like everyone else. Had a carefree life.

Ivanovna   Oh, just you wait. They'll send you to the Mentbase! A-choo! You'd best get some rest.

Smarty (*mumbles in a dream*)   "Best–rest"—an acceptable rhyme. Noted.

Bucky   Ivanovna!

Ivanovna   What do you want?

Bucky   What's the Ment . . . Mentbase?

Ivanovna   The scariest place on earth. Right below us. They send all the old defective pillows there. It's damp and dark, with rats and cockroaches . . . Brrr! Let's not talk about it.

Bucky   I want to have down and feathers. Like all pillows. I don't want to go to the Mentbase.

Ivanovna   Me neither. But I am weak. My health isn't the same anymore. This darn sciatica. A-choo!

Bucky   What?

Ivanovna   Sciatica! It's a disease. I sacrificed my health when I was young. And for what? They used me to block cracks in the windows! The wind and frost would blow through, whistling, howling, oooh-oooh! Well, here I am . . . a-choo! . . . caught a never-ending cold.

Bucky   Have you ever met someone like me? Filled with buckwheat?

Ivanovna   Not once in my very long life.

Bucky   And have you always been here, in the daycare?

Ivanovna   Yes, since I was young. Very young. I came straight from the factory. A-choo! I've seen more kids than you can count. Fat and skinny, bratty and sweet. I've seen 'em all. Even an albino kid.

Bucky   Who?

Ivanovna   An albino, white like your case. By the way, did you cover that hole of yours? 'Cause, you know . . .

Bucky   What?

Ivanovna   Pillows don't live long without filling, sweetie. A-achoo! (*She looks around, notices buckwheat scattered on the floor.*) Oh my, look what a mess you've made.

Bucky   It was my dream to get into a daycare when I was living at the store. And now they'll just send me to this Mentbase. Who sends the pillows there anyway?

Ivanovna   People. Teachers. But don't worry. Maybe you'll be fine.

Bucky   What if I pretend that I'm normal? Eh? Will you keep my secret?

Ivanovna *doesn't say anything.*

Bucky   Ivanovna!

But **Ivanovna** *is sleeping already; she sniffles and doesn't hear him.*

Bucky *comes closer to* **Smarty**'s *bed.*

Bucky   Hey, Smarty!

Smarty   It's rest time! Please follow the regimen.

Bucky   Oh, please . . . You are the smartest.

Smarty (*proudly*)   An IQ of 164. I substituted for a bean bag at the library for two weeks. Got real smart. Noted.

Bucky   Well, tell me. Why am I filled with buckwheat? Am I . . . wrong?

Smarty   All pillows are filled with down and feathers. But you aren't. This is a deviation from the norm. Therefore, technically, you are wrong.

Bucky   Can I do something to be like everyone else?

Smarty   First you have to follow the rules: lie on your tummy, follow the regimen of sleep and rest, change your case once a week. Don't talk to kids, even when they are asleep. And stop rustling, for pillow's sake! (*He watches buckwheat fall out of* **Bucky**.) Oh, and you are making a mess.

Bucky   I can't stop rustling. It's the buckwheat.

Smarty   The sound gives you away.

Bucky   Does this mean that people will send me to the Mentbase?

Smarty   Probably. Although . . . What if we have you undergo an operation? (*He touches* **Bucky***'s sides, examines him like a doctor.*)

Bucky (*laughs*)   Eek! That tickles!

Smarty   Alright, we've already got an access hole. We'll remove the buckwheat, stuff you with down and feathers. You'll be just like everyone else.

Bucky   And then I can stay here, in the daycare?

Smarty   The probability is high. And you don't have a choice anyway: you'll soon run out of buckwheat. And that would be fatal.

Bucky   Fa . . . what?

Smarty   Deadly. You'll be dead as a doornail.

Bucky   Oh, I don't know . . . An oper-ration! I need to think.

Smarty   Right. Thinking is good. Contemplation is rewarding. And I'll go back to my rest. After all, we have regimen! (*He flops onto his tummy and doesn't move anymore.*)

Bucky *wanders around the room, lost in thought. Without looking down, he sits on a bed.*

Cushy   Ouch!

Bucky (*jumps up; it turns out he sat down on the tiny* **Cushy**)   Oh, Cushy, I'm sorry, I didn't see you.

Cushy   That's alright, I'm used to it. It's easy to miss me.

Bucky   Cushy, tell me, why am I full of buckwheat?

Cushy   I don't know. I haven't seen anything like this before. But don't worry. Everything happens for a reason. Do you agree?

Bucky   When I lived in the store, I didn't think about it. I didn't know. I rustled though, unlike the other pillows. But so what? I've been like this since I was born. Why? Why am I not like everyone else?

Cushy   I'm not like others either. Look at me, I'd like to be bigger. Taller. Fatter. I'm the smallest here. The children throw me at each other. Because I'm light. And small.

Bucky   Well, not so small. Let's compare heights.

Bucky *and* **Cushy** *stand back to back.* **Cushy** *is several inches shorter than* **Bucky** *and much thinner than him.*

Cushy   You see. Half-pint, not even that. Do you agree?

Bucky   You could still grow.

Cushy   No, I can't. I'm a pillow. Pillows don't grow. I'll stay like this forever.

Bucky   You know . . . When I lived in the store, there were tiny pillows like . . . teeny-tiny pillows . . . (*Shows their size with his hands.*) Yes, small, like a cabbage . . . no, smaller, like a potato!

Cushy   No way!

Bucky   Pillow swear! Absolute tinies.

Cushy   I wonder who they make them for . . . There aren't any people that small.

Bucky   Well . . . they aren't exactly . . . for people.

Cushy   For who then?

Bucky   Well, for, what do you call them . . .? Dolls. Right, for dolls! Barbies and the like. They are so teeny-teeny-tiny. You are a giant next to them!

Cushy   Really?

Bucky   Of course.

Cushy   So, I am not the smallest? You agree?

Bucky   I agree! I agree one hundred percent!

Cushy   Cool. One hundred percent. I like that.

Bucky   The thing is, even those teeny-teeny-tiny baby pillows are surely stuffed with down. Whereas I'm . . .

Cushy   Did you talk to Smarty? He's smart, he knows everything.

Smarty (*mumbles in a dream*)   Knows everything . . . That's me . . .

Bucky   I did.

Cushy   And?

Bucky   He says I should undergo an operation. To swap the buckwheat for down and feathers. Do you think I should agree?

Cushy (*automatically*)   Agree. No, wait. I don't know. You should think about it.

Bucky   That's what he said, too—"think about it." (*Steps aside.*)

Cushy *looks at him, and then lies down again.*

Bucky *prods himself, buckwheat rustles inside him.*

Bucky   Why is there buckwheat in me? I'm not a pot, for pillow's sake!

He tries to shake out the buckwheat—jumps, twists, stands on his head, gives himself a few good shakes, rustling loudly all the while. **Fuzzy** *wakes up.*

Fuzzy   Bucky, what are you doing there? Stop it. You'll lose all your filling and die, you know.

Bucky *stops and tries to catch his breath. He sighs. Stumbles away slowly— buckwheat keeps trickling out of the hole.*

Bucky (*sad*)   Why live like this? Nobody needs buckwheat . . .

Fuzzy   Well, that's not true. Buckwheat's not so bad. Better than barley, that's for sure.

He sniffs the air.

Mmmm . . . Do you smell that? Coming from the cafeteria?

Bucky (*deep in thought*)   They'll send me to the Mentbase, to the rats. I deserve it.

Fuzzy   What? Stop talking about the Mentbase. Do you smell cookies? And milk? Means that the kids are having snack time. Then they'll go for a walk, you know. They'll come back frozen, their cheeks rosy from the cold.

Bucky   Fuzzy, you're so big.

Fuzzy   Special design! For exceptionally large kids.

Bucky   You must have seen many dreams . . .

Fuzzy   Four hundred and ninety-four dreams. Almost an anniversary, you know—no kidding. When I get old, I'll write a memoir.

Bucky   A meow what? Meow-mew?

Fuzzy   A memoir. That is, my memories, you know. I'll write down every single dream that I'll have seen into one big book.

Bucky   I probably won't ever have a shot at that meow-mew. What could a buckwheat pillow write about?

Pause.

What dreams have you seen? Tell me.

Fuzzy   Oh! All kinds!

Stands tall on his bed.

Once I dreamt of a magic land. It's in the sky, among the clouds. There, the grass is blue, the trees are orange, and the rivers are white, just like milk! Cloud folk live there.

Bucky   Which folk?

Fuzzy   Cloud folk. Their arms, legs, and bodies are all made of clouds. They're soft and warm, like cotton. Every day they fly out of their homes and push clouds back and forth. They can fly!

Bucky   Cool!

Fuzzy   I also saw striped monkeys once. We . . . I mean, the boy who dreamt of them, was fighting underground tigers. Just imagine, the jungle, the sun, and there, from under the ground, huge tigers come crawling out, just like moles, you know. And you jump from one tree to another with striped monkeys and throw bananas at the tigers. If you hit them, they disappear. We threw bananas all night long, you know—woke up soaked in sweat.

Bucky   Fascinating.

Fuzzy   And once I saw the same dream three days in a row. Different kids dreamt one and the same thing! Three days in a row!

Smarty (*mumbles*)   Three days . . . Three days . . . Noted.

Bucky   What did they dream about?

Fuzzy   Berries. A huge field of berries, and the children were wandering around, picking berries, and eating them. And then the berries came to life and started rolling away from the kids, you know. And they had to catch them, catch them! They were hiding under leaves, behind flowers, next to mushrooms. They jumped, bounced, rolled away, and hid. Petya caught thirty-two berries, Masha got thirty-six, and Sashka—forty-eight. Oof, I got so tired!

Bucky   I would also like to catch berries . . .

Fuzzy   And I've dreamt of ice cream so many times, I've lost track! Strawberry, cookie dough, chocolate, vanilla—something for everyone! And once, well . . . once I saw an ice cream city. Everything was made of ice cream there—houses, trees, cars, even garbage bins, you know! And it wasn't cold at all there!

The sun was shining, everyone was in T-shirts and shorts, but the ice cream didn't melt at all. You could come up to a bench, bend over, bite off a piece, and keep going, you know—that's how it was.

Bucky   Wow!

Fuzzy   Oh yes! The things I've dreamt about! A million toys! Toy cars and Legos, dolls and blocks, balls and marbles. I've seen real animals—a pillowzillion! Kittens, doggies, hamsters, parrots, you know. Elephants, foxes, lions, eagles, and partridges. Seagulls. And a kangaroo.[2]

Bucky   A kangaroo?

Fuzzy   Yep, a kangaroo. With a pouch on its belly, you know. Ahh, and the food I've seen . . . I love these dreams more than anything . . . Just yesterday, I dreamt of cake.

Bucky   Was it yummy?

Fuzzy   So yummy. With cream filling, pieces of banana and orange on top, covered with strawberry glaze, you know . . . (*Licks his lips.*) Dreamt of pastries of all sorts. Scones, tarts, danishes. Filled with jam, custard, chocolate. Seen my fill of pies too—apple pies and cabbage pies, cherry pies and rice pies, mushroom pies and potato pies.

Bucky   Have you ever dreamed of buckwheat? Cream of buckwheat, maybe?

Fuzzy   Nope. No buckwheat. Or oatmeal. Children don't really like porridge, you know. Borscht, on the other hand—saw that in a dream once. And a shish kabob—still steaming, with onions and tomatoes, you know. But more often than anything else I've seen candy! Caramel, toffee, chocolate, jellybeans, lollipops, gummy bears.

Bucky   Ooh . . . gummy bears.

Fuzzy   I also love the moment right after lunch, when the kids lie down for their naps . . . They lay their heads on me, smelling . . . soups, pies, pastries! Once, a boy even dropped a doughnut on me, you know! Can you believe that? He brought it from the cafeteria, sat on the bed and dropped it right onto me! It had cream filling! Oh, I wished that case could stay on me forever. It smelled so good.

Bucky   Your life is so exciting, you've seen so many things. And I am totally useless! Neither down, nor feathers!

Fuzzy (*jumps in, hearing the last words*)   No down, no feathers—no pillow! (*He catches himself.*) Oh, I mean . . . Never mind. It's just your first day. You need to, you know . . . acli . . . alchi . . . alchimate . . .

Smarty (*still dreaming*)   Acclimate!

Fuzzy   Right! That's what I meant. Acclimate.

Smarty (*still dreaming*)   That is, to get accustomed.

Fuzzy   Right. Get accustomed, you know. One can live with buckwheat, too.

He watches **Bucky***'s filling trickle out of him.*

Fuzzy (*notes apprehensively*)   Whereas without buckwheat, one could easily die . . .

Bucky   But I am wrong! People will send me to the Mentbase!

Rose *stretches softly.*

Rose   Bucky, why are you making so much noise?

Bucky *comes over to* **Rose** *and sits down on her bed.* **Fuzzy** *goes back to sleeping on his tummy.*

Rose *notices that* **Bucky** *is losing buckwheat.*

Rose   Just don't make a mess on my bed, please.

Bucky (*jumps up from the bed*)   Oh, sorry.

Rose   So why are you making so much noise?

Bucky   I don't know, Rose. It's just, I'm wrong, that's all.

Rose   Why think about it? Pretend that you have down and feathers. We won't remind you how you really are inside.

She brushes buckwheat grains off her bed.

Well, of course, if you don't make it so obvious all the time.

Bucky   They'll find out anyway. The people. The buckwheat just keeps coming out of me! Children throw pillows all the time.

Rose   They spare me. I am too refined for these kinds of games.

Bucky   By the way, they say you have the most beautiful dreams around here.

Rose   Who is "they"?

Bucky   Cushy.

Rose   Ah, Cushy . . . Dear sweet Cushy.

Bucky   I agree. Dear and sweet.

Rose   He is nice. But tiny. I wish he were a bit bigger, just a little bit bigger.

Bucky   Like Fuzzy?

Rose   No, to be honest, Fuzzy is way too big. He isn't my match either.

Bucky   Your match for what?

Rose (*smiles*)   Bucky, tell me, have you ever dreamt about your pillowmate?

Bucky   A pillowmate? What do you mean?

Rose   Every pillow in the world has a pillowmate—another pillow, who suits them perfectly.

Bucky   Why do you need one—this other pillow?

Rose   Because . . . because it's nicer together, when you have someone. It's cozier, happier. It's wonderful. People call it "love."

Smarty (*mumbles in his dream*)   "Love" . . . Encyclopedia, letter L . . . A feeling of deep affection . . .

Bucky   Never heard of it.

Rose   I've seen it so many times in dreams. Mom and Dad. Dad and Mom. Love . . .

Bucky   Lovey-dovey. Dovey-lovey.

Rose   You know, I have a dream. I want to get into a real home, into a bedroom, in the parents' bed.

Bucky   Parents' bed? What's so special about it?

Rose   Well, first of all, there's lots of space in it—it's a really, really big bed. Mom and Dad sleep in there. Second, these beds always need two pillows. A couple. They are always together, forever. Day and night. They are meant for each other. They are happy together.

Bucky   What if they get bored? Forever, in one bed, with one and the same pillow?

Rose   They won't. Never, ever. This is how tight the connection between them is. They even dream the same dreams. Even their pillowcases are the same. Can you believe it?

Bucky   Wow. Wow.

Distracted by the story, **Bucky** *sits down on* **Rose**'s *bed. The grain from his hole starts falling on her bed again.*

Rose   Bucky!

Bucky (*jumps off* **Rose**'s *bed*)   Ah, right, right.

Rose   When I lived at a pillow factory, my girlfriends and I would dream about going to real homes, to real apartments. We wanted to get into the parents' beds. And some did get a chance to go there. Whereas I . . . well, I ended up here.

Bucky   Don't you like it here?

Rose   I do. The kids are sweet, the dreams are wonderful. But I want more . . . I want to finally see the adult world!

Bucky   But everyone loves you here.

Rose   Yes, but I'll grow old someday! And they'll send me to the . . . the Mentbase! To the bad place.

Bucky   And if you get into a home, into a bedroom?

Rose   They don't send pillows to the Mentbase! You live there your whole life. And when you get old, they just put you in a closet. Which is warm, cozy, and there are always others to talk to.

Bucky   Tell me then, does it mean that my pillowmate must also have buckwheat? Does it have to be not like others?

Rose   I don't know.

Bucky   What if I'm the only one like this in the whole world?

He steps aside, sits on another bed, sighs.

Suddenly, he hears barking. **Bucky** *starts, looks around—it is* **Emma** *who is sitting next to him.*

Emma (*satisfied*)   Aha, got you!

Bucky   Very funny. You scared the buckwheat out of me.

Emma   You've hardly got any left, anyway, as I far as I can tell. The samurai that you are. (*Laughs.*) Better death than disgrace, is that what you're going for?

Bucky   Maybe that's for the best.

Emma   You know, I heard everything. How you've been moping around. "Why am I not like the others? Why?" Whining and whining. When will you stop?

Bucky   I'm not whining.

Emma   Yes, you are. I've seen lots of kids, and even they don't whine like you. Trust me, I'm an expert on kids' tears.

Bucky   I'm not whining.

Emma   Every pillow in here gets its case changed once a week. Mine is changed every other day. You know why?

Bucky   Why?

Emma   Well, think about it—what kinds of dreams do I get to see? Spiders, cockroaches, snakes of all sorts. Forest beasts, bogeymen, monsters. I am an expert on nightmares. On horror. Kids cry when they nap. And my cases get wet.

Bucky   Are you mean?

Emma   Not at all. I'm normal. It's just that there's more to life than flowers and sunshine. Where did you live before you got here?

Bucky   In a store. There were a lot of other pillows there. We never went anywhere, just lay all day on the shelves and in baskets. And at night, we chatted—we wondered who'd buy us, and where we'd end up. (*Sighs.*) I just didn't know back then that I was full of buckwheat.

Emma   That's what I'm talking about. You and everyone else here, you know nothing about real life. Grew up in comfort. Rose, Fuzzy, Smarty, and Cushy also came here straight from the factory. Ivanovna hasn't been anywhere else but this daycare, ever. And these stupid rules that they made up.

Bucky   They are all terrified of the Mentbase.

Emma   There's nothing terrifying about it! Don't listen to them.

Bucky   Should I listen to you?

Emma   You should. I always tell the truth. Some pillows, they tell you one thing when they actually have a different thing in mind. They want to seem nice. I speak my mind. I'm honest.

Bucky   Is that good?

Emma   "Good—not good." Doesn't mean anything. Have you heard that all pillows should sleep on their tummies?

Bucky   Yes. That's the rule.

Emma   Well, I sleep on my back. Because that's what I want. You don't have to listen to anybody.

Bucky   Smarty says we should sleep on our tummies, observe the hours of sleep and rest, change our cases, never talk to kids. That's how it should be.

Emma   "Should be." What if you don't want to? Sometimes, it's naptime and I don't want to sleep. I just lie on my back and think.

Bucky   And the kid?

Emma   Well, he also lies awake. He doesn't want to sleep!

Bucky   Can we really do whatever we want to do?

Emma   Yep. Anything. Do whatever you want. Be naughty, disobey, go rogue.

Bucky   I was taught not to do these things.

Emma   You are just like Chacha. She's my only friend. She is so shy, scared of everything. I've been telling her, do whatever you want. And I'm telling the same to you.

Fuzzy *jumps up in his bed.*

Fuzzy   Hey! Emma! What are telling Bucky there?

Emma   Chill out, chubster.

Fuzzy   Don't listen to her, Bucky. She gives this talk to all new pillows. She wants to turn them astray. Do you know where she lived before?

Bucky   At a pillow factory?

Emma   Go on, chubster, go tattle.

Fuzzy   No, it's not only from there that pillows come. Emma used to live . . .

Rose   She used to live . . .

Bucky   Where?

Ivanovna   She lived . . .

Fuzzy, **Rose**, **Cushy**, **Smarty**, **Ivanovna** (*all together*)   In the Mentbase!

Smarty   Which is damp and dark, with rats and cockroaches. Brrr! Well, of course, she got washed and cleaned. But you can't clean the soul. So her soul stayed the same. (*Whispers.*) A basement soul.

Emma   At least I know life. Real life.

Rose   With monsters and snakes? Life is not like that, Emma. It has lots of light, joy, and happiness.

Fuzzy   Rose is right. Emma, you want Bucky to be bad and naughty. Just like yourself.

Smarty   We should teach our little ones to be kind. That's noted.

Cushy   I agree.

Ivanovna   A-achooo!

Fuzzy (*reacts to the sneeze*)   Oh! That means it's true.

Emma   Oh, you all think you're so smart. Yet none of you can solve Bucky's problem! What can you offer him? What? Only your sweet words? Or you can terrify him with the basement? Just look at him—a little more time, and there'll be no filling in him at all!

Silence.

You only think about yourselves!

Silence.

Turns to **Bucky**.

Emma   Do you see now? You'll be like this forever! And nobody cares!

The room gets darker, quiet music is playing. The voice of a teacher talking to kids outside the room, "Get ready kids! Let's go for a walk!"

Something shuffles in the corner; the rat **Chacha** *enters again. She stands on her back feet, scared to move forward.*

Chacha (*whispers*)   Emma, Emma, where are you? Where are you? The concert is about to start—I can't do it without you!

Bucky *gets out of his bed, where the boy* **Kostya** *is sleeping; he looks around, doesn't say anything, sighs. This awakens* **Kostya**. **Chacha** *sneaks back into the baseboard hole.*

Bucky (*watches buckwheat trickle out of his "body"*)   That's it. The only thing I can do is die with honor.

Pause.

I never knew what it was like to be lonely. But now I know. It is when you are not like others.

Kostya   I am also not like others.

Bucky   Oh. Hi.

Kostya (*sits up on the bed next to* **Bucky**)   Hi! I'm Kostya.

Bucky   I know. You sleep on me.

Kostya   And what about you? Do you have a name?

Bucky   I do. My name is Bucky.

Kostya *notices the grain falling out of* **Bucky**.

Kostya   Hey, what's that?

Bucky   It's buckwheat. My filling.

Kostya   Hold on a second!

He removes a pin from his pajamas, which holds his shirt together at the bottom. He pins the hole on **Bucky**'s *"body." The buckwheat stops falling out.*

Bucky   Oh.

Kostya   That's better.

Bucky *inspects himself with surprise and joy. He looks at* **Kostya** *gratefully.*

Bucky   To tell you the truth, I've never talked to people before. It's against the rules.

Kostya   Well, I've never talked to pillows. But don't worry. It's just a dream.

Bucky   What do you mean? It's not a dream! We aren't sleeping!

Kostya   Of course we are. Everyone knows that pillows can't talk. Which means it's a dream.

Bucky   Hmm. Alright. I'm not gonna argue with you. By the way, why didn't you go for snack time and for a walk like the other kids? Why are you here?

Kostya   I'm new here. It's my first day. And besides, I can't go.

Bucky   Oh wow. I'm new here, too, and it's also my first day. Why can't you go?

Kostya   I'm sick. I have a special regimen.

Bucky   What are you sick with?

Kostya   I have this . . . what do you call it . . . allergy.

Smarty (*mumbles in his dream*)   Encyclopedia, letter A . . .

Bucky   Al . . . al-legry? What is it?

Kostya   A bunch of things make me sneeze and cough. Flowers. Cats, dogs. Pillows.

Bucky   Why aren't you sneezing now then? I'm a pillow, too.

Kostya   I don't know. Maybe because it's a dream?

Bucky   It's not!

Kostya   Well, let's check. Pinch me.

Bucky *tries to pinch* **Kostya**. *He doesn't react.*

Bucky   I can't pinch. I'm a pillow. I'm too soft.

Kostya *tries to pinch* **Bucky** *too.*

Bucky (*laughs*)   Oh, it tickles! A-ha-ha-ha . . .

Kostya   Alright, I'll stop.

Bucky   Yep. Or we'll wake everyone.

Kostya   Everyone? There's nobody here, only pillows. Or do you mean they can talk, too, just like you?

Bucky   Well, of course. We all can. But I'm different anyway. Not like them.

Kostya   How do you mean?

Bucky   A pillow should have down and feathers. But I have buckwheat.

Kostya   Why?

Bucky   I don't know. Nobody here knows why. I've asked. Rose, Fuzzy, Emma, Cushy, Ivanovna . . . Even Smarty doesn't know, and he's the smartest here—he lived in the library for two weeks.

Kostya   Who's Smarty?

Bucky   Well, do you see the pillow with the grey case? That's Smarty.

Kostya   Wait, do all pillows have names?

Bucky   Of course. Every pillow can come up with a name for itself. It's much easier that way.

Kostya   Emma, Fuzzy, Smarty, Ivanovna, Rose, Cushy . . . and Bucky. How are girl pillows different from boy pillows?

Bucky   Boy pillows have their cases buttoned left to right, and girls—right to left.

Kostya   Just like people. Cool! I get you. I can get you. I'm also not like others.

Bucky   Because of this . . . what did you call it . . . alle-legry?

Kostya   Yes. I'm different. Everyone in this daycare is normal. They don't get me. They sniff flowers. They play with cats and dogs. And I can't do any of that. I can't even play with plush toys.

Bucky   Even with toys?

Kostya   I also get sick a lot. Cold, flu. I stay at home in my bed, take medicine. I have no friends. But to be fair, I only ever talk to doctors. I haven't been in a place where I can make friends.

Bucky   Well, if you want . . . I could be your friend.

Kostya   I do. Just . . .

Bucky   What?

Kostya   Well, I'll wake up and it'll all be over. You'll be an ordinary pillow again. One that doesn't talk. In the end, it's just a dream.

Bucky   Oh, will you stop saying that?! Why don't you believe me?

(*He looks around and sees* **Ivanovna** *nearby.*) Follow me!

(*Comes up to* **Ivanovna** *together with* **Kostya**, *says quietly.*) Ivanovna . . . It's me, Bucky . . . Can I talk to you for a second? . . . Ivanovna!

Ivanovna (*wakes up*)   A-achoo! What do you want this time?

Bucky   I found a friend. He saved me from death! Look!

Bucky *shows her the hole in his "body" that the pin now holds.* **Ivanovna**, *still sleepy, squints at it.*

Bucky   This is Kostya. But he thinks that this is all a dream. Tell him!

Ivanovna *looks at* **Kostya**. **Kostya** *comes closer to her.*

Ivanovna   A-achoo!

Kostya   Aa-choo!

Ivanovna   A-achoo!

Kostya   Aa-choo!

Ivanovna   Hey, stop teasing! It's not polite to tease elderly pillows. Shame on you, young man.

Kostya   I'm not teasing, I swear.

Bucky   He's not, Ivanovna. It's because of his al-legry.

Kostya   Allergy.

Ivanovna   Aller . . . What?

Kostya   Pillows make me sneeze. (*He steps away.*) I guess, I'll just stand here.

Ivanovna (*turns to* **Bucky**, *whispers*)   What are you doing? It's against the rules to talk to kids! Have you forgotten?! Are you trying to get thrown in the Mentbase?

Bucky   No. I just . . . He just . . . he doesn't have friends. There's no one he can talk to.

Ivanovna   How is that your problem? A-achoo! It's his, human problem. Pillows should mind their own business. We have our own life.

Bucky   But Ivanovna . . .

Ivanovna   Go to bed. And no more talking to kids. If Smarty finds out, you'll be in big trouble. A-choo!

Smarty (*mumbles in a dream*)   Big trouble . . . Right . . .

Bucky *returns to his bed, sits down on it.* **Kostya** *sits down next to him.*

Bucky   You see now that it's not a dream?

Kostya   I still can't believe it. But if it's true, it's awesome! It's so much fun talking to you. I haven't talked like this to anyone!

Bucky   Neither have I. But it's against the rules.

Kostya   What's against the rules?

Bucky   We shouldn't talk. Pillows have their life, humans have theirs. That's how it should be.

Kostya   Why? Says who?

Bucky   I don't know. But these are the rules. If I break them, they'll send me to the Mentbase.

Kostya   The Mentbase? What is it?

Bucky (*whispers*)   It's the basement. It's damp and dark, with rats . . . All defective pillows go there.

Kostya   The Mentbase, mentbase . . . That's a weird name. Aha! I see, it's basement backwards. But who sends pillows there? People?

Bucky   Yes. I'll double-check with Smarty. Stay here. Pretend that you're sleeping. Or he'll be angry.

Kostya   Okay. (*Gets into bed.*)

Bucky *comes up to* **Smarty**.

Bucky (*quietly*)   Hey, Smarty.

Smarty   Regimen, hours! Do not disturb!

Bucky   It's important. It's very, very important.

Smarty (*sits up*)   What is it?

Bucky   Well, you know, I met a boy . . .

Smarty   What?! Did you talk to him?

Bucky   Well, Smarty, dear . . . He's special. Not like other kids. And he closed my hole with this thing, whatever it is. I'm not going to die anymore.

Smarty (*inspects* **Bucky***'s hole, fastened with a pin*)   It's a pin. Not a bad idea. (*Angrily.*) But you know it's against the rules to talk to kids. Absolutely, resolutely! You have broken the rule of rules that pillows have. Do you understand that? He will tell the teachers, and they'll send us all to the Mentbase!

Bucky   He's very smart. Very.

Smarty   Smart? Smarter than me?

Bucky   Yes. Oh, I mean, no. I don't know. See for yourself.

Smarty *goes to* **Kostya**. **Kostya** *sits up in bed.*

Kostya   A-achoo! I'm sorry, could you stay where you are?

Bucky   He has this thing . . . al-legry.

Smarty (*steps away*)   Allergy. Hypersensitivity of the body's immune system.

Bucky   Pillows make him sneeze.

Kostya   And cough. Only Bucky doesn't, somehow.

Smarty (*ponders*)   Well, well . . . Bucky has buckwheat. I see now! It's hypoallergenic! Noted.

Bucky   Hypo . . . what?

Smarty   The boy is allergic to down and feathers. But not to buckwheat. Buckwheat is hypoallergenic, it helps neutralize allergies. Now I see why you're here. The daycare must have bought you specifically for cases like this. We have all sorts of kids. Kids with allergies, too.

Bucky   Cool! Kostya also likes being with me. That's why we're friends.

Smarty   A pillow cannot be friends with a human.

Bucky   Why?

Smarty   Do you have a Mentbase-wish? These are the rules. No one should break them.

Kostya   Every rule has an exception!

Smarty   The boy is smart, I can't deny that. Tell me, why is 10 afraid of 7?

Kostya   Because 7, 8, 9?

Bucky   Told you he was smart. Can we please be friends? Please!

Smarty   No. It's against the rules.

Smarty *returns to his bed and very carefully gets into it.*

Smarty   When I wake up, everything should be like it was before. Noted!

Bucky (*to* **Kostya**)   That's alright. It's not over yet. Stay here.

Goes to **Rose**.

Bucky   Rose, Rose dear.

Rose (*gets up in her bed*)   Bucky, is that you? What is it this time?

Bucky   Rose, do you remember our talk about pillowmates?

Rose   I do.

Bucky   I found mine.

Points at the sleeping **Kostya**.

Bucky   There he is.

Rose   He's cute. Just one little problem: he's a person.

Bucky   And? I don't have friends. He doesn't have friends. Nobody gets us. We get each other very well. So why can't we be friends?

Rose   A pillowmate should be a pillow. And he is a person!

Bucky   Is that so important?

Rose   Of course it is! A pillow and a person . . . They are too different!

Bucky   But we are so similar. We get each other.

Rose   Bucky, stop talking nonsense. Just wait for a normal pillowmate. A pillow like you.

Bucky   There aren't pillows like me. I like spending time with Kostya.

Rose   Oh goodness, why are you so stubborn? It's against the rules to be friends with a person.

Bucky   Who made this rule?

Fuzzy (*sits up in his bed*)   Our ancestors made this rule. Ivanovna, tell him!

Ivanovna   Right, right. I remember, when I was young, older pillows told me about it, right here, in the daycare. Do as Fuzzy says. A-achoo!

Bucky   Why did they make this rule?

Fuzzy   A long time ago, let me tell you, pillows and people talked to each other all the time. They were friends and would not leave each other's side, day or night, you know. It was a relationship of equals. Until, once, came the Day of Great Cold.

Smarty (*mumbles*)   DGC . . . DGC . . .

Bucky   The Day of Great Cold?

Fuzzy   That day, terrible frost descended on earth. It was, really, really freezing, you know. Pillows tried to keep people warm, but they couldn't. And then people decided to turn all pillows, with no exceptions, into warm quilts . . . They took the pillows and . . .

Her hands start tearing invisible pillows in the air.

Rose   The horror, the horror.

Fuzzy   People used these quilts to cover their houses. Finally, it was warm. But there wasn't a single pillow left in the world . . .

Rose   Just horrible.

Fuzzy   From that day on, the relations between people and pillows changed. People turned us into objects. And pillows stopped talking to people. There is no trust between us anymore.

Ivanovna   We aren't friends anymore, that's what I'm saying. A-achoo. We are just things to them.

Smarty   People are mean. They use us, and then they throw us away. That's why we have to stay fit all the time. We have to obey the rules. The Mentbase . . . is a terrifying place.

Rose   Tell us, Smarty.

Smarty   It's the basement. Right below us. Many pillows found their death there, ones that had given their lives to serve the daycare. People sent them there, despite everything they had done.

Bucky   Is it really so terrifying?

Fuzzy   Very.

Rose   Very.

Smarty   We are people's partners. But not friends. We help them rest and dream. Nothing personal, just business. So it is noted.

Bucky   But I don't want it to be this way. I want a different life.

Rose   Bucky, we all wish you well.

Fuzzy   It's true. We do mean well.

Bucky *comes up to* **Cushy***'s bed. The latter sits up in his bed.*

Bucky   Cushy, do you also think this way? Why can't we be friends with people?

Cushy   I got accustomed to it. So will you. Do you agree?

Bucky   No, I don't. I don't agree. You know, you agree with others way too much. Does it make you happy?

Cushy   I don't know.

Smarty   Bucky, you want to be a real pillow, don't you? With down and feathers?

Bucky   It's impossible. You know that.

Smarty   Not true. Do you remember when we talked about an operation? I have given it more thought, and I've got a great idea.

He comes up to **Bucky***, pulls up his case and reveals buttons.*

Smarty   Do you see? You have buttons on the inner side. We'll unbutton you, take the buckwheat out, and put down and feathers in there instead. It's very simple.

Bucky   Where would we get down and feathers?

Smarty   I've got it figured out. Fuzzy will give you some of his.

Fuzzy   Yeah. I have a lot of down. Way too much. I need to lose some weight.

Rose   Right, right. Fuzzy should lose some weight.

Cushy   I agree.

Smarty (*to* **Bucky**)   And you'll be just like us.

Bucky   But then I won't be able to talk to Kostya anymore . . . I'll make him sneeze and cough, just like you do.

Smarty   Well, yes, but you'll also be a real—proper—pillow! Do you see what I mean? That's what you hoped for!

Rose   Oh, it will be wonderful. When naptime is over, you'll share the dreams you saw with us. We'll all discuss our dreams together. You won't be lonely. And nobody will send you to the Mentbase!

Cushy   Agree, Bucky.

Bucky   But he saved my life!

Ivanovna   So go live it in happiness just as we do. A-achoo!

Bucky   I need to talk to Kostya. I need to think.

Smarty   Right. Thinking is good. Go, think about it.

To **Fuzzy**, **Rose**, *and* **Cushy**.

Smarty   Pssst! . . . Noted.

Fuzzy, **Cushy**, **Rose**, *and* **Smarty** *return into their beds.* **Bucky** *stumbles to his bed and sits down on it.* **Kostya** *sits next to him.*

Bucky   Kostya . . . Here's the thing . . .

Kostya   I know. I heard everything.

Bucky   So, what do I do?

Kostya   Well, you want to be a normal pillow, don't you?

Bucky   But we won't be able to be friends anymore . . . Because of your al-legry. I'll be like everyone else; we won't be able to talk.

Kostya   Well, there wouldn't be much talking anyway. I don't come to the daycare that often. I'm too sick.

Bucky   Why would you say that? Don't you want to be friends?

Kostya   I do want to be friends with you. But I don't want you to get hurt.

Bucky   I won't get hurt. Because if you aren't in daycare, I'll just be waiting for you. And I'll be happy.

Kostya   That's if you have to wait a day, or a week. But what if it's a month? Three months? It will hurt you, I know!

Bucky   But why?

Kostya   I had a favorite toy once. A blue plush dolphin. When we moved to a new place, we shipped our things. We arrived and started waiting for our stuff. Furniture came first. The TV set and our computers came a day later. Books, clothes, and kitchenware also arrived. But the toy box didn't show up. I waited for three months . . . But it never came. They told my parents it got lost during shipping. That's it.

Pause.

Bucky, I know what it means to wait. You start with joy, but it always hurts in the end.

Bucky   Well, I'm ready to wait even three months.

Kostya   But I can't promise you even that. Once I was out of daycare for six months. You see?

Bucky   I will still be waiting for you . . .

Kostya   You can get another friend.

Bucky   I don't want another friend. I want to be friends with you!

Kostya   He will be healthy. Unlike me. And when they swap your buckwheat for down and feathers, you'll be able to make friends with him. You see? You'll get everything you need.

Bucky   I don't want that! I don't, I don't want that! Don't say that! Don't!

Emma (*sits up in her bed*)   People these days.

Kostya   What?

Emma   You are a smart boy. But you're wrong.

Kostya   I'm doing my best to figure something out. So that Bucky has a good life.

Emma   He won't. He will have a bad life. And you too.

Pause.

Let me tell you my story. I used to live in the basement . . .

Bucky   In the Mentbase?

Emma   Yes. It's not scary at all, don't believe the stories they tell you. So, there I lived, lying on the hot water pipes. I was warm in summer and in winter, all year round. It was damp, but warm. And I had a friend.

Kostya   A friend? In the basement?

Emma   Yes. I've been telling everyone about her. The rat Chacha. Very smart. Speaks English. Good at math. And she's read so many books in the basement— Smarty could only dream about it! She's just quite shy. I taught her to dance—that helps. Chacha was supposed to perform at the rat concert and wow everyone there! But the janitor found me . . . And now I'm here. Couldn't even say goodbye to Chacha. I lost a friend. It hurt a lot. And even now, it still hurts.

Bucky   But it's so much better here than in the basement! Everyone is terrified of the Mentbase!

Emma   What does "better" actually mean? It's true, people take care of me here, clean me, and change my cases. It's a cozy and beautiful place. But I'm lonely here, nobody gets me. I'm bored and sad. I realized that the basement is where I was the happiest. Because my friend was there with me.

Kostya   You mean . . .

Emma   It doesn't matter where you live. It doesn't matter how you look. What matters is that there's someone next to you who gets you and accepts you as you are. I would give anything to go back to the basement. The Mentbase.

Bucky   But how can Kostya and I be together? He'll leave, and I'll stay here.

Emma *reaches into her case and gets out a marker.*

Bucky   What's that?

Emma   A marker. I saved one. Just in case. I guess, this is the case.

Bucky   What do you suggest?

Emma   I know how to help you stay together. Forever.

Smarty (*mumbles in his dream*)   Forever . . . Noted.

Emma *glances at* **Smarty**, *beckons to* **Bucky** *to come closer, and whispers something into his ear. Then, she hands him the marker.*

Bucky   Awesome!

He runs to **Kostya**, *whispers him* **Emma**'s *idea and hands him the marker.*

Bucky   Got it?

Kostya   Yep. That's so simple.

Bucky   Shall we do it?

Kostya   Let's do it.

They hug. **Emma** *looks at them proudly.*

Emma   Kostya!

Kostya   Yes, Emma?

Emma   Can I ask you to do something?

Whispers something into **Kostya**'s *ear.*

Kostya   Sure! You got it.

The noise outside the room grows louder with the voices of kids coming back from their afternoon walk. Somebody shouts, "Kostya, your mom is here!"

Kostya (*to* **Bucky**)   Shall we?

Bucky   Sure.

Kostya *grabs* **Bucky** *and runs out of the door. Meanwhile, the pillows in the room get up, and sit in their beds.*

Fuzzy   Oh, that was good!

Cushy   Good. I agree.

Rose   Good, good!

Fuzzy   I could get some more sleep.

Ivanovna   Our dear sleeping beauty. A-achoo!

Smarty   Noted.

Looks around.

Hold on. Where's Bucky?

Rose   Oh, right. Bucky! Where are you?

Everyone looks around, puzzled. The door opens, and **Kostya** *comes back with* **Bucky** *in his arms.* **Bucky** *doesn't have a case anymore.* **Kostya** *puts* **Bucky** *on a bed.*

Bucky   Hi everyone!

Fuzzy   And?

Rose   So?

Smarty   Are you ready? Shall we swap out your buckwheat?

Cushy   Do you agree?

Ivanovna   A-achoo!

Bucky   No. I'll stay just as I am now.

Ivanovna   Where's your case? You'll freeze to death.

Bucky   I don't need it.

Rose   Are you out of your mind?

Fuzzy   Bucky, what's going on?

Smarty   I don't get it. Explain the current situation to us.

Kostya   Bucky is coming home with me. He'll be living at my place. I've arranged it with my mom already. And the teachers have approved it, too.

Smarty   Is this a joke?

Rose   Bucky, where are you going?

Emma   To a place where he'll be happy.

Fuzzy   Emma, was this your idea?

Emma   Goodbye, Bucky! Good luck. Be happy!

Cushy   Is this boy taking you with him? Can he actually do that?

Smarty   You can't just leave this place! It's against the rules! That's how it's noted!

Bucky   Every rule has an exception.

He turns his back to the pillows. They can see "KOSTYA" written on it in bold letters.

Rose (*gasps*)   Ah!

Cushy   Whoa!

Smarty   A disruption! An infraction! Remove this right now! Wash it off, get it off!

Fuzzy   What is it?

Kostya   It's permanent marker. Sorry.

Smarty   This is destruction of public property!

Kostya   We'll pay for it. And take him with us. I'm bringing Bucky home with me. As a defective pillow that the daycare doesn't need anymore.

Bucky   And we'll always be together. It was Emma's great idea.

Fuzzy   Emma!

Ivanovna   Bucky, what have you gotten yourself into? A-achoo!

Rose   Think this over!

Smarty   This is just gross insolence! Going against the rules!

Cushy   I disagree!

Rose   What?

Fuzzy   Cushy, you disagree? With Smarty?!

Cushy   I do. Bucky is doing the right thing.

Ivanovna   Why?

Cushy   Because Bucky needs Kostya, and Kostya needs Bucky.

Fuzzy   But they are different!

Rose   Bucky, don't you want to stay with us?

Smarty   It's nice, warm, and cozy here! They change our cases every week.

Bucky   That's not what matters. Now I know that. It doesn't matter where you live. It doesn't matter how you are inside or outside. What matters is that somebody gets you. And accepts you. Right, Emma?

Emma   That's right, Bucky. You can be happy even in the basement.

Smarty   In the Mentbase?!

Bucky   I don't want to change who I am. I don't need to change.

Smarty   I disagree. This is wrong. I'll file a formal complaint!

Bucky   Don't be mad, Smarty. Yes, maybe I am wrong. And maybe I'm doing wrong things. But I'm happy.

Rose   And you won't come back?

Bucky   Kostya will be coming to the daycare. And he'll be bringing me with him. We'll see each other again.

Smarty   This is just outrageous . . .

Rose   Does it mean he's your pillowmate?

Bucky   He is.

Rose   I envy you so much . . .

Bucky   You'll find your pillowmate, too. Just wait.

Ivanovna   Oh, these young pillows! A-achoo!

Cushy   I'll miss you.

Bucky   I'll miss you too.

Smarty   Are you all just going to put up with this, just like that?

Fuzzy   I thought you'd be here to celebrate my anniversary . . . Five hundred dreams!

Bucky   I'll be here. I'll come. And we'll celebrate six hundred, a thousand dreams!

Fuzzy   A thousand? You think, I can live to see a thousand dreams?

Bucky   Absolutely!

Kostya *comes up to* **Bucky** *and touches him slightly on the side.*

Kostya   Bucky . . .

Bucky   Yes. Alright.

To everyone.

We have to go . . .

Ivanovna   Let me give you a kiss, sweetie . . . As a farewell . . .

She kisses **Bucky** *and wipes off a tear.*

Bucky   Ivanovna, don't worry. I'll come back.

Rose   Bye, Bucky.

Fuzzy   See ya.

Cushy   Thank you, Bucky.

Bucky (*to everyone*)   Thank you all. (*To* **Smarty**.) I have to go now . . .

Smarty   Noted . . .

Kostya *takes* **Bucky** *into his arms. He turns to the door.*

Emma   Kostya, do you remember that thing I asked you to do?

Kostya   Of course! I'll do it. As promised.

Fuzzy   What are you talking about?

Emma *smiles.*

P.S.

The basement, aka Mentbase. **Emma** *is sitting on the pipes.* **Chacha** *is sitting next to her.*

Emma   I'm so happy to be with you again, Chacha.

Chacha   And I'm so happy to see you again, Emma. I looked for you all over the daycare. The concert is in just two days! All the basement rats will be there. I'm the first to perform! Who is the boy that brought you here?

Emma   Kostya. A great boy. And you and I will be together forever.

Chacha   Because we are pillowmates.

Emma   Of course we are pillowmates.

Chacha   Are the other pillows still scared of the basement?

Emma   They are. Fear makes mountains out of molehills.

Chacha   Someday they'll get it, too.

Emma   Well. Shall we start the rehearsal, my dear friend?

Chahcha   Shall we dance?

Emma   Let's dance!

Chacha *and* **Emma** *step dance on the pipes.* **Emma** *has "CHACHA" written across her back.*

Curtain.

2012

Notes

1 Ivanovna is a Russian patronymic. Normally, when you address someone of an older age, you use a patronymic alongside their first name (e.g., Anna Ivanovna). The use of the partronymic without the first name indicates an informal context of communication between old friends.

2 "Lions, eagles and partridges" is an allusion to Nina Zarechnaya's monologue in Anton Chekhov's *The Seagull* (1895): "Men, lions, eagles and partridges, antlered deer, geese, spiders, silent fish which live in the water, starfish and organisms invisible to the eye–in short, all life, all life, all life has been extinguished after completing its sad cycle . . ." Quoted here after Anton Checkhov, *Plays*, trans. with notes by Peter Carson (London: Penguin Books, 2002).

Every Shade of Blue[1]

PLAY (BASED ON A TRUE STORY)
(21+)[2]

Vladimir Zaytsev

Vladimir Zaytsev was born in 1985 in Orenburg, where he still lives. He started writing prose when he was twelve and expanded his repertoire to drama and film scripts during his studies at the Gerasimov Institute of Cinematography in Moscow. He is a member of the Moscow Writers Union. His plays include *With a Hammer. With a Shovel* (appeared in the journal *Contemporary Drama*), *Moscow-Noginsk* (appeared in *Contemporary Drama* and in *10 Best Plays of the Drama Competition "Characters"*), *Just Yura* (appeared in the magazine *Gostinyi dvor* and in the collection of plays by the Foundation SEIP), as well as *Hammer. Brick. Shovel* (came out in the collection *Eight*). The play *Every Shade of Blue*, featured in this anthology, has run at the Satirikon theater in Moscow since 2015 and was also staged in English in 2016 by Northern Illinois University School of Theatre and Dance as *Out of the Blue* (in the translation by Tatyana Khaikin and Robert Duffley).

Author's address
There is no animal more frightening than man.

Characters

Boy—*a teenager, high school student*
Mom—*Boy's mom, Sveta Biketova*
Dad—*Boy's dad, Kolya Biketov*
Grandma—*Boy's grandma*
Vika Malakhova—*an eighth-grader*
Yegor Averyanov—*a sixteen-year-old*
Lena Nevzorova—*Boy's classmate*
Chemistry Teacher
Taxi Drivers: One, Two, Three
Natasha—*Boy's classmate*
Classmates: One, Two, Three, Four
Exorcist
Princess Leia
Luke Skywalker
Frail Guy
Fashionably Dressed Guy
Viola
Nurse

Part One: The Die Is Cast

Boy   It all started with the simple "Mom, Dad, I'm gay." Of course, it wasn't that simple. "Simple" would have looked like this:

Boy   Mom, Dad, I'm gay.

Mom   Oh, great! And I made meat piroshki for dinner. Let's eat!

Boy   That's what "simple" looks like. But that's not how it went . . .

First, it wasn't simple for me to figure out that I liked boys and was not into girls at all. It's not like you can just go shopping, buy a pink button-down shirt, and everyone immediately realizes that you have no taste. Or a fortune teller looks at you and says, "This one's gonna grow up to be gay." And you just grow up, and everything's clear already. Here you have to dig deep, you have to figure out who you really are.

Take daycare, for example. I was friends with two Sashas: a boy Sasha and a girl Sasha. So, do you think I liked the boy Sasha more than the girl Sasha? Not at all! I liked them both, and I liked spending time with both of them. Sasha and I even had a fight once over the other Sasha; you know, the girl Sasha. And, by the way, I won. (*Pause.*) So how should I have figured out that I was gay? Feel it in my bones?

Or, when I started school, they seated me next to Sveta Buravleva. Blonde hair, a big nose. Should I have protested and told them I wanted to sit next to a boy? Of course not! I was fine sitting next to Sveta, I copied Russian off her, she cheated off me in math. We also walked to school together 'cause we lived close by. I even kissed her once. Sure, it was just on the cheek, but it still counts. I can't say it was incredibly amazing, but it wasn't gross or anything. I mean, I'd kissed my grandma on the cheek just like that before. So it was pretty much the same, just the skin was just less wrinkled. I mean, it was not wrinkled at all . . . anyway, at the time, there were no clues of my sexual orientation either.

And then, in the seventh or eighth grade, everyone started dating, and (*pause*) I tried it too. Not with Sveta, though—by that time she'd changed schools. There was a girl in my class, her name was Vika Malakhova. A girl just like any other, with thick glasses and braids. Not a stunning beauty, but I liked that she had dimples when she smiled. In fact, if it hadn't been for the dimples, I wouldn't have even thought about her, but there I went and wrote a note and during the break, when she wasn't looking, I slipped it into her backpack. "After school, come to the pavilion, alone." Of course, I didn't sign it.

We have this pavilion thing behind the schoolyard, a big one, where everyone hangs out when they skip class. Or, if they want to have a smoke, they also head there, so they don't get busted by the teachers. It always stands empty after school 'cause nobody needs to hide there anymore, obviously, and it only gets busy again at night, when the local winos hang out there and drink.

Anyway, Vika found my note, read it, and gave me such a look at once that I freaked out and hid behind a textbook. There it was, I thought, she'd see right through me, figure out I wrote that note, and wouldn't come; but when I dared to look over the physics textbook, I saw her scanning all the guys, so I calmed down. Good, she didn't know it was me—well, of course, I made sure to change my handwriting. And there she came.

Vika Malakhova   Oh . . . so it was you . . . I racked my brain trying to figure out who'd do something that weird? I was sure it was Mishka Semenov—he's always playing pranks. I was even thinking of not coming, but I was curious— what if it wasn't a prank? What if somebody else wrote it? And it turns out, it was you.

Boy   Yep, it was me.

Vika Malakhova   So, what do you want?

Boy   Not beating around the bush, are you?

Vika Malakhova   Why drag things out? (*She pushes her lips forward ready for a kiss.*)

Boy   Can you smile, please?

Vika Malakhova   What?

Boy   Smile.

Vika Malakhova   Why would I?

Boy   Is it hard for you or what?

Vika Malakhova   No.

Boy   Well, then smile. (*Pause.*)

Vika Malakhova   Like this?

Boy (*wistfully*)   Dimples . . .

Vika Malakhova   What?

Boy   Eh, nothing . . . I mean, thanks.

Vika Malakhova   You're funny. Is that all you wanted?

Boy   I don't know . . . I guess so.

Vika Malakhova   Well, I'm gonna go then . . .

Boy   Uh-huh . . .

And we started dating. Well, I mean, we went places together. Cafes, concerts, long walks around the city, or we hung out at the park. By the way, the concerts . . . Vika's older brother was in a retro cover band, or whatever they're called. A boy band, kind of, only they sang lots of old stuff, like "Some Dreams Come True, and Some Don't," "When She Got on the Train," and this other one, "We Wish You Happiness in this Truly Wide World"—Soviet retro, you know.

I can't even stand these songs anymore, but Vika loved them. Every week she took me to another concert, always sat in the front row, and sang along. I can picture her face even now . . .

Vika Malakhova (*sings*)

We wish you happiness![3]

Boy   Crazy . . . I didn't even think these bands could be as popular as Stas Mikhailov or Kasta . . . Well, even more popular, for that matter . . . Anyway, we went out together, held hands, but I wasn't really into it. Or rather, I felt weird. Not because her hands were sweaty, or because she squeezed my hand too tight—no, it wasn't that. Her sweat levels were normal.

It was something else. Somehow, nothing was ever enough for her: she called me all the time—to invite me out, or just for no reason, to chat. The handholding was always her idea too. Basically, she wanted our relationship to be serious, like grown-ups. She probably even had our wedding planned already. A wedding? Really? Give me a break! We were only thirteen, I just wanted to try dating because everybody was doing it . . . but the thought that Vika actually expected something from me, that she believed our relationship was a real mutual love—that stressed me out a lot.

Vika Malakhova   Oh, so it stressed you out, huh?

Boy   It did.

Vika Malakhova   So there was no love among us then?

Boy   No, there wasn't.

Vika Malakhova   Oh really?

Boy   Yes. And one more thing, you were too clingy! (*Pause.*) But of course, I would never have told her that. Besides, it was my first relationship, I had no idea whatsoever what to do, what to say . . . So I decided to go with the flow and see what would happen.

Vika Malakhova   Guess what?

Boy   What?

Vika Malakhova   Today is our two-month anniversary, can you believe it?

Boy   No way.

Vika Malakhova   Yep. I got you a present, here you go!

Boy   Thank you.

Vika Malakhova   Aren't they sweet? They look just like us, don't they? Don't they?

Boy   I guess . . .

Vika Malakhova   Well, aren't you fun . . . what did you get me?

Boy   Well, I kinda . . .

Vika Malakhova   Did you forget? Oh, you men, you never remember anything . . . Well, that's alright, you can give me your gift tomorrow. You will, won't you?

Boy   Sure . . .

Vika Malakhova   Two months . . . I can't believe it. What about you? Do you want . . . to kiss me?

Boy   To kiss you?

Vika Malakhova   Well, yeah, we've been walking together forever, I keep smiling at you like a fool, but you haven't even kissed me once . . .

Boy   I don't know . . . (*Kisses her.*)

Vika Malakhova   Is this your first time?

Boy   Well, on the lips, yes. And what about you?

Vika Malakhova   Mine too. Why did you make a face?

Boy   I just . . . I don't know . . .

Vika Malakhova   If you want, you can touch my breasts. Do you want to? (*Silence.*) So, do you like them?

Boy   I think so . . . (*Silence.*) Actually, I didn't like it . . . not at all . . . maybe it would have been nicer if they were bigger . . . I mean, I couldn't even really tell where the breasts started and where they ended . . . but I couldn't tell her the truth, obviously. As for the kiss, well . . . it wasn't really right either . . . I didn't even feel anything other than that she had had potatoes and mushrooms for lunch. And I don't really like mushrooms.

So that was the first time I wondered, do I even like girls? I knew for sure that I didn't feel anything for Vika. I could easily picture our future together: kisses that would taste like mushrooms or borscht, songs like "We Wish You Happiness," never-ending phone calls and questions, "Do you want to? Do you?" No, I don't.

I guess, the dimples were the only thing that I liked about her. But the dimples couldn't make up for everything else. So I decided to break up with Vika. It took me two weeks, though, before I could actually go through with it. My mom says that if you have to break bad news to someone, you can't drop it on them right off the bat. You should lead with doing something nice for them first, to sweeten the pill, you know. She works in HR, so she's good with this stuff . . .

Vika Malakhova   Did you get me a cake?

Boy   Well, yeah . . .

Vika Malakhova   A mille-feuille, my favorite! Are we celebrating something?

Boy   Well, it depends . . . (*Pause.*)

And we broke up. I thought it'd be easier from then on; I even started checking out Lena Nevzorova. I mean, I figured the first crepe always comes out wrong, so I had to give this relationship thing at least one more shot. Lena already had breasts. To be fair, I wasn't the only one who'd noticed that, so she wasn't exactly suffering from loneliness. Even guys from high school hit on her no problem. But, as it turned, out peaceful existence was just a dream. Vika completely lost it after our breakup, she really went full on nuts. She'd call me over and over again.

Vika Malakhova   Call me back, it's Vika, I really need to talk to you.

Boy   Or she'd threaten me.

Vika Malakhova   You're as good as dead, got it? My brother promised me he'd beat you up so bad, you'll be jealous of cripples after he's done with you.

Boy   Or she'd beg me.

Vika Malakhova   I'm begging you, come back to me. I can't live without you, you're so cool, my life is meaningless without you!

Boy   Or she'd blackmail me.

Vika Malakhova   If you don't come back to me, I'll tell everyone that you knocked me up, and you'll have to marry me!

Boy   Or she'd beg me again.

Vika Malakhova   Please, please, please, please . . . I'll change, I'll do everything you want! Come back to me!

Boy   Actually, I was just about to get back together with her and go to those dumb concerts again when Vika's parents decided they couldn't see her suffer so much and transferred her to another school. She went to therapy for eighteen months after that. Fuck . . .

And that completely killed my interest in dating anyone else. I mean, what is this circus? If every girl goes bonkers like this every time, why do I even need all this? Love . . . what kind of love is that? Of course, it's possible that Vika was just crazy. Glasses, dimples, braids—go figure what's hiding behind those glasses.

Anyway, it made me stop thinking even about Lena Nevzorova. What was the point? I decided to bail on the whole relationship thing . . . yep, that's how it went. And all this doesn't really shout you're gay either. I mean, you might get suspicious, but it's not that obvious . . . the next two years I didn't date anyone. I didn't even go out once. Other guys were all dating girls, and Pashka Pavlov almost became a dad, but I still couldn't get over the whole thing with Vika.

That's when they sent me to a competition. The Russian national intellectual competition among students of the tenth and eleventh grades. Russia's creative potential and all that. I was gonna go to Saint Petersburg, for an entire week! It was hilar, actually: half the students in our school were in AP physics—real nerds with glasses—but they sent me—for literature. I had won the city essay competition and taken third prize in regionals. I mean, lit is no sweat. You just need to have a big mouth. You skim an article about Pushkin, latch onto a couple of sentences, and you're all set—keep writing until the class is over. It's a bit harder with essays, though. The thing about them is not to write stuff like "like," "kinda," "I mean," and "anyway," but that's not always easy to do. This time I managed, and that's how I got the first prize. "I love you, my God blessed Motherland." Not that I really do—it was more of a white lie, to avoid failing the assignment. Anyway, they sent me to a national competition in Saint Petersburg, and our lit teacher with me. She was supposed to be my advisor, or something. The program there was packed with all sorts of seminars, conferences, workshops, quizzes—boring as hell, you get it. If it hadn't been for the lit teacher, I wouldn't have showed up for any of these . . .

We stayed in a hotel. In a double room. Not with the lit teacher, of course. She shared a room with another lit teacher. And I shared mine with Yegor . . . Yegor was a year older than me, but he looked like he was twenty. He was tall, well built, a real Batman. He'd been doing swimming since he was five, so he got real toned—I could die of envy! Girls were all over him. Actually, when I entered the room, I saw them before I saw him. Sitting all around the room, catching his every word. What a guy—not even five minutes since check-in and he'd already brought girls to the room! But Yegor quickly got rid of them. He said, let the guy (that is, me) settle in peace. Told them to drop by later. And I really liked that about him. And then he started to change, and I saw him shirtless and liked that even more. I mean, I was in awe of his body. Everyone wants to have a great body, even just an okay body, but his body was a dream. And he was only sixteen. So you get it, I was in real awe, you could even say I envied him. At that moment, I also thought that he probably was a good kisser. How could he not be? He'd had so many girls that I could only dream about with no one but Vika Malakhova on my own track record.

Vika Malakhova

We wish you happiness!
In this truly wide . . .

Boy   Oh, just go away, will you? (*Pause.*)

Then we went to dinner, and the girls drooled over Yegor. I was even a bit flattered; I mean, you know, flattered that this handsome guy was my roommate. Yegor, on the other hand, didn't seem to care much about their staring; it's like he couldn't care less who was drooling over him, even if it was the Queen of England. He had this vibe, like they weren't worth his attention. Played it cool, you know. So I liked him even more because of that. I *really* liked him . . .

After dinner, they held a few speeches, told us how amazing we all were and how lucky we were to have gotten that far and invited a bunch of university professors and writers on stage to open the competition. Well, the usual welcoming blah blah blah, I won't even bother retelling that . . .

All evening I couldn't take my eyes off Yegor, staring at him like a nutcase. He was sitting a row ahead of me with his lit teacher, and I was sitting next to mine. I knew it was kinda weird, like why would I stare at him when there were so many girls around. But I only looked at Yegor. And even if it was weird, so what? All of us are a bit weird . . . by the way, he also glanced at me from time to time, you know, giving me friendly winks, as if to say, hold on man, this "blah blah" is gonna be over soon. And when it was over, all the attendees started walking around and introducing themselves, and Yegor was once again besieged by girls. Every guy in the room was green with envy, but he was cool as a cucumber, as if he couldn't care less about these girls. What a guy—a rock!

Pause.

When we were getting ready to go to sleep, we started to chat. Yegor told me about the place he was from, Ulyanovsk, about his love of reading, and suddenly, before I even realized it, I asked him: "Are good at kissing?"

Yegor   Why?

Boy   I don't know . . . just wondering . . . never mind.

Yegor   Wanna find out?

Boy   What?

Yegor   Find out. Do you want to? (*A kiss.*) So, what do you think?

Boy   A good one . . .

Yegor   But you aren't. You bit my tongue.

Boy   I'm sorry . . .

Yegor   That's alright, you'll learn.

Boy   I'll learn?

Yegor   Well, yeah. Or are you gonna just keep biting people's tongues?

Boy   No, of course not . . .

Yegor   Awesome, so, we'll practice. (*Pause.*)

Boy   You're making a face right now, and many people do—I should have made a face as well. I should have, but I couldn't . . . because I liked it, dammit. With Vika, I didn't; with Yegor, on the other hand . . . I was, like Sergey Zverev says, "in unreal shock."[4] I couldn't even imagine that a kiss with a guy could move me like that. And it did move me, in a major way . . . my world turned upside down, I was just standing there and staring at Yegor, and couldn't say a word.

Yegor   Why aren't you saying anything? Or maybe, you don't want to do it?

Boy   Me? . . . Wait, but what about the girls?

Yegor   What about them? Girls won't be in our way.

Boy   They won't? Wait . . . are you (*whispers*) gay?

Yegor   Well, you could say so . . . you are too, by the way!

Boy   Me?

Yegor   Well, who's been staring at me all night? Or are you gonna try to tell me you weren't?

Boy   I was, but . . .

Yegor   No buts . . . we can spot one of us from 5 miles away.

Boy   One of us?

Yegor   That's right, one of us. Gays.

Boy   I don't get it—gays? Wait, and the girls? They're all over you.

Yegor   And that's good. It's a great cover. You bought it too, you see.

Boy   Whoa man, fuck . . .

Yegor   Wait, are you upset? Don't be! Or maybe you didn't like it?

Boy   I did . . . I guess . . .

Yegor   Well, you see. It was inside of you already and would have gotten out anyway, sooner or later.

Boy   Fuck . . . so what do I do now?

Yegor   Nothing. What can you do? Relax. And relax your jaw too, let's continue your training.

Boy   Wait . . . what training? All this, it's not normal . . .

Yegor   "Not normal" is when you love dogs and goats; to love a person is absolutely normal, no matter their sex.

Boy   That makes no sense . . .

Yegor   It does, actually. And don't you dare tell me that you felt gross, or I'll smack you!

Boy   Actually, at that very moment I did feel gross. Not because I'd kissed a boy, but because I liked it and even wanted to kiss him again . . . It was disgusting, it was scary and repulsive . . . I was already picturing my classmates, friends, acquaintances, relatives, the whole world, really, ready to drown me in an ocean of hatred.

—Are you gay?

—I am.

—Are you a sicko? Aren't you disgusted?

—I am, I guess . . .

—He guesses, what an idiot! You should have played sports, or something.

"An idiot," they say . . . Idiots are people who think that poutine is named after Vladimir Putin.

Of course, I immediately started stressing because of that. I mean, it wasn't the kind of situation when people just call you crazy and have a good laugh about it one day, just to forget about it tomorrow. It was for goddamn life. So, I tried to talk myself out of it. Like, who cares that you tried it with a boy, you tried it with a girl too after all.

It was just a kiss . . . One kiss doesn't mean anything. And that I liked it—well, it was just because Yegor was a good kisser.

Vika wasn't, neither was I. And that stupid old song of hers didn't help either.

Vika Malakhova

We wish yo . . .

Boy   Stop it! (*To* **Yegor**.) Do you like to sing?

Yegor   Not really.

Boy   Do you like this song?

We wish you happiness . . .

Yegor   I hate it.

Boy   Thank God! (*Pause.*) Of course, things didn't end at just one kiss. Yegor did good on his promise to teach me. The better I was getting, the more I was into doing it with Yegor.

Yegor   Told you you're one of us. Don't worry! I won't tell anyone. We're not in Holland or something. You know how scared shitless I am that people will find out? If somebody figures it out, I can't even imagine what would happen . . . but you know what's funny? I actually got into swimming to get girls. I mean, my parents signed me up for swimming to follow in my brother's footsteps. He's eight years older, a swimming champion, my folks are real proud of him, an example to follow, and yada yada. I was only five when he was already beating everyone else in the city-wide competitions. He was the pride of our neighborhood. And there wasn't a single girl who wasn't into him. So my parents led me into swimming, too. Like, swim, Yegor, swim!

My brother started to give me advice right away. Sport is a serious thing; you need to work your ass off. Even if you can't, even if you don't want to, you have to power through every training session and do what the coach says because he knows what's best. So, I did what the coach said, and worked my ass off, and trained. It was fricking hard. That much harder because I couldn't tarnish my brother's name. I just had no right to let him down. I had to be winning, had to be strong and confident. I wanted to drop everything so many times, but the idea that one day, everybody would respect me, and girls would straight-up adore me, made me stay. I mean, what's better than being respected and adored? And so I didn't go easy on myself. I knew what I was suffering for and stayed strong. Even my brother was proud of me. One day after a competition, he came up to me with some blonde—Snezhana or Anzhela, I can't remember. There was always a new girl, I couldn't keep track of their names. So, he came up to me, looked at me, you know, with pride, smiled, patted me on the shoulder and said, "Well done, bro, I'm proud of you!" And it was really cool.

I realized then that I should never quit swimming and started waiting to get older. Like how everyone waits for New Year's Day, I was also waiting. Just the presents would be different—girls. Of course, they'd already started to show an interest in me, but what kind of love could there be when I was only nine years old? I had to wait until I was at least thirteen.

So, the day after my thirteenth birthday, I made out with Dilya. She was a Kazakh girl living in our block, really pretty and really dumb, I would even say stupid. Don't get me wrong, I know I'm no Schopenhauer myself, but she was really something. I had the feeling that her folks met each other as contestants on *Big Brother*. I held out for ten days somehow, and then I dumped her and started dating Alissa.

All Alissas are crazy, but this one was the craziest of them all. She was completely obsessed with *Twilight*. She used to say, "I'm such a lucky girl, you look just like Edward!" I'd ask her, how on earth do I look like Edward, and she'd say that I was like a copy of him. Isn't that something? "Pity you aren't a vampire though," she'd say, "that would have been so cool." It was also just around the time when the sequel came out. So of course, she dragged me to the movies. But how can anyone watch that garbage? So I dumped her right there, at the movie theater . . . and then there was Tanya.

Vika Malakhova (*sings*)

   Ah, Tanya, Tanya, cutie, there is so much to tell!

Boy   Vika, I'm begging you, just leave, please!

Yegor   Tanya had this fat friend, Tonya, and it was impossible to get rid of her. She was always hanging out with us for some reason, and her mom would call her all the time, asking where she was and what she was doing. You get it, it was just crazy.

It felt like I was dating all three of them . . . I lasted a week. And then there was Olya, Rita, Polina, Zhenya, Natasha, Liza, Ira, Dina, Masha, another Masha, and another Tanya, and many others. It's a really long list. Don't get me wrong, I'm not showing off, it's just I really don't even remember half of them anymore. There could have been fewer of them, if I had actually liked any of them. Like really fallen in love, you know. But it didn't happen. They were all kind of the same. Each of them was weird in some way, but still the same as each of the others. They all ate alike, got mad and happy alike, looked at me alike, talked alike, dreamed about the same things, and even fucked alike, if it ever got to that.

Many of them, just like you, couldn't even kiss. I thought it was just an age thing, and started dating older girls, like a year or two older. They were a bit better at fucking, obviously, but other than that, they weren't much different. And the weird things they did were like a whole another level of nuts. Of course, I realized that it wasn't normal to get all bummed out about it at fourteen. Most guys my age (and not just my age) only dream of having someone to fuck, whereas I was having sex almost every day; but you know what, it was about love for me. It doesn't really matter if you're fourteen or seventy—if you don't click, you feel it. What matters is feeling good with another person, and I just didn't feel anything. So, I would get bummed out, dump the girl I was with, and find another one.

I was an athlete, you know, so I felt like I had no right give up. I trusted that sooner or later I'd start liking this whole thing or that I'd find a girl who would make me feel right. My brother found a girl like that and even married her. I mean, it mostly happened because he knocked her up, as it often does, but he stopped dating everyone else and became a real family man. He even quit swimming, which Dad never forgave him for. But my brother is still glad it worked out like this. He works as a security guard now and seems pretty happy. (*Pause.*)

So, I was hoping that something like that would happen to me, but instead, Kirill happened to me . . . when he kissed me in the shower room, I was shocked at first, just like you were, and I almost hit him, but all week after that I couldn't think about anything else but him and that kiss.

And when it got serious between us, I realized that that was it. I felt good around Kirill. Good, you get it? I hadn't felt like that with any girl before. The time spent with all of them combined wasn't worth even three minutes spent around Kirill. Simply put, life was interesting with him. We always had something to talk about, we finished each other's sentences, which, I guess wasn't surprising because his head wasn't full of girly stuff, you know. But what mattered most is that he actually liked *me* and not just my body, like all those girls. If it weren't for swimming, they wouldn't have even looked my way, but Kirill didn't care, he would have fallen in love with me even if I were not an athlete, even if I were fat. Eventually, I realized that swimming, and all aquatics for that matter, are the gayest sports. How could they not be? Where else do you have to spend that much time staring at beautiful male bodies with nothing else but Speedos on? Well ok, the caps, too.

Boy No idea.

Yegor Nowhere. Only in swimming. It's impossible not to admire them. The hardest thing is to keep yourself from getting a boner. You know, it's like with the nudists. If you get hard, everybody will figure out that you're no nudist. Here, it's the same. Go and try to convince them that you were thinking about your girl and not staring at the coach. Especially because the coach really is the reason. But I managed. I just needed to train myself, and training was something I was good at.

Pause.

And then I got hooked on literature. I started looking online for all kind of gay stuff, 'cause I was curious, you know, and I found out that Oscar Wilde even went to prison for that. You know Oscar Wilde, the writer, don't you? So I started reading *Dorian Gray*—a totally gay novel. Then switched to Stephen Fry. It turns out he's also one of us. Well, there're lots of us, even Chuck Palahniuk, though *Fight Club* isn't gay at all. And don't even get me started on the Silver Age,[5] where everybody who wasn't gay was a lesbian, and I am not talking just about the writers.

Take Tchaikovsky, for example, he was also gay. Although, this shouldn't come as a surprise: a straight guy couldn't have come up with *The Swan Lake* even if he tried, no way. So, as you can see, there are lots of talented folks among us. And it's always been like that. Since antiquity. Actually, back then people considered it normal to have an experienced adult mentor who'd teach you everything and fuck you from time to time. At the time, nobody gave it much thought, everybody fucked everybody, and nobody was called a pervert. And then they ended up with all kinds of Platos and Aristotles. But nowadays we have all these intolerants who are ready to tear apart everyone who isn't hetero. Damn freaks yourselves! It's a private business, how and who to fuck and who to love. And in antiquity, they knew that. Free love and yada yada. But then fuck knows what went wrong with humankind, they decided that it was a perversion, and that was it.

So I browsed lots of websites, read all sorts of novels and realized there were loads of us. It made me feel better. I mean, it still sucks to feel like you're different from the majority of people, especially when that majority really hates you. They even treat junkies with more humanity. But when it comes to us, they act like we're fucking kids or murdering old ladies to get their apartments. But that's alright, I can live with that. The thing is not to get busted and not to blab to anyone, especially to your folks, 'cause they'll get upset. I mean, I'm not denying that there are real perverts out there, sickos and fags, you know, like this (*demonstrates*), queeny, kind of effeminate, with their fucked-up voices. They always show them in movies. If there's ever a gay character, he's always like that. It's because of them that everybody thinks that gays are like that. But we aren't. We are normal! Do you get it?

Boy I get it.

Yegor Well, maybe not completely normal, but for sure not like that. (*Demonstrates.*) And there are plenty of perverts and idiots among heteros too, even more than among us, I'd say. Also, we're not forcing anything on people, we're not trying to make them love men; if you like chicks then be my guest, fuck the whole herd of them if you want, I couldn't care less, but if you're gay, that's it, dammit, everybody wants to fucking fix you, make you change your mind, especially girls. "How come? That's not possible! We need to do something about it." No, it is fucking possible, no need to do anything about it!

Boy I guess so . . .

Yegor Or how about this one. You often see it in films, in bad comedies. Two guys end up alone somewhere, you know, like get stuck in an elevator or locked up. And of course, one of them has to be gay, naturally, it's not even a question. And since he's gay, he kind of automatically must want to fuck the other guy. Like he wants to do it so bad that he can't restrain himself and throws himself on the guy, while the other twitches helplessly under him and cries for help. And that's supposed to be funny. Because we're real predators, aren't we? Just spending all our time plotting whose straight ass we're gonna fuck. Because relationships, love, feelings—we don't know what any of those are. Our only goal is to fuck somebody's ass. But no, heteros think that's funny, they write scripts like that and crack each other up. Like what is this nonsense? What kind of person would fuck someone who hates him by definition?

Or, it can also go like this:

—Oh, you're gay? No shit . . .

And covers his asshole with his hands. (*Demonstrates.*) Kind of like, "Fuck, he's gonna rape me right now." They really think we're like fascists. In any World War II movie, try and find a single German who acts like a human being, every single one of them is a bloody monster. Because they're the enemy, they're goddamn Nazis. But gays haven't occupied any countries, haven't slaughtered anyone. Whatever, forget it. Just don't get busted.

Boy   It really threw me for a loop. Revelations from Yegor, chapter one. Yesterday, I was living a carefree life—or mostly carefree—but now it turns out I'm gay and that from now on, my life's gonna be hard as hell.

Yegor   I mean, it's up to you. Nobody's making you do anything. You can keep living your life as you were; maybe you'll even convince yourself you're straight, and will be lying to yourself and everybody else for the rest of your life. You'll have to lie either way.

Boy   Great . . . so now what? This isn't some kind of virtual reality, this reality is more than real and in it, I have to make a real choice. Maybe the most important choice in my whole life. *The* choice. As soon as I thought about it, I wanted to go home—or anywhere else—just to get as far from that room as possible, to not to have to make that choice. And I closed my eyes. Like, when I was a child, whenever I didn't like something, I would just plainly close my eyes and stand still. I'd pretend I wasn't there, that whatever was happening had nothing to do with me, that it was all a dream. And when I opened my eyes, things would really feel a bit simpler, I think.

That day I also opened my eyes and I saw Yegor . . . and he was looking at me like, you know, I don't even know how to describe it, with sympathy, I guess. I mean, it was obvious he was actually worried about me. He might have been the first person ever to worry about me. Not Mom or Dad—they just kept fighting and picking at each other. Nor Grandma or my friends—not that I even have friends. Nor anybody else. Yegor . . . so, I made my choice.

Pause.

It was the best week of my life. We spent our days in conferences and workshops, sat apart in different rows, and didn't even look at each other. We even had to act like we were dating girls.

Well, that was no problem for Yegor, but things weren't going so well for me. Her name was Marina, she was slim and had a long braid. And her hands were sweaty, actually. But it didn't even matter, the hands weren't the problem. The thing was that I had just made up my mind to date a boy and here I was, with a girl. And she kept trying to kiss me, you know. Yikes. (*Shudders.*) But at night, we were alone in our room, having a great time.

And then it was the time to say goodbye.

Yegor   Okay so, don't look for me. I'm not on Vkontakte,[6] and I won't give you my phone number, or you'll keep calling and texting me.

Boy   Wait, I don't get it.

Yegor   What's not to get? What happened here stays here.

Boy   But why? Did I do something wrong?

Yegor   You did everything right. It's not about you. It was awesome, well, almost awesome. And I do like you, I just have a boyfriend.

Boy   What?

Yegor   Now you're going to think I just used you, but it's not like that. I opened your eyes, now you know who you are and what to do next.

Boy   Fuck you!

Yegor   Don't get all upset and take it out on me. I wish you well, I really do. You'll realize that soon.

Boy   Does your boyfriend know you're cheating on him so boldly?

Yegor   He does. And he sees other guys too. We have an open relationship. And that's another advantage we have over heteros. They always face the risk of having children from cheating. But not in our case. The worst that can happen is catching an STD . . . but Andrey and I love and trust each other, so if one of us likes someone else, then there's no reason to deny him that pleasure.

Boy   That's fucking . . .

Yegor   Please, don't get mad, I really had a nice time with you. And I sincerely wish you to find a person with whom you'll have true love, like me and Andrey. Even if that ends up being a woman. Maybe, that'd be even better if it's a woman. At least nobody will hate you. And now, goodbye, I really enjoyed our time together.

Boy   And he left . . . fuck, I was so mad . . . have you ever been dumped? Of course you have. I even started to get Vika Malakhova.

Vika Malakhova

>A lonesome pigeon flew by my window one day,
>It wanted to come in, it wanted to stay,
>I hope you'll come back to me
>And you will see, and you will see . . .

Boy   It's just that I felt much worse. I found out this big thing about myself and was left alone with my discovery.

Pause.

When I returned home, I felt so shitty that I decided not to date anyone at all; neither boys, nor girls. My parents, as always, didn't even notice that something was off. Back at school, I saw Lena Nevzorova again, but now I even felt somewhat repulsed by her breasts. I kept thinking about my time with Yegor; I felt that if I could just see him one more time, I'd . . . beat the crap out of him. But after a while, I wanted love and the warmth of another human being again, and I started checking out boys—my classmates, I mean.

In the locker room, after PE class, they all paled in comparison to Yegor, of course. And they talked exclusively about girls anyway. So, I signed up for swimming, but even there was no one to stare at. Whenever I had a training session, the pool was full of fat ladies with cellulite who jumped in, splashed around, grabbed water weights, and made circles around the pool. (*Shudders*.) Ugh . . . But when I finally met Vitaly, who was four years older than me, I realized that it was for real and forever. You can't fight your nature. Yegor was right: I'm gay and I just have to accept it.

Of course, I didn't tell any of that to my parents. I wouldn't have ever told them, if it hadn't been for that day . . . I mean, I was used to them fighting all the time, it was never anything serious, but this time . . . well, see for yourselves.

Part Two: Dad, I'm Gay

Scene One: Coming Out

Boy's *apartment. Evening. Living room.*

Boy *is playing a GameBoy on the sofa; he looks grumpy.* **Dad** *is standing in front of him;* **Mom** *is a bit further away. They are clearly worked up and are staring at* **Boy**; *he feels their stares but does not look up at them.*

Dad (*sternly*)   Son!

Boy *doesn't react; he pretends to be too immersed in the game.*

Dad   Put that damn thing away, for God's sake! Your father is speaking to you!

Boy *lets out a grumpy sigh but puts the GameBoy down and looks at* **Dad**.

Boy   What now?

Mom   Honey, Dad and I need to talk to you about something.

Dad   Enough baby talk. You're raising him to be a wimp!

Mom   Well, do it yourself, raise him not to be a wimp, nobody stands in your way.

Boy   And here we go again . . .

Dad   Sveta, now is not the time. You know perfectly well why things are the way they are. Right now, we need to talk to our son.

Boy   Oh, really? I'm fine. School's fine, nobody's kicked me out or anything. My grades in chemistry are better, I don't have fights with anyone. If it's about college, I have no idea yet where I'll be sending applications. Is that all?

Mom   Honey, choose literature as your major. Then at least you'll always be at home, safe, and with your wife by your side.

Mom *and* **Dad** *give each other angry looks.*

Dad   Alright, enough of this debate. (*To* **Boy**.) Answer me straight: Who do you love more—me or your mother?

Boy   What kind of question is that? I'm not a five-year-old.

Mom   Honey, just think carefully and tell us the truth. Dad and I really need to know.

Boy   Wait, are you getting a divorce? Are you nuts?

Dad (*sternly*)   Nuts?! Watch your mouth, you little twerp. This is not a way to talk to your father and mother. Answer quickly, who are you going to live with?

Mom   Kolya, take it easy! You'll traumatize the kid.

Dad   The kid could easily traumatize anyone himself. Look how big a guy he is, up to the ceiling already.

Boy *gives the ceiling a puzzled look and then returns it to* **Dad**.

Dad   Stop tiptoeing around him!

It is clear **Boy** *is unhappy with the news. He is silent, tries to grapple with what he's just heard.* **Dad** *and* **Mom** *are anxious to hear his decision.*

Dad   Well?

Boy (*jumps up*)   Don't do this! You shouldn't get a divorce!

Dad   And why is that?

Mom   Yes, honey, tell me and Dad why we shouldn't get a divorce?

Boy   Why, why? Well because . . .

He desperately scans the room for an answer. He looks at **Dad**, *at* **Mom**, *then again at* **Dad** *and tries to think of a reason to stop them but cannot come up with anything.*

Pause. **Mom** *and* **Dad** *are anxious to hear what he's got to say.*

Finally, the **Boy** *utters timidly:*

Boy (*blushing*)   I am gay! (*With a desperate look on his face, he sinks back on the sofa.*)

Dad (*shocked*)   Who?

Boy (*quietly, timidly*)   Gay . . .

Mom   Gay?

Boy (*scared*)   Well, yes . . . I mean . . .

Dad   Wait, what do you mean "gay"? Like "gay" gay?

Boy   What other kinds of gay do you know?

Mom   Oh God, honey . . .

Dad   Hold on! (*To* **Boy**.) Are you messing with us?

Boy   Yes . . .

Mom *and* **Dad** *exhale with relief.*

Mom   Thank God!

Boy   I mean no . . . I guess . . . I . . . mean it.

Silence. **Mom** *starts sobbing.*

Dad (*to* **Mom**, *enraged*)   See? That's all your coddling! Now our son is *gay*.

Every time **Dad** *utters "gay" in this scene and throughout the play, he places a special emphasis on this word.*

Mom's *sobs grow stronger.* **Boy** *shrugs guiltily.*

Boy   I'm sorry . . .

Dad   I swear, I could kill you right now . . . Go to your room!

Boy *obeys, but on the way out he stops and turns around to* **Mom** *and* **Dad**.

Boy (*cautiously*)   But you aren't gonna get a divorce now, are you?

Dad (*sternly*)   Did you hear me? Go to your room! Get out of my sight before I flatten you into wallpaper!

Boy *runs away, frightened.*

Dad *watches* **Boy** *until he's gone; he tries to grapple with what he's just heard and paces the room silently.*

Mom (*cautiously*)   Kolya . . .

Dad   Just be quiet for a minute! (*He grabs his head and sits down on the sofa.*) Fucking hell . . .

Mom *sits down next to* **Dad**. *They are silent.* **Dad** *is still holding his head, rocking it slightly back and forth.*

Mom   Maybe he'll change his mind?

Dad *doesn't respond. He gives* **Mom** *a look that says she couldn't have uttered a more stupid thing in this situation. It's a look that makes you want to put a bullet in your head.* **Mom** *lowers her head. They sit.*

Dad (*quietly*)   Fuck . . . (*Pause.*) Fucking hell . . . gay . . .

He is so disgusted that he cringes.

Mom *cautiously puts a hand on his shoulder.*

Lights fade to black.

In the darkness, **Mom** *'s voice is heard.*

Mom   Hi, Mom, do you hear me? Right now! You have to come here right now!

Scene Two: Reinforcement

Boy *'s apartment. Evening. Kitchen.*

Grandma (*seventy to seventy-five years old, a sophisticated lady of mature age*) *is sitting on a chair and drinking tea.* **Mom** *stands in front of her. A half-empty bottle of heartdrops is on the table.*

Grandma   What did he say?

Mom (*loudly*)   That he is gay!

Grandma   Gay? What kind of gay? You mean, happy?

Mom (*loudly*)   The usual gay. The I-love-boys gay, you know?

Grandma   Does he also love boys?

Mom (*loudly*)   He said he does.

Pause. **Grandma** *drinks tea.* **Mom** *is silent.*

Grandma   I must say, though, that I suspected it! Haven't you noticed how affectionately he looks at other boys?

Mom   Not really . . .

Grandma   That's because you're a bad mother.

Mom (*loudly*)   Mom!

Grandma   Don't "Mom" me! I would never have let you pull something like that.

Mom (*loudly*)   Don't start this again! I'm already barely keeping it together. Kolya almost had a heart attack. He's been taking heartdrops ever since. What should we do now?

Grandma   What can you do? You've done enough already.

Mom (*loudly*)   Mom!

Lights fade to black.

Scene Three: The Talk

Boy's *apartment. Morning. Living room.*

Boy *enters the room; he has a backpack on.* **Dad** *is sitting on the sofa, lost in thought. When he sees* **Boy**, *he abandons his thoughts and looks at him with revulsion, but then gets control of himself and speaks to* **Boy**.

Dad   Where are you going?

Boy   To school.

Dad (*sternly*)   I see . . . come over here!

Boy *stops. He looks at* **Dad** *with fear and can't bring himself to walk up to him.*

Dad (*softer*)   Come here, don't be afraid.

Boy *approaches him cautiously.* **Dad** *pats the sofa next to himself.*

Dad   Sit down.

Boy *sits down a bit away from him and observes* **Dad** *cautiously.* **Dad** *is trying to smile, but his facial expression rather comes off as frightening.* **Boy** *feels uneasy.*

Dad   How're you doing?

Boy   I'm going to be late for school.

Boy *wants to get up, but* **Dad** *stops him. He grabs* **Boy** *by the hand but quickly lets it go, revulsed.*

Dad　School can wait! Let's sit and talk, father to son! (*He overcomes his revulsion and hugs* **Boy**.) Just chat.

Boy *gives* **Dad** *a highly surprised look.* **Dad** *keeps forcing a smile. An awkward pause.* **Dad** *takes his hand off* **Boy**'s *shoulder.*

Dad　So, you say you're gay?

Boy (*quietly*)　Yeah, I am . . .

Dad (*pretends to sound approving*)　Uh-huh . . .

Boy　Dad, I'm gonna be late for school.

Dad (*with pretend tenderness*)　You have to understand, son, I'm not judging you, I'm just trying to sort everything out. I want to get you. You must agree, it's not every day your son tells you he's gay. Came completely out of the blue.

Boy　Dad, we're not living in the Stone Age. A lot of people live in same-sex relationships.

Dad *is infuriated—there is practically steam coming out of his ears—but he tries to control himself, although it's obviously difficult for him.*

Dad　Alright, alright, son, have it your way. Just tell me, aren't you ever planning to get married?

Boy *ponders the question; it seems that he hasn't given it much thought before.*

Boy (*is silent for a while*)　I don't know. I might.

Pause. **Dad**'s *eyes light up hopefully.* **Boy** *continues.*

Boy　If some day same-sex marriage is legalized in our country and I meet someone who I'd like to marry, then . . .

Dad (*enraged*)　Are you telling me you don't like women at all?

Boy (*in a guilty voice*)　Not at all. I realized a while ago that I liked guys more. Especially muscular ones.

Dad *is getting gloomier; he seems to regret starting this conversation. He is breathing loudly, panting with rage.*

Dad　And what about children?

Boy　What about them?

Dad　Your mother and I were hoping for grandchildren, or at least a grandchild. Someone has to continue the family line.

Boy　So, you and Mom aren't going to get a divorce anymore?

Dad (*clenches his teeth*)   Not right now.

Boy   Well, children aren't a problem . . . I guess.

Dad   How do you mean?

Boy   We could always adopt, there are so many kids in orphanages these days. A surrogate mother could work, too.

Dad *loses his patience. He puts his arms over his head and groans with anger.*

Dad (*groans*)   Go away!

Boy   What?

Dad   Go to your fucking school! Now!

Boy *jumps off the sofa, frightened, and runs away.* **Dad** *yells, then gets up and starts smashing the furniture, repeating* **Boy**'s *words.*

Dad   He'll fucking marry! (*Pause.*) He'll fucking adopt kids! (*Pause.*) He fucking loves guys! Fucking muscular guys! Fucking prick!

Lights fade to black.

Scene Four: Too Much Stress

School. Morning. Classroom. **Boy** *stands in front of the class; he is silent, looks at his feet, then looks up and starts to quietly recite a poem. He puts emotion into every word he utters.*

Boy

    Elysium of shades this soul of mine,
    Shades silent, luminous, and wholly severed
    From this tempestuous age, these restless times,
    Their joys and griefs, their aims and their endeavours.
    Speak, O my soul, Elysium of shades!
    What bonds have you with life? Speak, phantoms summoned
    From out a day whose very memory fades—
    What have you with this heartless mob in common?

Fedor Tyutchev.[7]

The classroom bursts into hysterical laughter. Baffled, **Boy** *looks around; his eyes stop on the* **Chemistry Teacher**.

Chemistry Teacher   Why Tyutchev, Biketov? What's wrong with you? This is Chemistry. We're talking about Mendeleev and the periodic table of elements here.

Boy's *classmates laugh loudly.*

Boy   Uh-huh . . .

Chemistry Teacher   I asked you a question about the physical properties of aldehydes. Have you done your homework?

Boy *is silent.*

Chemistry Teacher   Are you alright, Biketov? Why aren't you answering? Are you not feeling well?

Boy   I'm sorry. (*Rushes out of the classroom.*)

Chemistry Teacher   Biketov, come back! Or I'll give you an F!

Boy*'s classmates laugh loudly.*

Lights fade to black.

Scene Five: Busted

Boy*'s apartment. Afternoon. Hallway.* **Boy** *comes back home.* **Grandma***'s voice is heard from the kitchen.*

Grandma   Art! It's the only thing that can cure him!

Mom   Yeah, sure. The things you say sometimes . . .

Boy *heads for the kitchen, where* **Mom** *and* **Grandma** *are sitting. He walks through the living room, which is already free of any traces of the storm that raged in it this morning.*

Grandma   There's a reason they say *artes emollit mores*—art refines morals! I remember the time your father . . .

Boy *walks into the kitchen. When* **Grandma** *notices him, she cuts her speech mid-sentence; she and* **Mom** *exchange looks.*

Mom   Honey, you're back already? We didn't hear you, you startled us. Did school finish early today?

Boy   So, what were you saying about Grandpa?

Grandma   What about him? He was a drunk.

Boy   Uh-huh. So, who was it you wanted to cure then?

Mom   Who? Oh, you know . . . Oh God (*Pause.*) your Grandma's friend—Yury Mikhailovich.

Boy   Yury Mikhailovich?

Mom *goes up to the cupboard, takes out a plate and sets it on the table.* **Boy** *is patiently waiting for an answer.*

Grandma   Yes, you know, the bald one, with the cap, like Lenin.

Boy (*nods*)   Right, and with plans for the revolution! Sure. (*Turns around to leave.*)

Mom   Honey, aren't you gonna have lunch?

Boy   Nope. (*Walks out.*)

Mom *and* **Grandma** *rush to the door to listen, but* **Boy** *goes to his room and locks the door.*

Grandma   I've never known any Yuri Mikhailovich . . .

Mom *and* **Grandma** *exchange looks again.*

Lights fade to black.

Scene Six: Take a Ride with your Grandma

Boy's *apartment. Afternoon.* **Boy**'s *room.* **Boy** *is sitting in front of his computer. He opens the browser and types "came out as gay to my parents" into the search line.* **Boy** *presses Enter. His eyes grow large with surprise.*

The browser shows him a lot of results for this query. **Boy** *puts on headphones and clicks on a link to a video. A* **Frail Guy** *is sitting at a table against the background of light-colored wallpaper with dolphins. His face is hidden behind a black square.*

Frail Guy (*clears his throat and speaks*)   I used to think my mom was cool; we never even fought, so I decided to come out to her, "Mom, I'm gay!" She was shocked, but she didn't yell at me or anything. I was excited, I thought it meant she could accept me for who I was. The next day she asked to meet my boyfriend. It seemed nice—she was smiling as she said that to me. So, I bought it, and brought him over to meet her. As soon as my mom saw him, she attacked him and started giving him punch after punch. I had never seen her like that. She was like a rabid wolf. She kept punching him and wouldn't stop; she broke his nose and three ribs. THREE! What the fuck! What am I supposed to do now?

Boy *shakes his head sympathetically. He looks up and sees the door open slowly.* **Mom** *enters the room with a plate of fruit and cake.* **Boy** *frantically moves the mouse on the mousepad.* **Mom** *looks at him, forcing a smile.* **Boy** *hastily takes off his headphones and turns off the computer screen.*

Boy   What is it now?

Mom   I just wanted to check in on you. You didn't want any soup, so at least have some fruit. (*Puts the plate in front of* **Boy**.)

Boy   I don't want any.

Mom (*sternly*)   It's not "I don't want," you say thank you! (*Softens.*) Oh well, you can eat it later, honey. I've put cake in there too, your favorite kind.

Boy *pushes the plate away from him.* **Mom** *won't leave.*

Mom   Honey, what were you doing on the computer? Homework?

Boy   Mom, just tell me—what do you want from me?

Mom (*mysteriously*)   Take a ride with your grandma.

Boy   Where?

Mom   To an exhibition. She's been talking my ears off about Baroque or Rococo or whatever.

Boy   Well, why don't you go with her yourself?

Mom   I can't . . . I have to finish some things . . .

Boy   Do I really have to?

Mom   You really do, honey. Come on, go change, she's ready to leave, and you know how she is. Our grandma doesn't like waiting for others.

Boy   Damn! . . . why is she even here?

Mom   What kind of question is that? She missed you, so she came to see you. Aren't you glad?

Boy   I guess so . . .

Mom   So, take a ride with your grandma, just like old times . . .

Boy *reluctantly stands up, comes up to the wardrobe, opens it, and looks around inside.* **Mom** *is standing where she was, trying to see what's on the screen, but it's turned off.*

Boy   Mom, do you mind?

Mom   Right, sure honey. I'll leave you to it.

She slowly walks out of the room. **Boy** *follows her with his eyes and sighs.*

Lights fade to black.

Scene Seven: The Ride

In a taxi. Evening. **Boy** *and* **Grandma** *are sitting in the back.* **Grandma** *has a big, ridiculous hat on. She is looking at* **Boy** *with interest while the latter is engrossed with his GameBoy.* **Boy** *has headphones in his ears and diligently keeps his head down. The taxi driver turns on the radio. Boris Moiseev is singing.*[8]

Taxi Driver One (*displeased, loudly*)   Son of a . . .! Him again! Fags everywhere! Are they cloning them or something?

Boy *raises his head from the GameBoy and gives the taxi driver a frightened look; the driver switches the radio station. A primitive guitar melody fills the car; a gruff voice is singing Russian chanson (a kind of song about life as a criminal).*

Taxi Driver One (*approvingly*)   Now we're talking, that's a real man!

The **Taxi Driver** *turns on the volume and rocks his head to the music.* **Boy** *winces,* **Grandma** *notices his reaction, and* **Boy** *promptly plunges his head back into the game.*

Lights fade to black.

Scene Eight: Give Me Some Vodka

Boy'*s apartment. Evening. Living room.*

Dad *is sitting on the sofa, and moans loudly while clasping his head.* **Mom** *walks in, looks at him in silence for a while. He keeps groaning.*

Mom   Take some heartdrops or something.

Dad   I don't want to. (*Pause.*) Give me some vodka.

Mom *leaves the room in silence.* **Dad** *returns to groaning.* **Mom** *comes back with a glass and a bottle of vodka. She puts the glass on the table, pours a shot, and offers it to* **Dad**. *He doesn't take it.*

Dad   Give me the bottle.

Mom *hesitates, but* **Dad** *is groaning so pitifully that she has no choice but to give him the bottle.* **Dad** *gulps thirstily from the bottle for a while, then sniffs his sleeve.*[9] *He is silent.*

Mom *looks at the glass, sighs, drinks the vodka that was in the glass, winces, exhales loudly and sits down on the sofa.* **Dad** *takes another gulp from the bottle.*

Mom (*winces*)   Kolya!

Dad   Don't "Kolya" me! Don't! I've been putting up with your "Kolya this Kolya that" for twenty years already. "Kolya, I'm pregnant." "Kolya, I'm tired of staying at home, I want to go back to work." "Kolya, how much longer will we keep moving from one military base to another? The bases are all I've seen in my life." "Kolya, I want to live—not to be fearing for you all the time." "Kolya, retire from the army or I'll retire from you . . ." Damn. (*He spits and swears.*)

Mom   Oh yeah. And you're so much better. "Sveta, it's all gonna be fine, we just have to stick through it a little bit more!" "Sveta, everybody lives like this! Think about the Decembrists' wives—do you think they had it easy?"[10] "Sveta, why do you need to work? A woman's job is to make the house cozy and keep the hearth fires burning!" "Sveta, don't tell me you didn't know who you were marrying." Well, I *did* know, but what the hell did I *really* know then?

Dad   Oh, here we go again: "I was only twenty. I was a naïve girl, charmed by your lieutenant rank." Sveta, it's been five years since I retired. Five years that we've been living in an apartment—no military bases, no war zones. For five years you've been back to work, and nothing has changed, NOT A THING.

Mom   Back to work, sure . . . as an HR admin. What a fantastic career! Can you even imagine what I could have done if I'd stayed in finance?

Dad   Yeah, yeah, your college professors thought highly of you, promised you a brilliant future, I've heard this all before . . .

Pause.

Mom   Give me that bottle.

Dad *gives* **Mom** *the bottle; she drinks right out of it, finishes it, winces, coughs, hits herself on the chest, sniffs her sleeve, coughs again.*

Dad   Need some water?

Mom   No.

Pause.

We've waited so many years. We stayed together, sticking it out until our son grew up.

Dad   And here we are. Our son grew up. Gay.

Mom   Maybe it's not true, Kolya?

Dad   It is . . .

Mom   Well, maybe it was just a bad joke?

Dad   It wasn't.

Mom   How do you know?

Dad   How? I see these freaks who're doing their best to avoid the draft every single day. Trust me, I know who's really gay and who's just faking it.[11]

Mom *sobs loudly.* **Dad** *groans loudly.*

Mom   Maybe my mom will manage to do something about it?

Dad   Manage to do what?

Mom   Change his mind.

Dad   And how's she gonna do that?

Mom   With the power of art.

Dad   The power of what?

Mom   The power of art . . .

Dad   She's been stuffing him with this "power of art" stuff since he was five. And what's the result? The kid is neither fish nor fowl.

Mom   Well, you could've raised him to be a man, nobody stood in your way.

Dad   It was your decision to leave him with his grandma. "We shouldn't drag the child from base to base all over the country."

Mom   That's right. A child has no business on a military base.

Dad   Well, here we are . . .

Pause.

He gives the empty vodka bottle a sad look, sighs bitterly.

I am an officer of the Russian Army.

Mom   Retired.

Dad   Retired. And with a faggot son! I swear I'd kill him if I could . . .

Mom   Kolya!

Dad   Kolya what? Kolya what? I'm sick of you all!

Mom   Well, everyone is sick of you, too!

Dad   Fine!

Mom   Fine!

Dad   I hate you!

Mom   I hate you too!

Dad   And there's no more vodka . . .

Mom   And there's no more vodka . . .

Dad   Great talk. (*Leaves.*)

Mom *stays alone. She is crying.*

Lights fade to black.

Scene Nine: Nature Wins

Art gallery. Evening. The gallery is almost empty. In fact, **Grandma** *and* **Boy** *are the only visitors.* **Grandma** *is standing before a Rubens. The painting is of a voluptuous nude woman.* **Grandma** *is looking at the painting with awe.* **Boy** *has stopped before another painting, "Bathing of a Red Horse," and is studying it.*[12]

Grandma   Just look at it! Pure beauty! The passion, the emotion, the colors! Rubens is a genius! No one had such fine understanding of true female beauty like he had . . . Kid, why are you silent? I'm talking to you.

She turns around and notices that **Boy** *is studying another painting. She comes closer and realizes that it is "Bathing of a Red Horse."* **Grandma** *shakes her head mournfully.*

Grandma   Oh, devil's work . . . you're possessed . . .

The **Boy** *is fascinated by the painting and doesn't hear* **Grandma***. She grabs him by the hand.*

Boy   What is it?

Grandma   Run! We need to get out of this hell!

She pulls poor **Boy** *with her away from the gallery.*

Lights fade to black.

Scene Ten: Report

Boy's *apartment. Evening. Living room.*

Mom *is sitting on the sofa, lost in thought.* **Grandma** *and* **Boy** *walk into the room.* **Boy** *is smiling,* **Grandma** *is frowning. Both notice an empty vodka bottle lying at* **Mom**'s *feet. When* **Mom** *realizes this, she jumps off the sofa and tries to discreetly push the bottle under the sofa.*

Mom   Well, hello! How did it go?

Grandma *shakes her head and sighs.*

Mom   Mom!

Grandma *is silent. She walks out of the room.*

Mom (*worried*)   Oh God! Why is she acting like that?

Boy (*directs his gaze under the sofa*)   Everything's fine. Don't you know how Grandma can be?

Mom   I do. So, how was the trip? (*She grabs the remote control from the table and turns on the TV. A blue screen lights up.*)

Boy   I'll tell you later. Mom, are you alright?

Mom   Why are you asking, honey?

Boy *and* **Mom** *both look under the sofa in silence.*

Mom   Oh, this? I . . . just wanted to make some meat pierogis.

Boy   But we've got a rolling pin.

Mom   Oh, I gave it to our neighbor, Auntie Kapa.

Boy   If you say so . . . and why were you drinking?

Mom   Well, you know . . . wait, are you trying to tell your mother what to do?

Boy (*guiltily*)   No, of course not. I'm just worried about you.

Mom   Thank you, honey, but don't worry, I'm okay.

Boy   Are you sure?

Mom   I'm sure.

Boy   Is Dad ok?

Mom   He is.

Boy   Alright then.

Pause.

Mom   So, how was the exhibition? Did you like it?

Boy   I did. Wonderful colors. The brush work is very lively.

Mom   So why is Grandma upset then?

Boy   Mom, you know her, she's a perfectionist and a Caravaggio fan. Realism is her thing. This was all too metaphoric . . .

Mom   I see. Of course. Maybe you're right . . .

Boy   Alright, I'm gonna go.

Mom (*anxiously*)   Where?

Boy   To finish my homework.

Mom   Oh, sure, go, go, honey.

Boy *heads out of the room but stops mid-way.*

Boy   Mom.

Mom   Yes, honey?

Boy   Don't drink anymore, please.

Mom (*after a while*)   I won't, honey.

Boy   Yeah, and don't worry about pierogis. I don't like them anyway. (*Exits.*)

Mom *follows him with her eyes until he is gone, then turns around, sits down and stares into the blue TV screen.*

Lights fade to black.

Scene Eleven: Dream Number One

School. Morning. Classroom. **Boy** *is standing in front of the class, answering from the homework. His classmates are talking loudly.*

Boy   And finally, I would like to add something before I finish my talk. I have been so successful in learning the properties of aldehydes because I am gay—I mean a genius—no, actually, I mean it—because I am gay.

The room goes dead silent.

Boy *closes his eyes and breathes quickly and loudly.*

Vika Malakhova, *who is sitting at one of the desks in the classroom, rises.*

Vika Malakhova   You know, I am not surprised. I thought so.

Boy (*opens his eyes*)   Vika?

Vika Malakhova   Who did you expect to see, Justin Bieber?

Boy   What are you doing here?

Vika Malakhova   Oh oh oh. What am I doing here, what am I doing? Nothing anymore. (*Comes up to the door.*) Big deal! (*Exits.*)

Boy *is silent. There is a pause. The classroom is filled with the whispers of* **Boy**'s *classmates.*

Boy   So, what do you think?

Silence again.

Chemistry Teacher *walks up to the* **Boy**.

Chemistry Teacher   Biketov! (*Gives* **Boy** *a hug.*) Stay strong! (*Hugs him again.*) Attaboy! I am speechless. (*To* **Boy**'s *classmates.*) Let's say it together.

All   Atta-boy! Atta-boy! Atta-boy!

Boy   Why "attaboy"?

Chemistry Teacher   Not everyone can confess about such a thing—but you have; and on top of that, you're also exceptionally good at chemistry.

Boy   Thank you. I didn't expect you to be so nice about it. I thought you'd bully me.

Chemistry Teacher *and* **Boy**'s *classmates laugh.*

Chemistry Teacher   That's hilarious. You really crack me up. Biketov, you know we're all educated people here. (*Exits the classroom, shaking her head like she's hurt by his words.*)

One by one, classmates come up to **Boy**, *shake his hand, pat him on the shoulder, and so on.*

Classmate One   What a speech, man! "Because I am gay!" What a strong finish. Really strong! (*Exits the classroom.*)

Classmate Two   Now I get why you were staring at me in the locker room. I hope I'm not your type?

Boy   You aren't.

Classmate Two   Thank fuck, awesome! Good luck! (*Exits the classroom.*)

Classmate Three And I really don't care. As long as you're a good person. You seem alright.

Boy Thanks.

Classmate Four Ciao! (*Exits the classroom.*)

Classmate Natasha You know, I even like you more now. I mean, as a person. You don't lie and chicken out, like some other people.

Boy Thank you, Natasha.

Classmate Natasha *exits the classroom.*

Classmate Four Yo! Respect, man!

Boy Damn! Thanks, man!

Classmate Four I mean, come on. I'm gonna post on VKontakte, "Biketov, bro—you're Number One!" (*Exits the classroom.*)

Lena Nevzorova Does this mean that you aren't into my breasts?

Boy Your breasts are great. I'd even say outstanding. But breasts aren't the most important thing about a person.

Lena Nevzorova Idiot! (*Exits the classroom.*)

Boy (*runs after* **Lena**) Wait! Where are you all going?

The classroom door slams shut. **Boy** *rushes to it, pulls it and tries to open it, but in vain. The door is locked. Loud voices of* **Boy**'s *classmates can be heard behind the door. They are noisy, shouting out something indistinguishable, laughing.*

Boy Let me out! Hey guys, this isn't funny!

The voices get quieter, it's harder to discern them.

The lights fade to black.

Hey! What's going on?

It gets really quiet. The spotlight shines on a set of swings that is rolled in to the center of the classroom. **Vika Malakhova** *is sitting on them, swinging and singing.*

Vika Malakhova (*sings*)

    I had a dream of falling snow,
    The world was filled with peace and light,
    Light and peace, silence and snow,
    Pity it was just a dream last night.

Boy I don't get it; what's going on?

Vika Malakhova What is there to get? You're dreaming. This is a dream.

Boy So?

Vika Malakhova   So this is the end!

Lights fade to black.

Scene Twelve: A Ticket to the Ballet

Boy's *apartment. Evening.* **Dad** *and* **Mom**'s *room.* **Dad** *is sitting on the bed; he is looking tenderly at the wedding photo album that lies on his lap. He opens it, looks at a photo, turns the next page, smiles, turns a few more pages, sighs. He hears* **Mom**'s *steps in the corridor. He freezes, listens in. The steps come closer.* **Dad** *looks at the album, alarmed, hides it behind his back, realizes that this is not a good hiding place, grabs it again, jumps up, frantically runs around the room, then quickly stuffs the album under the bed covers, puts a pillow over it, then throws the pillow off again, and sits himself down over the place where the album is.* **Mom** *walks into the room.* **Dad** *hastily tries to assume a natural pose.* **Mom** *notices* **Dad**'s *fidgeting.*

Mom   What's wrong with you?

Dad   Nothing.

Mom   Kolya, have you been drinking again?

Dad   No, I haven't! Why would you think that?

Mom   I see it written all over your face.

Dad   Well, clearly you can't see very well, Sveta! I haven't had a sip. And everything is great.

Mom   Really?

Dad (*mimicks her*)   Really.

Pause.

Mom *sighs, silently pulls three theater tickets out of her pocket, looks at them, puts them on the nightstand and steps back.*

Dad   What have you got there?

Mom   What are you talking about?

Dad   You just put some tickets on the nightstand.

Mom   He's only sixteen, Kolya, we shouldn't give up hope. Everyone's like that as a teenager. I mean, difficult and sensitive.

Dad   So, what are the tickets for?

Mom   He's seen us fighting, so he's gotten the wrong idea that a marriage between a man and a woman leads to fighting. We have to show him otherwise; that we're happy, that we can live together and not fight. We just need to be nicer to each other, and to him above all, Kolya . . .

Dad (*enraged*)   For God's sake, will you tell me what those tickets are?

He gets up from the bed, takes the tickets, studies them.

(*Surprised.*) Ballet tickets?

Mom   Well, yes. We'll go out tomorrow—together, like a normal family, so that he sees that we love him, that we love each other.

Dad   Sveta, are you out of your mind?

Mom (*hurt*)   Kolya, that was mean. I didn't call *you* names . . .

Dad   That's not what I'm talking about, Sveta! The goddamn ballet? Grandma already took him to an art exhibition.

Mom   So? He won't change overnight. Anyway, ballet is a totally different thing.

Dad   Oh, it sure is. It's even worse, it's full of them!

Mom   "Them" who?

Dad   Well, you know . . . (*Gestures with his hands who "they" are.*)

Mom   What do you mean?

Dad   Homos, goddammit!

Mom (*alarmed*)   Oh, God . . . I didn't even think about it. You're right, of course . . . (*Pause.*) Well, maybe we could go to the opera?

Dad   Right, to see Tchaikovsky.

Mom   Why not, Tchaikovsky seems good, he's not boring.

Dad   No wonder our son grew up gay.

Mom   Oh God! What's wrong with Tchaikovsky?

Dad   The same thing. (*Repeats the hand gesture for "them."*)

Mom   Oh God! So, what do we do now? (*Sits down on the bed with a doomed expression; she feels around with her hand.*) Oh, what's this?

Dad   Nothing . . . an encyclopedia.

Mom   What encyclopedia?

Dad   Well, you know, a normal one . . . on history.

Mom   Why is it under the covers? (*Tries to get the album out.*)

Dad   Sveta! (*Rushes to* **Mom***, takes her hand.*)

Mom (*puzzled*)   What is it, Kolya?

Pause.

Dad   This! (*Sweeps* **Mom** *up and carries her away from the bed.*)

Mom (*gasps*)   Put me down!

Dad *obediently puts* **Mom** *back down.*

Mom   What's gotten into you, Kolya?

Dad   Nothing . . . just . . . you're the one who commanded to act like a happy family. So, I'm practicing.

Mom   Practicing . . . you could have warned me. I bit my tongue in surprise, you know.

Dad   Sorry. Does it hurt?

Mom   It's fine, I'll live . . . you know, you used to carry me around once upon a time . . .

Dad   Should I do it again? I could carry you to the kitchen.

Mom   Don't bother.

Dad   Want some tea?

Mom   No.

Dad   I'd have some. I am parched.

Mom   Well, make some. (*Turns towards the bed.*)

Dad   Sveta! (*Turns* **Mom** *back to him.*) Maybe to hell with all this art?

Mom   What do we do, then? Take him to a therapist?

Dad   We'll send him to a military school for boys. I can arrange that. He'll man up there, leave all this faggotry of his behind.

Mom   No. One "real" man in the family is more than enough for me . . . and what if they find out about him? That's gonna be awful.

Dad   That's true . . . we don't generally like people like this. He'd get beat up.

Mom   What were you doing with an encyclopedia?

Dad   Maybe therapy isn't such a bad idea? Or—hell—art might work after all.

Mom   Kolya!

Dad   You know what, let's go to the movies together. I haven't gone for ages. And if I remember correctly, both of you love movies.

Mom   Movies?

Dad   Yeah. I think I saw a flyer for a movie theater in the hallway.

Mom   It's in the living room.

Dad   Great, see, you know where it is. Can you bring it over?

Mom   Why?

Dad   I want to have a look. Come on, Sveta, Chop-chop. Forward, march! Two, three! Four, five!

He literally pushes baffled **Mom** *out of the room, shuts the door behind her, rushes to the bed, gets out the album and puts it back on the shelf in the closet, sits down on the bed again, and exhales loudly.*

Lights fade to black.

Scene Thirteen: Russian Cinema Is Fucked

Movie theater. Evening. **Boy**, **Dad**, *and* **Mom** *are standing in the lobby.* **Boy** *looks around, smiling,* **Dad** *is frowning,* **Mom** *jabs him with her elbow when* **Boy** *isn't looking.*

Boy   I'm so glad you two made up!

Mom *smiles artificially.* **Dad**'s *face doesn't change.*

Boy   You remember Sveta Petryaeva in my class? When her parents got a divorce, she slit her wrists.

Mom (*shocked*)   Jesus, that's horrible! Honey, maybe you want to get yourself something before the film starts? Popcorn, water?

Boy   No, I'm good.

Mom   Well, get something to drink for me and Dad. (*Hands* **Boy** *some money.*)

Boy   Coke?

Mom   Anything.

Dad   I'll have water.

Boy   Uh-huh. (*Leaves.*)

Mom   Kolya, did you hear that?

Dad (*grim*)   I did.

Mom   Kolya, hold my hand.

Dad   Why?

Mom   For God's sake! Do you see how sensitive they all are? Let's show him that we're fine, so he can be fine.

Dad *takes* **Mom**'s *hand.*

Mom   Oh.

Dad   What?

Mom   This is nice.

Dad *is silent.*

Mom   It's been a long time since you held my hand.

Dad   You haven't asked.

Mom   Well, apparently, you didn't need it either.

Dad *is silent.*

Mom   Or maybe you have somebody else whose hand you can hold?

Dad *is silent.*

Mom   Why aren't you answering me? Is there another woman? Tell me.

Dad   Where did he go? The movie is about to start.

Mom   I see. So, there is another woman. (*Frees her hand.*)

Dad   There isn't another woman! Stop nagging me. You didn't ask me to hold your hand, so I didn't, that's all there is to it. Don't overthink it.

Mom   There he is.

Dad *promptly grabs* **Mom**'s *hand.*

Boy *enters with a bottled water. He hands it over to* **Dad**.

Dad   What were you doing, getting a physical over there?

Boy   A physical? What are you talking about?

Mom   It just took you a while. Dad is worried that we'll miss the start of the movie.

Boy   Oh, I see. There was a line. Hey, look, Princess Leia and Luke Skywalker are kissing.

Mom   Who's kissing?

Dad   Where?

Boy   Right there! (*Points.*)

Mom *and* **Dad** *turn around and look in the direction* **Boy** *is pointing. They see a young couple dressed as* **Princess Leia** *and* **Luke Skywalker**. **Princess Leia** *is shorter, so they only see her back. The couple is kissing loudly and passionately.*

Mom   That's real love!

Dad   We can do that too.

Mom   Really? Oh, I don't think that's very appropriate . . .

Dad   What's inappropriate about it?

Mom   We aren't twenty anymore, you know.

Dad   As you wish.

Mom (*to* **Boy**)   Honey, don't look at them. It's rude to stare.

Boy *doesn't move. He keeps looking at the kissing couple.*

Mom   Honey!

Dad   Leave him alone, he needs to watch and learn! He should see what a normal relationship looks like. Maybe then, he'll want to have something like that too. (*To* **Boy**.) Yes, son, watch and learn!

Princess Leia *and* **Luke Skywalker**'*s kiss is getting more and more passionate. Hands get involved. Luke is groping* **Princess Leia**'*s bottom.* **Princess Leia**'*s hands are also all over* **Luke Skywalker***. Both are moaning with pleasure.*

Mom   Oh God! Well, this is already unacceptable! (*To* **Princess Leia** *and* **Luke Skywalker**.) Excuse me, do you mind toning it down a bit? You're in a public place after all.

Princess Leia *and* **Luke Skywalker** *stop kissing, turn around, and give* **Mom** *a disgruntled look. Now it is clear that* **Princess Leia** *has quite an impressive beard.*

Mom   Oh God!

Dad   Fucking hell! Great trip to the movies! (*To* **Boy**.) Stop staring, you creep! We're leaving right now! Go, didn't you hear what I said? (*To* **Princess Leia** *and* **Luke Skywalker**.) Freaks!

Dad *rushes* **Mom** *and* **Boy** *out of the movie theater.* **Princess Leia** *and* **Luke Skywalker** *watch them leave with bewildered looks on their faces and suddenly burst out laughing.*

Luke Skywalker   See, Anton, I told you nobody would get the joke. You should have at least shaved your beard off.

Princess Leia   Come on, Tanya, it was fun! Let's go mess with the folks inside the theater.

Princess Leia *and* **Luke Skywalker** *exit.*

Lights fade to black.

Scene Fourteen: What We Need to Fix All This Is a Real Exorcist

Boy'*s apartment. Evening. Kitchen.* **Grandma** *is sitting there in a wide-brimmed hat and watching* **Mom***, who is aggressively kneading dough.*

Grandma   He's possessed by a demon!

Mom (*loudly*)   Why would you say that?

Grandma   You should have seen how he was staring at that painting.

Mom   I saw, actually! Had a live "painting" right in front of me at the movies. (*Loudly.*) You told me art would cure him.

Grandma   I didn't consider the demon. Art is of no help here. We need an exorcist!

Mom (*loudly*)   Come again?

Grandma   An exorcist. (*Emphatically lifts her index finger in the air.*)

Mom *freezes. She is silent.*

Grandma   Say something.

Mom   Oh, do whatever you want. (*Drops into the chair with a doomed expression on her face, buries her face in her hands.*)

Lights fade to black.

Scene Fifteen: I'm Happy We're Together

Boy's *apartment. Evening.* **Boy**'s *room.* **Boy** *is sitting at his table, staring at the computer. A video is playing.*

Outside. A park. Afternoon. A young, **Fashionably Dressed Guy** *is sitting on a bench. He's wearing colorful skinny jeans and an equally colorful top. His face is hidden behind a black square.*

Fashionably Dressed Guy   It was hard for me to hide my nature. And when my father . . . (*pause*) started yelling again that he couldn't understand what was wrong with me, I just lost it. I told him I liked guys and that I had hooked up with them a few times already.

I thought he would tear me apart, like a true homophobe, but he didn't raise a hand or yell. Instead, he turned to my mom . . . I mean, his wife, and said, "We should have adopted a different rat." Turns out they took me in fifteen years ago. Of course, I had no memory of that. And that's how I found out. I couldn't stay in that house anymore. It was so cruel and it hurt so much. It would've been better if he'd just beaten me (*his voice drops*) but that . . . now I live with my boyfriend, and he's really supportive, and I'm happy we're together . . .

Boy's *apartment. Evening.* **Boy**'s *room.*

Boy (*frightened*)   Shit! (*Runs out of the room.*)

We can hear him rifling through drawers in the other room. He runs back in with a bunch of photo albums, sits down in an armchair, and puts the albums on the floor next to the armchair. He takes the first one, opens it, and anxiously flips through it, studying every photo. It's **Boy**'s *childhood photos. One is a picture of him next to a cartoon character, one is on a merry-go-round, and another shows him together with his parents.* **Boy** *puts the album aside, picks up another one. He's at the seaside, on the beach; another photo shows him riding an elephant—he's about five or six years old.*

He puts this album aside too and takes another one. Nervously, he goes through every page until, finally, he finds what he's been looking for. Relieved, he exhales. He's looking at a photo of him as a baby in his **Mom***'s arms in front of the maternity ward.* **Mom** *quietly walks into the room and silently looks at* **Boy** *with interest. He turns the page and sees himself as a baby in his crib, with young* **Dad** *and* **Mom** *joyfully leaning over him.* **Boy** *looks at the photo lovingly, then looks up and notices* **Mom** *standing in front of him. She's looking at* **Boy** *with a sad smile.*

Mom   Honey, why are you going through our photos?

Boy   No reason, just wanted to relive my childhood memories.

Mom *sits down on the arm of the chair and looks at the photos together with* **Boy***. She smiles lovingly.*

Mom (*gently*)   Oh, look at this cutie! Dad and I were overjoyed to have you!

Boy   You were?

Mom   Of course! Why would I lie? When you were born, your dad brought the whole squad to the maternity ward. They stood under my windows and sang (*singing*) "I love you to tears, I do," and (*singing*) "I'll ride my bike all the way into the fields." They woke up all the other women in the ward. Oh, the good old days . . .

She turns the page, looks at another photo.

And in this one, you'd just peed yourself. I'm changing your diaper, and you're lying there, all pleased with yourself, kicking your tiny legs and cooing, as if you were singing a song. Dad and I laughed so much; we joked that you'd become a performer when you grew up . . .

Boy *smiles.* **Mom** *turns the page, looks at a photo, smiles.*

Mom   You barely ever cried, never made a scene. Sometimes you'd have a poopy diaper, but you wouldn't even whimper.

Boy (*annoyed*)   Gross, Mom!

Mom   Oh God! You loved to be fed. You'd suck my breasts so hard that I couldn't tear you away!

Boy (*annoyed*)   Mom! Why are you even here?

Mom (*takes some time to answer him*)   Oh yes! Honey, you're not going to school tomorrow.

Boy   Why is that?

Mom   Because. You'll take a ride with your Grandma. (*Shuts the album.*)

Boy   Where are we going this time?

Mom   You'll find out tomorrow.

Boy   Mom.

Mom (*gets up, sternly*)   That's all you need to know! (*Pause.*) And anyway, I have no idea.

She goes away. **Boy** *carefully stacks the albums one on top of the other, and smiles.*

Lights fade to black.

Scene Sixteen: Trip Two

Taxi. Morning. **Boy** *and* **Grandma** *are sitting in the back seat.* **Grandma** *has her eccentric wide-brimmed hat on.* **Boy** *is looking at* **Grandma** *curiously, but she is gazing out of the window.*

Taxi Driver Two (*thirty-five to thirty-seven years old, short, plump, bald, with a week's stubble) turns on the radio. A gruff voice is singing Russian chanson.* **Taxi Driver Two** *tuts disapprovingly.*

Taxi Driver Two (*effeminately*)   Oh nooo, I wonder who was dumb enough to let you out on stage? You should've at least learned to sing first.

Boy *looks at* **Taxi Driver Two** *who promptly switches the station.*

DJ's Voice   Thank you, Anna, for your call, and just for you we're gonna play this hit by your favorite Nikolai Baskov.[13]

Taxi Driver Two (*effeminately, approvingly*)   Well, that's another story! What an artist, a real star!

Boy *looks at* **Taxi Driver Two** *and smiles.* **Grandma** *doesn't react at all. She is facing the window and seems to have fallen asleep.*

Lights fade to black.

Scene Seventeen: Door Sign

Street. Morning. **Boy** *and* **Grandma** *are at the entrance to a building. The sign on the door says Center for Legal and Psychological Assistance in Extreme Situations.* **Boy** *studies it carefully.* **Grandma** *walks past him, turns around.*

Grandma   Why are you just standing there? The doctor won't wait. These appointments are hard to come by. Hurry up!

Boy *follows* **Grandma** *into the building.*

Lights fade to black.

Scene Eighteen: He Exists, the Exorcist

Center for Legal and Psychological Assistance. Morning. The **Exorcist**'s *office.*

The **Exorcist** *is sitting at the table (he's fifty to fifty-five years old, tall, with a lush mustache). On the table in front of him,* **Boy** *notices a phone, a knife, a jar of water, and a jar of oil. He gives* **Boy***, who is standing in front of him, a stern look.* **Grandma** *is sitting on the couch behind* **Boy***.*

Exorcist (*sternly*)   Are you ready to get rid of your problems?

Boy *looks at* **Grandma***, she waves her hand at him, encouraging him to answer the question.*

Boy   Sure, I'd be happy to. I have a C in Math and some problems with Chemistry.

Exorcist (*shakes his head*)   No. Not these problems.

Boy   Which ones then?

Exorcist (*earnestly*)   We're now going to rid you of the demon of homosexualism.

Boy (*bewildered*)   What?

Exorcist (*puts his index finger to his mouth*)   Shhh! You've said enough.

The **Exorcist** *puts on music on his phone—it sounds like shamanic wailing—and grabs the knife.* **Boy** *takes a step back, frightened. The* **Exorcist** *slowly advances toward him, then suddenly starts bellowing as he runs at* **Boy***, circling around him and brandishing the knife.* **Boy** *stares at him, baffled. The* **Exorcist** *turns to* **Grandma***.*

Exorcist   You have to help! Repeat after me! Ommmmmmm!

Grandma (*stands up, waves her arms*)   Ommmmmmm!

The **Exorcist** *continues to circle* **Boy***, bellowing and blowing directly into* **Boy**'s *ears.* **Boy** *shakes his head, clearly displeased, but the* **Exorcist** *doesn't stop—instead, he keeps blowing.*

Exorcist   Demon, I exorcise you! Get out! Get out! Get out!

Grandma (*waves her arms*)   Get out, demon! Get out, demon! Get out, get out!

The **Exorcist** *rushes to the table and grabs the jar of water.* **Boy** *takes advantage of this pause and dashes towards the door, but* **Grandma** *blocks his way.*

Grandma (*waves her arms*)   Get out, demon! Get out, demon! Get out, demon!

Boy   Granny, let me go!

Grandma   No!

The **Exorcist** *comes up to* **Boy***, turns* **Boy** *to face him and sprinkles water on him from the knife.* **Boy** *shakes the water off his head in displeasure.*

Boy   What the hell? Granny, what is this place?

Grandma (*waves her arms*)   Get out, demon! Get out, demon!

Exorcist   Ommmmmmm!

Grandma (*waves her arms*)   Ommmmmmmmm!

Boy   Is this some kind of a prank or what?

The **Exorcist** *bellows and puts the jar of water back on the table.*

Exorcist   Do you hear me, demon? I command you to get out! Get out! Get out!

The **Exorcist** *takes the jar of oil, raises it in the direction of* **Boy**, *dips the knife into the oil and sprinkles it on* **Boy**. **Boy** *jumps away from him.*

Grandma (*waves her arms*)   Get out, demon!

Boy (*displeased*)   Have you lost your goddamn fucking minds?

He pushes the **Exorcist** *off him.*

Exorcist   Hold him! Don't let him leave!

Grandma   Stop! Stop, I'm telling you!

Boy   No way!

He slips under **Grandma**'s *arms and runs out the office.*

Grandma (*sighs*)   Oh, this demon . . .

Exorcist (*helplessly*)   He's gone . . .

Grandma   So, what do we do now, doctor?

Exorcist   I'm not a doctor.

Grandma   Pardon me?

Exorcist   Oh, right . . . you have to have faith. Hope for the best.

Grandma   That's it?

Exorcist   Do you believe in God?

Grandma   What?

Exorcist (*louder*)   Do you believe in God?

Grandma   Oh, yes, I do.

Exorcist (*loudly*)   Well, then pray. Take him to church or something.

Grandma   Yes, doctor.

Pause.

The **Exorcist** *starts to tidy up his office; he takes a mop and wipes the floor.*

Grandma *doesn't leave.*

The **Exorcist** *keeps wiping the floor.*

Grandma *doesn't leave.*

Finally, the **Exorcist** *comes up to the table, takes out a 16 oz plastic bottle with some liquid in it and hands it to* **Grandma**.

Exorcist (*loudly*)   Take this. Holy water. Three tablespoons a day.

Grandma   Thank you, doctor! How much do I owe you?

Exorcist (*loudly*)   Nothing. This is included in the séance package. And I'm not a doctor. I'm a psychic.

Grandma   Oh, thank you, thank you so much! And I'm sorry he was like this, doctor!

Exorcist (*waves his hand, giving up*)   I'm not . . . whatever.

Grandma *leaves.*

Lights fade to black.

Scene Nineteen: I'm Out, I'm Out . . .

Boy's *apartment. Evening. Kitchen.* **Mom** *is pounding pork steaks.* **Grandma** *is sitting across from her.*

Grandma (*waves her arms*)   Demon, get out! Demon, get out!

Mom (*loudly*)   And what did he do?

Grandma   He was just standing there, grinning. And then he got mad and shouted, "Have you lost your minds?" and ran away. There's a demon in him, a powerful one. You can't exorcise a demon this strong.

Mom (*loudly*)   Oh God! But you told me the exorcist was a sure thing.

Grandma   I wish! It's way too strong. He gave me this holy water, told to give him three tablespoons a day.

Mom (*loudly*)   Water? That's it?

Grandma   He told me to take him to church.

Mom (*loudly*)   Your exorcist is a fraud. (*Hammers the meat forcefully.*) How much did you pay him?

Grandma *is silent.*

Mom (*loudly*)   Tell me! Three? Five grand?

Grandma   Fifteen.[14]

Mom (*loudly*)   Come again? (*Drops into a chair.*) Mom, you really *have* lost your mind.

Grandma   Don't yell at me! "Lost my mind." No wonder I'm losing my mind. Such a tragedy in the family. I'd give my last ruble to fix him! Whatever it takes to help the boy.

Mom (*loudly*)   And how exactly was he of help?

Grandma   Oh, you . . . it's your fault the child is like this, and now you expect some stranger to fix all your problems for you.

Mom (*loudly*)   What do you mean, it's our fault?

Grandma   Exactly what I said. When he lived with me, he was a normal kid. Once he moved back in with you, he started to like boys.

Mom (*loudly*)   Mom!

Grandma   Don't "Mom" me! Am I wrong?

Mom (*loudly*)   Wrong, right—what does it matter? What do we do now?

Grandma   Do whatever you want! I'm out! I can't handle this much stress. My heart is too weak to take it. (*Gets up, about to leave.*)

Mom (*loudly*)   Mom, please, stay. I'm desperate. I'll go crazy with all this. I don't know what to do . . . Kolya is mad all the time, I tried to make peace with it, to accept it, but I can't. You're my only hope. You've seen a lot, you're wise!

Grandma   "Wise." When things are fine, you don't need your mother *or* her wisdom, but as soon as something happens, you come running, "Mom, help!" "Mom, tell us what to do." I won't tell you what to do. That's it! I'm tired! This is your doing, so deal with it. (*Turns around and leaves.*)

Mom (*loudly*)   Oh God! Mom! . . . (*Pause.*) Mom!

She slams the tenderizer into the meat; blood splatters all over the counter.

Lights fade to black.

Scene Twenty: Let's Not Talk About This

Boy's *apartment. Evening. Kitchen.*

Boy *is sitting at the table, cutting into the pork steak on his plate.* **Mom** *is staring at him intently.* **Boy** *pretends not to notice, but* **Mom** *won't stop staring. Finally,* **Boy** *gives up and turns to* **Mom**.

Boy   What is it now, Mom? Did Grandma complain about me?

Mom   No, I just . . . honey . . . (*Comes up to the table, sits down next to* **Boy**.) Do you like the pork?

Boy   It's good. Thank you.

Mom *reaches out for his hand, is about to take it, but doesn't.* **Boy** *notices and looks at her in surprise. She takes his plate instead.*

Mom   Want another one?

Boy   No thanks, I'm full.

He gets up from the table, walks to the door. **Mom** *gets up too, holding the plate in her hands.*

Mom (*cautiously*)   Honey, will you introduce us to your friend?

Boy   What friend?

Mom   Well, the friend . . . your . . . boyfriend or whatever you call him?

Boy's *eyes grow big with fear. He remembers the video he saw online.*

Boy (*scared*)   I don't have a boyfriend!

Mom (*rejoiced*)   Oh, God! Maybe you're not really gay?

Boy   What do you mean "not gay"? . . . I am . . . I just don't have a partner right now.

Mom   Right now?

Boy   Well, yeah. Right now, I'm not seeing anyone.

Mom   Oh honey, would you like to meet a girl then? My colleague Polina Ermakova has a daughter who's smart, and a real beau . . .

Boy   Mom . . .

Mom   Don't "Mom" me. Just don't. Dad and I are worried about you, you know . . .

Boy   Thank you, but I don't like girls. Do you understand that? I don't! What can I do?

Mom   Of course, honey, of course! There's no need to get upset. I understand. I am your mom, after all. I just thought that maybe you haven't made up your mind yet . . .

Boy   You don't understand anything! Neither you, nor Dad. Do you think it was easy for me to accept that I'm like this?

Mom   God, I don't know, I guess it wasn't . . .

Boy   Or that it was easy for me to come out to you?

Mom   No, of course not.

Boy   Or that my life is going to be easy? Everybody hates us, you know.

Mom   Honey, what are you talking about? Nobody hates you.

Boy   Right, of course. Even you and Dad can't stand me.

Mom   Honey, you're exaggerating . . .

Boy   I am understating it, Mom. It's clear that you and Dad won't come to terms with it, won't accept me for who I am. Dad didn't even want to have dinner with me.

Mom   Don't be silly. Dad just went to meet up with his old army friend.

Boy   Or you had another fight, didn't you?

Mom   No, we're doing fine.

Boy   Great! I'm happy for you! Because I love you.

Mom   We love you too, honey! And we wish the best for you.

Boy   Then why don't you want to understand me? That's the only thing I need now. Not your pity, or criticism. Your understanding.

Mom   Honey . . .

Boy   If you love me, you will understand me.

Mom   We're trying, honey, but it's hard. You know, other people . . .

Boy   Now I see . . . I'm sorry, Mom, for being such an asshole who grew up gay and now ruins your life.

Mom   Why would you say something like that? Honey . . .

Boy   I'm sorry, Mom . . . please, let's not talk about this anymore . . . please. (*Leaves.*)

Mom   Oh God, honey . . . (*Desperately drops into the chair.*)

Lights fade to black.

Scene Twenty-One: Dad Is Back

Boy's *apartment. Night. Hallway.*

It's dark. Commotion on the stairs outside, followed by the sound of keys falling on the floor outside the apartment door, then a key loudly scratching at the lock. The scratching doesn't stop. **Mom** *runs out of the bedroom, her bare feet thumping on the floor.*

Mom   Oh God . . . Kolya, is that you? (*Turns on the light.*)

No answer. The key in the lock gets more active. **Mom** *looks into the peephole and opens the door.*

Dad *is barely standing on his feet. He is smiling.*

Dad (*loudly*)   Sveta, I'm back!

Mom   Shhh, Kolya, calm down, you'll wake all the neighbors!

Dad (*loudly*) I don't give a shit about the neighbors! I haven't seen my army buddy for eighteen years, my wife doesn't love me anymore, my son is a fag . . . Forward, march! Two, three, four, five! (*Marches on the spot.*)

Mom Calm down, do you hear me?!

Dad Yes, sir, Commander-in-Chief! Halt two, three! (*Stops marching and drops on the floor.*)

Mom Oh God! Kolya! Kolya!

Lights fade to black.

Scene Twenty-Two: Dream Number Two

Park. Evening. **Boy** *is sitting on a bench; he's playing on his GameBoy.* **Vika Malakhova** *enters and heads towards* **Boy**. *She looks sad.*

Vika Malakhova Hi!

Boy You?

Vika Malakhova Who did you expect to see? Sergei Bezrukov?[15]

Boy Of course not, you just caught me by surprise. Hi.

Vika Malakhova "Caught him by surprise," right. Well, I can leave. Do you want me to leave? Do you?

Boy I don't, I guess. Stay.

Vika Malakhova Well, thank you. (*Sits down on the bench next to* **Boy**, *sighs.*)

Boy Why are you so sad?

Vika Malakhova Is it that obvious?

Boy Very.

Vika Malakhova My parents are getting a divorce . . . bummer . . .

Boy Sorry to hear that.

Vika Malakhova Yep . . .

Pause.

Boy Mine wanted one too.

Vika Malakhova They did? And now?

Boy And now they don't. Or rather, they do, but they're afraid to go through with it.

Vika Malakhova What do you mean afraid?

Boy They're afraid for me. I really freaked them out. I didn't mean to, it just happened. And now they're going crazy, trying to figure out how to change me.

Vika Malakhova   Why don't you put them at ease? You could tell them you changed your mind. Or do you enjoy seeing them suffer?

Boy   I don't. But you know, we're finally like a family. A normal—well, almost normal—family. We're spending time together, and they ask me how I'm doing and stuff.

Vika Malakhova   Was it different before?

Boy   It was.

Vika Malakhova   That sucks.

Boy   It does . . . but what really sucks is that for it all to change I had to tell them I'm gay.

Vika Malakhova   So, how is it, being gay?

Boy   It's mostly ok.

Vika Malakhova   I thought it was humiliating.

Boy   It's humiliating to hide from everyone, to live in the shadows, to feel like a freak—that's humiliating.

Vika Malakhova   Yeah, you guys aren't really loved, to put it mildly. I can imagine how your parents must feel.

Boy   Not great. I thought Dad would kill me, but I can tell that he's trying to keep it together. Although it's not easy for me either.

Vika Malakhova   Why are clinging to their marriage so much anyway? They don't love each other, do they?

Boy   Yes, they do. They just forgot they do. People tend to forget about good things. And then, if they didn't love each other, they wouldn't have stayed together that long.

Vika Malakhova   Well, a whole family is always better than a broken one. Let them fight, give each other the silent treatment, but stay together, together . . . enough parents break up in this country already.

Boy   Right. Some break up and some go broke.

Vika Malakhova   That's not funny!

Boy   I know.

Pause.

Vika Malakhova   Listen, what if I tell my parents that I'm a lesbian?

Boy   Why?

Vika Malakhova   Well, to have it like you. My folks will get scared, they'll start talking me out of it, they'll go out with me, they'll stop fighting. The "tragedy-unites" kind of story, you know.

Boy   But you aren't a lesbian.

Vika Malakhova   So what?

Boy   What do you mean so what? You'll just get caught up in your own lies and make things even worse.

Vika Malakhova   I don't know, maybe I'm some latent lesbian and just don't know about it.

Boy   No, it's really obvious that you're straight and that you want kids, and want to get married. You even look at me with desire.

Vika Malakhova   Wait, really?

Boy   Well, yeah.

Vika Malakhova   So what do I do?

Boy   I don't know. Try to make them feel something for each other again.

Vika Malakhova   Easier said than done.

Boy   You're a smart girl. Figure something out.

Vika Malakhova (*smiles*)   "Smart."

Boy (*smiles*)   Dimples.

Vika Malakhova   Sorry?

Boy   Never mind. It's fine. Well, almost. (*Pause.*) It turns out you're . . .

Vika Malakhova (*grumpy*)   I'm what?

Boy   Pretty cool . . . actually.

Vika Malakhova   Ohhh. Well, this is a dream.

Boy   So what?

Vika Malakhova   It's a dre-eam.

Boy   Oh, I get it.

Vika Malakhova   Uh-huh.

Boy   If you want, you can sing.

Vika Malakhova   For real? I can?

Boy   Knock yourself out.

Vika Malakhova   Cool. (*Clears her throat and sings.*)

The die has been cast,
Mom, I'm gay, Dad, I'm gay,
you don't have to tell me
what you think right away.

Boy   Oh, come on, Vika!

Vika Malakhova   Well, if you don't like it! (*Gets up and walks away.*)

Boy *is silent.*

Lights fade to black.

Scene Twenty-Three: I'll Beat All the Demons Out of Him

Boy's *apartment. Morning.* **Mom** *and* **Dad**'s *room.* **Dad** *is sleeping on the sofa. He's sprawled all over it and is snoring loudly.*

Mom *comes up to him, shakes him by the shoulder.*

Mom   Kolya, wake up! Kolya!

Dad *mumbles incoherently.*

Mom   You have to go to work! Biketov, come on, dammit! (*Shakes him even harder.*)

Dad *only mumbles incoherently in response.*

Mom (*loudly*)   Private Biketov, on your feet!

Dad (*jumps to his feet*)   Sir, yes, si . . . shit, Sveta, that's not funny.

Mom   Not funny, huh. It's already half past seven. Aren't you going to work?

Dad   I am. Shiiit! (*Grabs his head, sits back down on the sofa.*) What happened yesterday?

Mom   You don't remember, do you? You should drink less.

Dad   I remember everything. I had a couple of drinks with Zhenya Androsov. We chatted about the old days.

Mom   And how many bottles did you "chat"?

Dad   Sveta, do you think I can't hold my liquor? Shiiit . . . I am an officer of the Russian Army. Everything's gonna be fine.

Mom   Sure it is. (*Silently hands* **Dad** *a big mug.*)

Dad *gratefully takes the mug, chugs it all, and a miracle happens. A magical transformation.*

Dad   Oh, I feel so much better! Sveta, you are an angel! Get over here, I wanna kiss you.

Mom   Biketov, focus! You have to go to work.

Dad   Well, if you don't want a kiss, then fine. (*Arranges his hair with his hand.*)

Mom   Kolya, I feel so sorry for him. We talked yesterday . . .

Dad   Talked to whom?

Mom *nods in the direction of* **Boy**'s *room.*

Dad's *mood changes immediately.*

Dad   More tears for him? It's us you should pity. Us! Got this fucking idea that he's into guys. That's bullshit, real bullshit.

Mom   It's a demon, not bullshit.

Dad   I'll fucking show him a demon. I'll beat all the demons out of him!

Mom   Kolya, don't you dare raise your hand at that child! You have to be sensitive with him.

Dad   Sensitive. And how much progress did you make being sensitive? "Let's go out, like a family." "Mom will take him to a psychic." Did it help?

Mom   Kolya, he'll slit his wrists.

Dad   I'd rather he slit his wrists than suck cocks!

Mom   How can you say that?!

Dad   "How can I say that?" I'd disappear off the face of the Earth if I could, I'm so ashamed. I've never been so disgusted in my whole life.

Mom   Kolya, calm down, please! He's just a kid!

Dad   Just a kid . . . Don't you worry, I'm not going to beat him! I'll teach him to love women! (*He comes up to* **Mom***, lifts her up, puts her down on the sofa and starts passionately kissing her.*)

Mom   Kolya, what's all this? What're you doing?

Dad   I'm calming down, like you said.

Mom   Kolya, let me go, Kolya.

But **Dad** *won't stop. He kisses* **Mom**'s *neck, unbuttons her blouse.*

Mom   Kolya . . . Kolya . . . (*Stops fighting him.*)

Lights fade to black.

Scene Twenty-Four: You'll See Some Real Tits

Boy's *apartment. Evening.* **Boy**'s *room.* **Boy** *is sitting at the computer, typing something. The door opens and* **Dad** *enters the room. He is holding a colorful plastic bag with Disney characters on it.* **Boy** *tenses up but tries to act nonchalant, types energetically.* **Dad** *is silent; he's looking at* **Boy** *and waiting patiently, but* **Boy** *doesn't stop typing.*

Dad   Son!

Boy *doesn't react. He types even more energetically.* **Dad** *keeps waiting but then loses his patience and utters angrily:*

Dad   I'm speaking to you! Or have I become invisible?

Boy *shudders and looks up at* **Dad**, *frightened.*

Dad   Come over here!

But **Boy** *remains glued to the chair.*

Dad   Did you hear me? March, two, three! Four five!

Boy *comes up to* **Dad**.

Dad (*hands him the bag*)   I got you something.

Boy *looks at* **Dad**, *then at the bag.*

Boy   What is it?

Dad   Well, open it and you'll see.

Boy *cautiously takes the bag, opens it and pulls out a bunch of adult magazines* (Playboy, Maxim, Strawberry, *etc.*). *He gives* **Dad** *a perplexed look.*

Dad   Well, why are you standing there like an idiot? Or are you just overwhelmed with joy?

Boy *shrugs. Pause.*

Boy   Is that all?

Dad   Is that all? No, it isn't. Standing there like an idiot, fuck. Any other boy would be overjoyed, but this one just stands there, staring blankly. My God, do I hate you!

Boy *looks at* **Dad**, *frightened.*

Dad   Sit! Sit down, do you hear me?

Boy *obeys.*

Dad   Open the magazines! Open them, you hear me? That's an order!

Boy *opens a magazine and goes through its pages, glancing at* **Dad** *from time to time.*

Dad   There you go. Keep looking, keep looking, I'm telling you.

Boy *turns page after page, looks at them.*

Dad   Keep looking!

Boy *keeps turning pages.*

Dad   I'll join you. (*Sits down next to him.*)

Boy *and* **Dad** *are sitting silently, looking at photos of naked women.*

Dad   So? Do you like it?

Boy   I don't know . . . I guess . . .

Dad   "He guesses," geez . . . Sissy! Do you at least realize what you're missing out on?

Boy *is silent.*

Dad   Have you even seen real tits? Touched them? Held them in your hands? Answer me!

Boy   No, I haven't.

Dad   Are you crazy? How could you say no to all this if you haven't even tried?

Boy *jumps up scared and shrugs.*

Dad   What an idiot . . . what an idiot . . . (*Pause.*) You'll see some real tits. Thiiiiis big! And don't you look at me like that. You'll see some, I swear! (*He walks out of the room, determined, and slams the door on his way out.*)

Boy *stands without moving or saying anything for a while, then flops down on his bed. He pushes the magazines away and buries his face in his hands.*

Lights fade to black.

Scene Twenty-Five: Priestess of Love

Boy's *apartment. Afternoon.* **Boy**'s *room. On the bed sits* **Viola**, *posing lasciviously (twenty-three to twenty-five years old, a short but voluptuous woman with D-cup breasts). She is looking at* **Boy** *who is standing aside from her and is very surprised to see her. He's wearing his school uniform and a tie.*

Viola   Hello, handsome!

Boy   Hi! (*Pause.*) Who are you?

Viola   I'm Viola.

Boy   Nice to meet you, and I am . . .

Viola   I don't care. I'll just call you handsome.

Boy   Uhh . . .

Viola   So long as you aren't Gaylen. You're not, are you?

Boy   What do you mean?

Viola   Well, I had a Gaylen as a client once. He turned out to be real Gay-len (*Laughs.*)

Boy   Are you a prostitute?

Viola (*stops laughing, angry*)   I'm a priestess of love, not just some hooker, is that clear?

Boy   Yes. Did my dad hire you?

Viola   Dad, uncle, aunt—what difference does it make? As long as they pay.

Boy   And did they pay a lot?

Viola   Enough.

Boy   And you, ma'am . . . .

Viola   Don't ma'am me. I'm no old lady, am I?

Boy   No, you aren't.

Viola   Exactly, so quit talking to me like one.

Boy   Sure, ma'am, I mean, miss. Aren't you afraid?

Viola   Afraid of what?

Boy   Of going to jail?

Viola (*clicks her tongue*)   Oh dear . . . They don't put people in jail for love. Aren't you tired of standing? I don't bite. (*She pats the bed next to herself.*)

Boy *cautiously sits on the corner of the bed.* **Viola** *smiles flirtatiously,* **Boy** *scoots away slightly.* **Viola** *chuckles, grabs* **Boy** *by the tie and pulls him toward herself.*

Boy   I'm only sixteen.

Viola   Oh but that's good! You're so young, so inexperienced, so innocent!

Boy   I'm not even of age yet! (*Pulls the tie out of* **Viola***'s hands, gets up.*)

Viola   Me neither.

Boy   Really?

Viola   Of course not, I'm messing with you. What is this, an interrogation? Should I show you my ID? I'm nineteen, does that work for you?

Boy   I don't know, I guess . . .

Viola   Any more questions?

Boy *shrugs.*

Viola (*invites him to join her, with her finger*)   Come closer.

Boy *stands still.*

Viola   Are you just gonna stand there the whole time?

Boy *is silent.*

Viola   I mean, do whatever you want, it's your money, but time is running out. In fifty-three minutes, I'm outta here.

Boy *sighs loudly.*

Viola   I had this client once. Pays for two hours up front, and goes, "let's talk." And then he spends the whole damn time whining to me about his miserable life. He's had enough, nobody loves him, nobody appreciates him. So, I'm like, "I can love you. I'll love you so hard you won't know what hit you. You just gotta relax." But he's all, "I can't like this," and keeps dumping all his emotional garbage on me. Shit, I'd rather just make love.

Boy   Make love?

Viola   Well, yes, I'm a priestess of love, not some whore whose mind he can fuck with. That's what his wife is for. I'm here to love.

Boy   Uh-huh . . .

Viola   You're not going to mind-fuck me, are you?

Boy   I guess not . . .

Viola   So, what's holding you up then?

Boy *shrugs.*

Viola   Do you want me?

Boy   I don't know.

Viola   He doesn't know. Maybe you're sick?

Boy   No. I had a checkup. What about you?

Viola   What about me?

Boy   Do you have a health certificate?

Viola   Do you want me to show it to you?

Boy   Yes.

Viola   He wants to see the certificate. Oh, I'll show you one, and another one. (*She grabs* **Boy**'s *hand and puts it on her voluptuous breasts.*) You like that?

Boy   What?

Viola   Do you like my breasts?

Boy   Yeah, I guess . . .

Viola *pulls* **Boy** *to her, kisses him.* **Boy** *is struggling against her.* **Viola** *grasps* **Boy** *even harder but suddenly yelps and lets* **Boy** *go as she puts her hand up to her mouth, wincing from pain.* **Boy** *is standing there, looking flustered.*

Viola   Are you a moron? The fuck you bite me for?

Boy   I'm sorry.

Viola   Don't sorry me. Am I ugly or something?

Boy   No, I guess you're pretty . . .

Viola   So, what's the problem?

Boy   I don't know, I feel kind of disgusted . . .

Viola   "Oh, so innocent, look at me, I'm so disgusted." Is it because I'm, like, a prostitute?

Boy   I don't think so . . .

Viola   He "doesn't think so." I see what's going on here. But you know, I'm not just some cheap slut who has sex for money. I could do it for free. The thing is, I make everyone feel real good. And all good things come with a price. Don't you agree?

Boy *is silent.*

Viola   Don't you want to feel good?

Boy   I do.

Viola   Then stop dragging it out. Come over here, I'll do everything myself.

Boy *stands still.*

Viola (*sighs*)   Are you a virgin?

Boy   What?

Viola   Are you a virgin? Have you done it already?

Boy   Of course, I have. I'm no virgin.

Viola   Well, you're acting like one.

Boy   What? You know, I think you'd better go.

Viola   No way. You still have forty-five minutes paid for.

Boy   Well, then I'll go.

Viola (*blocks* **Boy**'s *way*)   You're not leaving either. Or I'll tell your daddy and he'll spank you. Like this, like this. (*Spanks herself on the bottom.*)

Boy   Geeez!

Viola   Well, if you want, we could try something unorthodox.

Boy   Anal?

Viola   No, anything but anal. My ass still hurts from the last client. He's all like, "let's do it there, in the back." And the next thing I know, he takes his schlong out. It was like a damn firehose.

Boy   Ohh . . .

Viola   Anyway, I offer lots of different services. Domination, trampling.

Boy   What's that?

Viola   That's where I walk on you.

Boy   I see.

Viola   Blowjob. With a condom, without, deep throating. Fetish, foot fetish, role play, golden shower—some clients really like that. Sex toys. But all of those cost extra.

Boy   What toys do you have?

Viola   Dildos, anal beads, handcuffs, vibrators, riding crops, whips, and so on.

Boy (*whispers*)   Do you have a strap-on?

Viola   Male? Oh, so you can't get hard?

Boy   No, God no! Female, so that you're like a guy.

Viola   Like, trans?

Boy   Well, yeah . . .

Viola   What the fuck. So, you're a fruit, aren't you?

Boy (*frightened*)   No, I just . . .

Viola   Damn, I'm so fucking tired of you. Only perverts around. Are there any normal people out there anymore? One wants a golden shower, the other wants me to step on his balls in heels, and now you want a strap-on up your ass! What more do you all need, huh? (*Grabs her breasts.*) Is this not enough? Freaks! Just fucking with my goddamn mind! I'm out, Gay-len!

Boy   I'm not Gaylen . . .

Viola (*waves her hand*)   Whatever. (*Leaves.*)

The **Boy** *stands there, trying to process what's just happened.*

Lights fade to black.

Scene Twenty-Six: That's It

Inside a car. Evening. **Dad** *is driving.* **Boy** *is in the back seat. The only thing* **Boy** *sees out the window are lush tree tops.*

Boy (*cautiously*)   Dad . . .

Dad *is silent.*

Boy   Dad . . . (*Pause.*) Where are we going?

Dad *is silent. Finally, he pulls over and, without looking at* **Boy**, *utters.*

Dad   Get out, that's it.

Boy *looks around, frightened.*

Lights fade to black.

Part Three: Some People Do Care

Yegor They were sitting on a bench. On their usual bench. They sit on it every day. What else have they got to do anyway? They swill beer and chew on sunflower seeds. And they were all friends. I mean, they hung out together, roamed the block, jacked people's phones, drank vodka, got in fights for each other—that too. And then one day, they found out that one of them was gay; I mean, really gay—as in he's into guys, for real, not a latent gay, or metrosexual, but *gay* gay.

He was hiding it, of course. You don't exactly share this with your boys—even though they'd been friends since they were five or ten, I don't know. And then, they found out. Somebody took a picture of him, or it was a slip of the tongue, doesn't matter anymore. They found out. And the boys got real mad. They just went nuts. They beat the crap out of their friend, didn't miss a single rib. He was lying on the road, spitting blood, but it wasn't enough for them. "So, you like it in the ass? Well, here you go." They stripped him naked and shoved a bottle into him. The guy was yelling, cussing at them, but they were his real friends, weren't they? "Oh, you like it, do you? Here's another one." And they shoved in another one. The guy went silent after that—he'd passed out. But it still wasn't enough for his friends—they'd had a lot of beer by then. They tried to shove a third one in, but they couldn't get it in all the way, everything was completely torn up down there. This son of a bitch had been drinking from the same bottle as them, sharing cigs with them, going to the sauna with them! No doubt he'd been looking at them, having his sick fantasies, asshole! Fucking cocksucker! So they left, leaving him out on the road, naked.

They came back soon though. They realized that if he came to, the homo would go to the cops and rat them out. After all, he wasn't even a human being, just a piece of shit. So, they finished the pervert. They took a boulder, 40 pounds, and bashed him on the head eight times. Just to be sure.

Nice people, aren't they. Both already had criminal records. And you know what else, it was Victory Day. Great way to celebrate, guys. Honoring our grandfathers who fought in the war, their incredible feats, their courage, because our grandfathers were no fags . . .[16]

So why the hell would you tell your parents?

The lights come on. A hospital room; **Boy** *is sitting on the bed in a hospital gown; he's staring blankly straight ahead of himself.*

Yegor *turns to* **Boy**.

Yegor Don't want to say anything? Well, fine, keep quiet. If only you'd kept quiet before. And don't look at me like it's all my fault. Didn't I warn you not to tell anyone? I did. Didn't I tell you it could all end badly? I did. Did I force you to change your orientation? I didn't. I told you the choice was all yours to make, that you had to look into yourself and figure it out. And you did. But life is cruel, you know, it's not like playing with toy cars. You chose this path. So sorry, but you should have kept quiet or been like others, be straight. Man, don't fucking look at me like that. I feel sorry for you, I do, but what else can I do? I'm in another town and haven't even thought about you in ages. Sorry. That's just how it is . . . anyway, stay strong, man. It's all gonna be fine. It should be . . . (*He pats* **Boy** *on the shoulder and exits.*)

The lights in the hospital room fade. **Vika Malakhova** *enters.*

Vika Malakhova   I couldn't bring myself to lie to my parents. You know, that I'm a lesbian. Just couldn't make the words come out . . . so they ended up getting divorced. It sucks, you know. But if you think of it, it was self-centered of me. I wasn't really thinking about their happiness, only about mine. I thought that if they stayed together, everybody would be happy, but that's not true. They are happy apart. The most important thing is for people to be happy, and this is what makes them happy. And by the way, I'm not doing too bad myself. I thought it would be worse. But actually, nothing's really changed.

I still have my dad and my mom, they just live in different homes, but they love me even more now. They have a kind of competition with each other, like who will give me more attention and care. You remember, my brother moved to Saint Petersburg, he lives there now. So, now I'm taking the blow. But it's actually good. I have them wrapped around my little finger now.

See these new jeans—Dad bought them for me, and this watch is from my mom. Next month Dad promised to use his credit card to get me an iPhone 5. Before the divorce, I wouldn't have gotten this many new things in a whole year. Also, they smile more now. And they don't need to fight. Mom even has a new love interest already. Our neighbor, Valera, has been hitting on her. He's constantly looking for excuses to drop by. And Mom blushes like a teenager when she looks at him. It's hilar.

A while ago a girl kissed me on the lips. She's in the same grade as me, but we don't have classes together. She wears black all the time and is really gloomy, you know, a goth. Nobody really talks to her. One day, she walks up to me, and says, "Vika, I'm sorry to hear that your folks are getting divorced, I've been through that too." And then she just started kissing me, totally freaked me out. And the thing is, she just kept squishing her lips on me and wouldn't let up. I was lucky somebody showed up at the end of the hallway, or she would have stuck her tongue in my mouth. Ugh, it still freaking cringes me. It's all those jokes, I totally jinxed myself. Now I'm sure I'm no lesbian—I like boys, and I'll always like them. As for that girl, I stay away from her now, I don't say hi or anything, and if I spot her, I run to another floor or hide. If it goes on like this, I might even have to change schools. Like how fucked up do you have to be to just start kissing another girl completely out of the blue? I would have even tattled on her, but I'm no snitch. She'll have a hard enough time anyway. I hope she doesn't land in a hospital, like you. Although maybe she'll smarten up before it comes to that.

The lights come on again in the hospital room. **Boy** *is still sitting in the same pose and with the same facial expression as before.*

Vika Malakhova *walks up to him.*

Vika Malakhova   You look like shit. What have they been giving you? (*Pause.*) Man, I told you, tell them you changed your mind, but you got stuck on your "We finally look like a family." A family my ass. Look, keep your head up. I'm sure it's all gonna be fine. They'll treat you, they'll let you out—just get better, you hear me? You have to. Or who will I talk to in dreams? (*Pause.*) Check out my watch, do you like it? It's cool, isn't it?

Boy's *mouth opens as if to say something, but he can't utter a word.*

Vika Malakhova   I didn't get that. What is it you want?

Boy *is barely audibly wheezing.*

Vika Malakhova   Oh. Want me to sing something? (*Singing.*)

> I wasn't like the others
> Since I was eight,
> It seems that being different
> Has always been my fate.

You know, I don't feel like singing . . . I'm gonna go. Get well, got it? Got it? (*She hugs* **Boy** *and exits*).

The lights fade again.

Viola *enters.*

Viola   So, I'm, like, a fallen woman and not exactly in a position to judge anyone. But I don't give a damn. I hate gays. I'd kill all of them. I'd take a machine gun and pull the trigger, let the bullets rain. Rat-a-tat-tat, Rat-a-tat-tat-tat! Every single one of them. I mean, come on! I'll be out of work because of you people. Me and other girls.

You multiply like fucking rabbits. I keep losing clients because of you, and among the few left, normal ones are almost impossible to come by. You are freaks—do the likes of you get it? Freaks. Fucking perverts. Even normal guys are getting perverted because of you. Nobody's satisfied with the classics anymore, they want to get peed on, to be humiliated, beaten up, tied up, handcuffed. Aren't they idiots? And it's all because of you assholes. You've mind-fucked everyone, do you get it? I'm a priestess of love, not a queen of perversion. I can make you feel good without all this shit, all these whips and anal beads. It makes me want to puke. I don't want to just sell my body like a cheap whore, I want to give men pleasure and get pleasure myself, too. I know what love is. It's when both people feel good; but these new types only fucking think about themselves. As long as they get what they want, as long as *they're* satisfied, they don't care about us at all. We get paid for it, so that's, like, supposed to be our satisfaction.

And why is it like this now? Because you people showed up. You've turned everything upside down. You could have screwed each other in private, but no, you wanted attention, you wanted respect. And once you crawled out of the woodwork, everyone else thought, if they can do it, why can't we try something else too? What if it's actually cool? And here we are, with all sorts of perverts on the loose . . .

You want respect? Why should I respect you? For going against the laws of nature? Didn't you have science in school? The birds and the bees, pistils and stamens, all that stuff. Or did you fail that class? Why are you only using pistils? Or are you afraid of stamens? Freaks. And don't look at me like that. I am saving humankind here. If all the men get infected with this shit from you, who'll make us babies? We'll all fucking perish. I am a guardian of normal love—normal, do you hear me?—without your perversions, so that at least some will not forget how it is—to love a woman. Got it?

The lights in the room come on again. **Boy** *hasn't moved; the expression on his face is the same.* **Viola** *turns around and looks at* **Boy**. *She walks up to him.*

Viola   You see what this does to you? You're just a boy—almost innocent—even cute, I'd say. Why the hell do you need any of this? Don't be stupid, listen to what I have to say. Be normal, find a chick, fall in love with her—just don't do any of these perv things to her—and if you don't find a girl, come to me. I'll love you so hard it'll blow your mind. Anyway, come on, get well. Here and here. (*Taps her finger on her head, making it clear that the other "here" referred to* **Boy**'s *body. Exits.*)

The lights fade to black for the third time.

Grandma *enters.*

Grandma   I know why this is happening to me. It's my punishment. I didn't think, though, it was going to be like this. But it is what it is. I guess I deserve it. It was a long time ago, a very long time . . . I was so young when it happened—a student of art history. I was pretty . . . had a braid this long, down to my waist . . . ah (*sighs*) . . . and a lad started courting me, you know. Vitya was his name. He was in the same school but another program, I can't recall what it was . . . doesn't really matter anyway. He was following me everywhere, walking me home, buying me cakes with frosting. I loved those cakes. Today you can find any cake you want, but you'll never find cakes like those. They were so tasty, so sweet, there was nothing sweeter in the whole world. Oh, where was I . . . yes, he was courting me, but wasn't really much of a looker himself. Small himself, he had a big nose, red hair, was covered in freckles, and was so puny, just skin and bones. Not husband material, right? I felt sorry for him, nothing else. But he wouldn't give up. He would take me out to the movies, or to dance. Oh boy, did I love dancing . . . oh those wonderful dances of the old days—it was such a joy even just to watch them. The whole country was dancing, everybody was happy. But nowadays . . . I can't make heads nor tails of these songs—bad lyrics, bad music; and the dances are no better. Just twitching and flinching, like crazy.

Anyway, it was at those dances that I met my first husband, my sweet dear Andrey. He was tall, almost six foot six, strong, a volleyball player—looked like a model. Compared to him, Vitya seemed like an ant. But as soon as he noticed that Andrey and I liked each other, he lost his mind. He dropped to his knees, took my hand, and said, "Tatyana, I beg you, don't look at anyone else. Be my life companion, for my love for you has no limits; you are the air I breathe; when I look at you, my heart skips a beat." And that was in front of everyone there. Oh boy, was it awkward.

I helped him up, but I didn't know what to tell him. I mean, his words were nice and everything, but I didn't love him, not a bit. And how can you be together without love? I didn't give him an answer then, I just led him away from that place so as not to embarrass ourselves. I told him I'd talk to him the next day, that I needed to sleep on it. I cried all night in my bed, thinking about it. Of course I felt sorry for the poor fellow, but what could I do? I didn't love him, that was it . . .

Anyway, the next day I walk out of my house and he's already there, waiting for me at the entrance. So, it all came pouring out of me right then and there: I didn't need him to walk me home anymore, I liked him as a comrade, but nothing more, and a future together was out of question. And although I felt sorry for him, it would be best for both of us this way. Of course, he was of a different opinion. He said he wouldn't give up that easily, that he'd fight for me until I "woke up" and found the courage to acknowledge that I also loved him with all my heart and that we were meant for each other. To be fair, he did fight for me. He even challenged Andrey to a duel. Crazy. Obviously, Andrey did not accept the challenge. He could have taken Vitya down with just his pinky. But Vitya was not afraid of him. Day after day I kept telling him, "Please, leave me alone, I don't love you." And he kept bringing me flowers. A bouquet of daisies from the fields, every day. I've hated daisies ever since.

He also wrote poems for me which, I must admit, were not that bad; he even painted my portrait. But my heart would not melt for him. One day, Vitya attacked Andrey after all, and Andrey hit him back—it wasn't a strong blow, but Vitya went down anyway. I thought that would stop him, but it didn't. Something else did. Andrey and I got married. He proposed literally the day after all that happened, and in three months, we were husband and wife. Only that made Vitya finally accept his defeat and move to Sverdlovsk[17] . . . quite a story . . . Andrey and I got divorced five years later. In all that time, I never even thought about Vitya. A few years later, maybe two, a girl who went to college with me and then moved to Sverdlovsk told me that there had been a huge scandal. That Vitya had been accused of this homosexualism of yours. That they even wanted to prosecute him, for, you know, being gay, or whatever you call it. Right. Gay, that's it. But then the case against him went quiet. Somebody testified in his favor. A girl turned up who claimed they were . . . in love and all those allegations were slander. So they let him go. And then he managed to emigrate to some place in Europe. Somehow, he left. They say he did in fact start to live with a man there, and that they're still together. Real filth, at its worst.

I had actually forgotten about all of this until now. Now I see that it was all my fault. My fault . . . if I'd just . . . if I hadn't rejected him, he would have stayed normal . . . instead, he had so much suffering, so much pain, that he found a way to escape it all . . . although maybe it was his fate all along. Who knows? But I am guilty anyway. And now I get my punishment . . . I understand that I deserve it, I'm old already, but why should the boy suffer? He grew up without parents, saw them once a year at most. And now all this suffering. Damn you, demon . . . damn you . . . damn you to hell!

The lights come back on in the hospital room. **Boy** *is sitting in the same pose; his face hasn't changed.*

Grandma   Oh Lord . . . oh sweet Mary Mother of God! What's happened to you, honey . . . oh dear, oh God . . .

Boy *doesn't react.*

Grandma   Why are you just sitting there? You're not even blinking. Can you hear me?

Boy *blinks with difficulty.*

Grandma   Oh God . . . oh dear . . . well, at least you can hear me. God, forgive me for my sins. (*To* **Boy**.) You can't just sit all the time, you hear me? You need to get up, walk around, or you'll never get better. Come on, honey, get up! (*She comes up to* **Boy**, *helps him up.*) Well, just look at that! Well done! Well done . . .

Boy *can barely stand—it seems that he'll fall back down on the bed any moment, but* **Grandma** *helps him stay on his feet.*

Grandma   Hold on, honey, hold on! Just look how weak you've gotten. You need to walk, walk around.

Boy *takes a small step with difficulty.*

Grandma   Great job! Come on! One more step! That's it! There you go!

Boy *takes another step, then another, and then one more.*

Grandma   All this sitting around does you no good.

Boy's *steps get firmer.*

Grandma   Keep walking, I'll walk too. (*Exits.*)

Boy (*as she leaves, with effort*)   Gran . . .

But **Grandma** *has already left.*

Boy *walks around the room a bit more. He stops. Starts speaking. Words come out with considerable difficulty.*

Boy   This is actually a rehab for drug addicts . . . I still can't figure out what I'm doing here . . . I mean, I understand that I am here to be treated, kind of, but I'm not a drug addict. I've never even tried drugs . . . and I don't want to start . . . now for sure I don't . . . and I don't know how long this is gonna last. It feels like it'll never end . . . like in prison . . . serving a life sentence . . . dammit . . . (*Winces with pain, silent for a while.*) What was I saying? Damn. My brain isn't working at all. I can't remember anything. No wait, I do remember something . . . I remember that Dad brought me here. We were in the head doctor's office; you know, the chief physician. He was asking me something, I think, something about drugs. If I had ever used, if I had an addiction. And so on. I answered no to all questions. You can tell just by looking at me that I'm not a druggie. He was taking notes, nodding, and smiling. Dad was silent. He was just frowning and not saying anything. And then . . . then . . . dammit. My head . . . (*He is silent, rubs his temples.*) the white lab coat. White, as white as snow . . . I hate . . . I hate lab coats . . . At some point, I think, he asked me to step out and wait in the corridor, and Dad stayed in there with him. I had a feeling they'd admit me here, and Dad would leave, but I didn't want to believe that. And I got this feeling . . .

not fear, no . . . I was really hurt and frustrated. Why would they do this to me? I'm not sick. We were like a family after all—well, almost. We talked to each other, didn't fight . . . almost . . . I never saw Dad leave that room. A nurse came and told me to follow her. We walked and walked. She was also in white. White is the color of angels, but these people are doctors . . . we came to the reception, or . . . what is it called? They took my phone and my GameBoy. My money too, I think, I don't remember, and brought me to the room, I mean, here . . . that's it. I don't know how long I've been in here. They've been giving me some stuff, and after I take it, I can't remember anything and want to sleep all the time. Wait. Somebody's coming. (*Listens.*)

The door opens, a **Nurse** *walks into the room, pushing a cart with medications in front of her.*

Boy   As I was telling you, here are the pills. Speak of the devil . . .

Nurse   Who are you talking to? There's no one here.

Boy   And they're drugging me again . . .

Nurse   Of course we are. Open your mouth.

Boy   I won't take it!

Nurse   Well, hello! What's gotten into you?

Boy   No pills, no injections, I don't want them!

Nurse   We only do injections in the morning.

Boy   Isn't it morning now?

Nurse   Now it's evening.

Boy   It doesn't matter, I won't take anything anyway.

Nurse   Alright, I've had enough of this show. You're not a baby. I have ten more patients to deal with.

Boy   Well, go do your rounds.

Nurse   Don't you get it? This isn't for my benefit. It's for you. If the doctor says you have to take this, then you have to take it, or you'll never get better.

Boy   There's nothing wrong with me. I'm not a drug addict.

Nurse   You all say that. Take it, or I'll call the doctor!

Boy   Don't call the doctor.

Nurse   Then take the medicine and I won't have to.

Boy   What are these pills? They make me feel bad.

Nurse   That's impossible.

Boy   What are these pills?

Nurse   Don't yell, or somebody will actually come.

Boy   What are these pills?

Nurse   Will you stop? Enzyme modulators. Are you happy now?

Boy   What kind of endtime modulators?

Nurse   Enzyme. That's enough. I don't have time to argue with you. Open your mouth.

Boy *opens his mouth. The* **Nurse** *puts a capsule and a couple of pills in his mouth.*

Nurse   Swallow.

Boy *doesn't swallow.*

Nurse   You have to swallow, you hear me?

Boy *swallows obediently.*

Nurse   Have some water.

Boy *drinks.*

Nurse   Open your mouth. (*Pause.*) Well, come on, open it. I can't wait for you all day.

Boy *opens his mouth again. The nurse checks his mouth with a spoon.*

Nurse   Good, close your mouth. That's more like it. None of this "I won't, I won't."

Boy *closes his mouth.*

Boy   Do you see how they treat me here? They check to make sure I swallowed the pills. I can't even hide them under my tongue.

Nurse   And there he goes, talking again. Who are you talking to there?

Boy   No one.

Nurse   Good. Now lie down. Come on, lie down. You have to rest. (*Puts the* **Boy** *in bed.*) Sleep, rest up, and you'll get better in no time.

Boy   Will I?

Nurse   Of course. Go on, sleep.

Boy *turns his face to the wall. The nurse looks at him for a while, then pushes the cart out of the room.* **Boy** *lies still and moans quietly; finally, he turns around, slowly sits up on the bed, holding his head.*

Boy   Dammit . . . this headache again. I keep telling them, these pills only make it worse, and they make me want to sleep all the time. Sleep . . . no, I can't, I shouldn't, I won't. (*He gets up, walks in circles around the room to keep himself from falling asleep.*) I don't understand what's going on. I'm not a drug addict, but they are treating me the same way as everyone else here. Every day they put some sensors on

my head. The doctor said they affect certain parts of . . . what do you call it . . . brain.
These parts are responsible for addiction. But I don't have it, this a . . . (*winces with
pain*) addiction. Then they put me in some kind of capsule. I think, I'm not sure . . .
Shit! Come on! You can remember! They put me, they put me where? They put me
in . . . in a capsule, right. In a capsule. I lie in there while a laser, some kind of laser,
cleans my blood or something. Damn. I can't fall asleep, I can't!

He does a few squats and walks around the room.

I have to keep talking. I can't be silent. If anyone hears me . . . 'cause someone must
be listening to me, right? I am really losing my . . .what do you call it . . . mind here.
No, no, no. I shouldn't, I can't. I was telling you about . . . about the treatment. Right.
The treatment . . . what else? I also have meetings with a therapist. I think he told me
that the course of treatment would take three weeks. Or did he say five? Damn, I can't
remember. I can't remember . . . every day is the same. How long have I been here? A
day? Two? A year? A month? Endtime modulators . . . I will never get out of here . . .
save me, please, somebody, anybody . . .

I tried to escape, but it's impossible to escape from this place. On the ground floor,
they have . . . those things . . . bars. . . on the windows—and here, you can't even
open the windows—they've removed all the handles. Besides, there are gu . . . gua
. . . guards everywhere, and sensors too, on the poles . . . infrared . . . (*Pause. His
head falls on his chest. He shakes it and continues.*)

I shouldn't, I can't fall asleep! Maybe the TV will help? Damn . . . it only makes it
worse. I think I may have tried it already. It has . . . it has only one channel. Nature.
Nature all day long . . . who watches this stuff? (*Does a few more squats.*)

They also take us somewhere . . . where do they take us? Oh, right, it's like an AA
meeting. Just they talk about something else here. About drugs, I think. Right, of
course about drugs, everyone around here is a drug addict . . . I'm afraid of them, they
have this crazy look . . . don't fall asleep! Don't! (*Slaps himself on the cheeks.*) Where
was I? Damn, I forgot . . . was I telling you about the TV? No, I think I already
mentioned the TV . . . damn . . . oh, right, of course! Support groups . . . and
everybody kind of . . . you know, tells their stories . . . how they got hooked. But I
never say anything. I don't have anything to tell. I haven't even tried drugs once, I
think . . . don't fall asleep! Don't!

How long have I been here? When will I get out? Nobody comes to visit me . . . I
can make one call a day . . . five minutes, I think . . . maybe six . . . but I don't call
anyone . . . I don't. I can't remember any phone numbers, damn . . . I can't . . . I have
a mom . . . and a dad, I think . . . why don't they . . . visit me? Why? How are they . . .
there? (*Drops on the bed and falls asleep.*)

Lights fade to black.

Boy's apartment. Evening. The room of **Boy**'s **Mom** and **Dad**.

Dad   What else could we have done? What?

Mom   I don't know. You told me you'd handle everything.

Dad Sveta, I tried. I did what I could. But I can only take so much, you know, I'm not made of steel.

Mom Your heart is made of stone, Biketov.

Dad Sveta . . .

Mom Don't "Sveta" me, just don't. Oh God, that's not life, it's just hell . . .

Dad You just underestimate medicine. Everything is gonna be fine.

Mom Fine? It'll never be fine again.

Dad It will be. The doctor told me that they'd had a similar case. They'd treated a patient . . . also a teenager.

Mom And did they cure him?

Dad I guess . . .

Mom You guess?

Dad Well, he didn't exactly tell me that they had cured him, but why would he even mention that case if there was no result?

Mom Oh Kolya, Kolya . . .

Dad What?

Mom What if they make things worse?

Dad Worse? There's nothing worse . . . I brought him such a babe, but even then he turned his nose up at her. He only likes guys. Moron!

Mom What babe?

Dad What?

Mom What babe are you talking about?

Dad Why are you looking at me like that, Sveta?

Mom What babe are you talking about?

Dad "What babe"? A hot one . . . A priestess.

Mom What kind of priestess?

Dad A priestess of love, Sveta, of love . . .

Mom Are you telling me you brought him a prostitute?

Dad Well, not a prostitute. A priestess. Of love.

Mom Biketov, are you insane?

Dad It's hard to be sane next to you people . . .

Mom Where do you think you're going? Halt, two, three! Did you bring a prostitute into our home?

Dad   Well, I didn't bring her for myself . . .

Mom   Biketov, I'm gonna kill you, you asshole!

Dad   Sveta, what's gotten into you? Calm down!

Mom   I'll fucking calm down. I'll be so calm I'll knock your teeth out, asshole! (*She slaps* **Dad** *in the face, punches him in the chest, then slaps him on the face again a few times.*) You asshole! Jerk! Bastard!

Dad *does not resist her.*

Dad   Go on, do it! Hit me again! Keep it coming . . . (*He grabs* **Mom** *by the shoulders and hugs her tight.*)

Mom *keeps punching* **Dad** *on the back. Each punch is weaker and weaker. Finally, she stops and sobs into his shoulder.* **Dad** *strokes* **Mom**'s *hair.*

Dad   Sveta . . . you have to understand, Sveta . . . I am desperate . . . every morning I wake up and face the fact that my son is gay . . . I want to forget it, I want to stop thinking about it, but how can you forget something like that? The worst thing that can happen to any parent is to resent their own son.

Mom   Kolya . . .

Dad   Wait Sveta, let me finish. I am afraid of him, do you get it? Afraid. I am not afraid of anything: of death, of killing people, but I am afraid of him. I have no idea how to look him in the eyes, I immediately picture how he's doing *that* with others like him, it makes me cringe. And yet, he's my son. My son . . . my flesh, my blood, my family line . . . and so yes, I did bring her over. I thought, "He's human after all, a man. He should at least try it with a real woman." He didn't even have to do anything, just try, I paid for everything . . . and yes, she was a prostitute, but I'd bring him the devil if it could help. Anything that could help . . .

Mom   You could have told me.

Dad   You wouldn't have agreed to it.

Mom   Oh God, of course, I wouldn't have. And I never will.

Dad   That's what I'm taking about, Sveta. In fact, we should have done it much earlier. Much earlier. If he'd tried it earlier, everything would be fine now.

Mom   What are you talking about?

Dad   What? That's what we should've done. Better at home with a prostitute than doing God knows what with some kind of freak. They're not human at all. They're freaks, perverts.

Mom   Shut your mouth!

Dad   What?

Mom   Shut your mouth! You and I are hardly human! We are the freaks! He's just a child. A child. It's our fault. He's like that because of us . . . because of us . . . and we just keep torturing him. Drag him to the exorcist, lock him up in a psych hospital.

Dad   It's not an insane asylum. It's a rehabilitation clinic.

Mom   You know what I mean.

Dad   What if they do cure him?

Mom   He's the one who should despise *you*. Forty years old, afraid of his son.

Dad   Sveta . . .

Mom   We don't even know how he's doing there . . .

Dad   How *can* he be doing? It's a hospital like any other. They'll discharge him in three weeks.

Mom   Oh God, I can't do this anymore. What kind of mother am I? God, forgive me . . .

Dad   You're a normal mother, calm down. He's fine. He'll stay there for a while, rest, get a few treatments. If it doesn't help, we'll think what to do next when he comes back.

Mom   What is there to think about? Where else to put him? Will you send him off to a deserted island or something? Enough already!

Dad   Where are you going?

Mom   To our son. And you can get the hell out of here. We'll do fine without you . . . he's "afraid," he says.

Dad   Sveta, wait! Wait, do you hear me?

Mom   What is it, Biketov?

Dad   You don't know the address.

Mom   I'll find it.

Dad   I'll come with you. I can drive you there. You'll see for yourself that he's fine.

Mom   Biketov, I hate you . . .

Dad (*quietly*)   I hate myself too . . .

They exit.

Lights fade to black.

Mom *and* **Dad**'*s voices, in the darkness.*

Dad   Well, you see, he's alive. Sleeping.

Mom   Sweetie, do you hear me? Wake up.

Dad   Look, there's even TV here. (*Turns on the TV.*)

The lights in the room come on again.

Boy *is in bed.* **Mom** *and* **Dad** *are standing in front of him. The TV shows incredibly beautiful landscapes.*

Mom   Wake up, come on. Mom and Dad are here.

Boy *makes an effort to open his eyes. He's half asleep and can't understand what's going on. He blinks, rubs his eyes. Winces with pain.*

Mom   Oh my God, what have they done to you?

Boy   Mom? Is that you?

Mom   Of course it's me, honey. Who else would it be? Have you been missing us, my dear? Oh, dear God . . .

Dad   Enough of these tears! (*To* **Boy**,) So, how have you been doing here?

Mom   Don't ask stupid questions! Don't you see for yourself? He's barely alive! He looks like hell, pale as a ghost, no spark in his eyes, he'll pass out at any moment from the looks of it. "He'll stay there for a while, rest"!

Boy   You came!

Mom   Of course, we did. Did you think we were going to leave you here? We're not monsters, honey. Of course, we came. (*She hugs* **Boy**, *strokes his head.*) Our dear, our only boy.

Boy   I hoped so much that you'd come . . .

Mom   Oh God . . . our child has been waiting for us. My heart is breaking. I am so sorry, sweetie, so sorry, my darling, my love. Dad and I made a mistake, a horrible mistake . . . (*To* **Dad**.) Say something, will you?

Dad   Son, listen . . . I didn't mean to, you know . . . I ask you . . . to forgive me . . .

Boy   I'm so glad you came!

Mom   We are too, honey. We are too . . . you're our good, smart, handsome boy . . .

Dad   Well, let's not get carried away . . .

Mom   Say that again?

Boy   You'll take me with you, won't you?

Mom   Of course, we will, honey. Of course, we will. We came to take you home. We'll go together right now. Won't we, Kolya?

Dad   Yes, we will. (*To* **Boy**.) Pack your stuff, you're coming back home with us.

Mom *helps* **Boy** *stand up. He can barely stand.*

Mom   Oh God . . . we almost lost you. This is all our fault.

Boy   That's alright, Mom, I'm happy we're going back home now . . . this place is bad. Dad?

Dad   What, son?

Boy   Everything's gonna be okay, right?

Dad   Yes . . .

Boy   You sure?

Dad   I'm sure. Let's get out of here.

They exit.

Lights fade to black.

The only light on the stage comes from the TV that is still on.

Silence.

Suddenly, we hear the **Nurse** *speak.*

Nurse   Biketov! Biketov! Biketov. Wake up, you hear me?

The lights in the room come on again. **Boy** *is in the bed, sleeping. The* **Nurse** *is standing by the bed, shaking him by the shoulder.*

Nurse   Wake up, Biketov!

Boy *struggles to open his eyes; he looks at the* **Nurse**, *baffled.*

Nurse   Don't look at me like that, you've got visitors.

Boy   Who is it?

Nurse   How should I know? Go and see for yourself, hurry up. I've been trying to wake you up for ten minutes now.

Boy   Are you sure they're here for me?

Nurse   Yes, for you. Get up. (*Helps* **Boy** *stand up.*)

Boy *takes a few steps, stops, looks at the* **Nurse**, *turns around and walks out of the room.*

Nurse (*sighs*)   Poor people. Why could they not just live like everyone else? He didn't even turn off the TV. (*She stands in front of the TV and looks at the screen. Ten seconds, twenty, keeps staring.*)

Curtain.

April 2013–January 2014.[18]

Notes

1   "Blue" in the play title refers to the Russian word "light blue," which, apart from indicating a hue, is slang for "gay."
2   Age restriction "21+" was put by the playwright in response to the infamous "gay propaganda law" adopted in Russia on June 29, 2013, as the play was in the making.

Officially registered as Federal Law 135-FZ, the law penalizes the so-called "propaganda of non-traditional sexual relations to minors." The age of majority in Russia is eighteen; the use of the 21+ age limit is arbitrary and underscores the consent of this law. It also mirrors the obligation to mark all events and products with LGBTQ-related contents with "18+" under the 2013 law.

3   This and other songs that Vika will be singing throughout the play mostly come from the Soviet and post-Soviet years and are all melodies and lyrics widely known to speakers of Russian. Anyone who grew up in Russia in the 1990s and 2000s would be immediately familiar with the songs mentioned in the play. This note contains all songs that appear in the play, with their original titles in Russian and YouTube links.

"Some Dreams Come True, and Some Don't"—Мечта сбывается by Yuri Antonov (1981), https://bit.ly/385dwLP.

"When She Got on the Train"—В свой вагон вошла она, aka Люди встречаются by VIA Veselye rebiata (1971), https://bit.ly/2LvWjn6.

"We Wish You Happiness in this Truly Wide World"—Мы желаем счастья вам, счастья в этом мире большом by Stas Namin and band (1983), https://bit.ly/34wC3IX.

"Oh, Tanya, Tanya, cutie, there is so much to tell"—Таня, Таня, Танечка, from the film *The Carnival Night* (1956, dir. Eldar Ryazanov), https://bit.ly/3qZ5TiJ.

"A lonesome pigeon flew to me one day"—Одинокий голубь by Yana (1998), https://bit.ly/2KIv9ZI.

"I had a dream of falling snow"—Снилось мне: неожиданно выпал снег by the band Voskresenie (1990s), https://bit.ly/37laCDJ.

"I love you to tears, I do"—Я люблю тебя до слез by Alexander Serov (1995), https://bit.ly/2KtjGgw.

"I'll ride my bike all the way into the fields"—Я буду долго гнать велосипед aka Букет by Alexander Barykin (1997), https://bit.ly/3ak2vJv.

"The die has been cast, Mom, I'm gay, Dad, I'm gay"—Все решено by Valentin Strykalo (early 2010s), https://bit.ly/3mliaKW. This song is the least known as well as most recent among the selection for the play; it was performed live on Russia's state Channel One on the talk show *Pust'govoryat*.

"I wasn't like others / Since I was eight, / It seems that being different / Has always been my fate"—Быть таким как все с детства не умел aka Прыгну со скалы by Korol' i Shut (around early 2000s), https://bit.ly/3qYxgJM.

4   Sergey Zverev is a prominent Russian stylist, known for his extravagant looks, flamboyant personality, and the catchphrase "The Star is in shock."

5   The Silver Age refers to a period of Russian culture around the turn of the twentieth century (1893–1921). It was characterized by the flourishing of poetry and the arts. It was the time when the first Russian literary works (which we know of) that explore same-sex desire among men and women were written and published (*The Wings* by Mikhail Kuzmin (1906) and *Thirty-Three Abominations* by Lidiya Zinov'eva-Annibal (1906)).

6   A popular Russian social network, modeled on Facebook.

7   Quoted after: Fyodor I. Tyutchev, "Elysium of Shades This Soul of Mine," in *Poems & Political Letters of F. I. Tyutchev*, translated with introduction and notes by Jesse Zeldin (Knoxville: University of Tennessee Press, 1973), pp. 51–52.

8   Boris Moiseev is a Russian pop singer who plays with the image of a gay man, which is also reflected in the lyrics of his songs, such as "The Light Blue Moon."

9   Sniffing the sleeve is part of the Russian vodka drinking ritual, to "help the vodka down."

10   The Decembrists were a group of officers in the Imperial Russian Army who started an uprising in Saint Petersburg against the ascension of Tsar Nicholas I to the throne in December 1825 (after his elder brother Constantine had renounced his claim to the

Russian crown). The uprising was suppressed; the officers who led it were exiled to Siberia. Their wives followed them voluntarily into the exile—the story that engendered a long-lasting trope of a faithful wife in Russian culture.

11   Russia has obligatory military service for all men between eighteen and twenty-seven. Conscription can be avoided in a number of ways, including by pursuing higher education (until over the age of twenty-seven) or by claiming you are a homosexual. While there is no official ban on military service for gays in Russia, the medical board usually takes claims of homosexuality into account and disqualifies the drafted from service on the ground of psychiatric disorder (the same is true for trans persons). This practice has inspired young men who want to avoid military service to fake homosexuality in front of the medical board.

12   *Bathing of a Red Horse* (1912) is the iconic openly homoerotic painting by the Russian painter Kuzma Petrov-Vodkin that depicts young naked boys riding red horses into the lake to bathe them.

13   Nikolay Baskov is a popular Russian opera and pop singer, assumed to be a closeted gay.

14   In 2013/14, when the play was written, 15,000 rubles was around 500 US dollars. To put this number in perspective, even as this book comes out in 2021, most pensioners in Russia receive a pension that is below this amount. Therefore, Grandma must have not only sacrificed her monthly pension to pay the exorcist, but also reached into her savings.

15   Sergey Bezrukov is a Russian television and film actor, assumed to be a closeted gay.

16   The story narrated by Yegor is based on real-life events that took place in 2013. It happened on Victory Day, celebrated annually on May 9 in Russia to commemorate the end of the Second World War. For more details on the story, see, for example, a report by the *New York Times*, https://www.nytimes.com/2013/05/13/world/europe/homophobia-linked-to-murder-in-russia.html (accessed May 24, 2020).

17   Sverdlovsk is the Soviet-era name of Ekaterinburg.

18   The plot of the play, according to the playwright, was inspired by a real-life story of a young Russian gay teenager who came out to his parents and was subjected to conversion therapy and exorcism. After moving in with his boyfriend, he published an open letter online, in which he shared his traumatic experience. Zaytsev saw the letter and used it as inspiration for *Every Shade of Blue* (interview with Zaytsev, https://www.satirikon.ru/news_press/press/beseda-s-vladimirom-zaytsevym/, accessed December 15, 2020). The events in question possibly refer to Ivan Kharchenko, whose forced admittance to a psychiatric clinic was widely publicized in April 2012. See, for instance, a news story by major Russian channel NTV from April 25, 2012 at https://www.ntv.ru/video/310921/ (accessed December 15, 2020).

A City Flower

A CONFESSION STORY

A STORY OF A LIFE

Elizaveta Letter

Elizaveta Letter is an actress, theater director, playwright, and dancer. She is a founder and artistic director of the theater of social drama Garcia and of the production company Vzglyad (Glance). She was born in the early 1990s in the Siberian city of Achinsk, near Krasnoyarsk, and grew up there. As her parents were not into arts, she availed herself of the books at the local library and read passionately. Her writing has been influenced by William Shakespeare, Federico García Lorca, Maurice Druon, Juliette Benzoni, Georg F. Born, and Alphonse Daudet, among others. She has authored several plays, including *Dear Time, I Want to Live* (2013), *In the Wind* (2016), and *A City Flower* (2018), which all explore moral foundations of human relationships. Her works are stories of love and growth, pain and betrayal, and search for happiness. They always explore journeys of accepting one's sexual and gender identity and are informed by her personal experience as a trans woman who has traveled a long road of self-acceptance and has reached her destination.

Author's address
I have always believed in my life, in the necessity of being myself, of loving and being loved, and I wish the same to my readers.

Character

Erik/Erika *nineteen years old*
twenty-two years old
twenty-four years old
twenty-eight years old

Scene One: Becoming. Childhood. School

A dark room. By the wall—a teenager. Wet clothes. It's cold. Scary. Eyes full of fear. Disappointment. It happened.

Erika   It's over. Yet another thing, over. What's wrong with me? Even the river won't take me . . . Who asked him? A good person. Kind. What do you know about my life? About me? It was my cry into the void. Into inevitability. I couldn't stand the pain. I had to stop this nightmare. A mistake. A disgrace to my family. I want to be with my grandma. She's the only one who never thought I was a mistake.

"Erika, sweetie, you'll make it. It's a test. You can do it. With grace. I believe in you."

It was years ago, but I still remember her words as if she'd just said them. Where are you? Why did you have to pass away that November night? Why? A terrible injustice. Today. We were supposed to finally see each other again today. You would have put on your pink dress, the lace one.

Recollects.

You'll never put it on again . . . My dolls got buried next to you. Snowy November wind took my happy childhood away. "Propaganda." That's what my mom says. That I'm a mistake, that I'm "Western politics." How can a human being be propaganda?

One can't just make people up, make them believe, make them love. My closest people, Mom, Dad. You used to hurt me every day. And these wounds grew to be too many. I can't even remember a single morning when I wouldn't see regret in the eyes of those closest to me. The regret that I even existed.

"I gave birth to a son. A handsome boy. Everyone envied me. Everyone told me it was going to be a girl. But I knew—it was a son! And now, what is this . . ."

A question into the void . . . Nobody will ever explain to my mother why fate played such a cruel joke on her. Nobody will tell you. I am who I am. And there won't be another me.

I wanted to free you both of myself. Last resort, I know. This fisherman got in the way.

When I was little, I didn't think that something was wrong. That I was different somehow. At my grandma's, I only knew love, affection, and care. My sweet grandma never let me feel lonely or get hurt. She worked at a big factory. So, I had to go to daycare. I remember us entering a room. There were a lot of kids in there. My grandma told them, "This is Erika, be nice to her."

I had long ashy-gray hair. So, they called me a little squirrel. Sometimes, I didn't get enough sleep during the naptime, so I would just go to the playroom and sleep there on the couch. In the girls' corner. Everybody called me either Erika, or little squirrel, or sleepyhead. Girls would braid my hair, and boys would sneak me marshmallow from snacktime. Our teachers thought it was sweet.

In the morning, they'd say, "Oh, our little Erika has had her eyebrows painted, again," and wet a finger to check. Because of my light hair, dark brows always drew attention. There was just this one teacher, Alyona Ivanovna. Fat, in an orange suit. She always walked around like an usher at the circus. And looked at me with undisguised contempt, judging me all the time. Once, my grandma even had a fight with her. Nobody could get why she hated me. Although sometimes it felt like she just hated all kids.

Boys always sought my attention. They would bring me marshmallow or pull my hair. Dima was always by my side. He played with me, brought me a blanket when I wanted to have a nap. When we watched cartoons, I would sometimes lie down on the floor and put my head in his lap. One day, they showed us a new cartoon. It was beautiful. *Pocahontas*. After watching it, Dima and I pretended we were Pocahontas and Jack. We braided ribbons into my hair, and he put on a cowboy hat. Like a little hero. Who would always stand up for me, who would protect me. Even from Alyona Ivanovna. Who would have thought that harmless games would cause the Problem.

I was bound to be at this problem's very heart. One morning, we were exercising. We were walking in a circle, stretching our arms, necks. Suddenly, Dima ran up to me and gave me a big kiss. Just like in *Pocahontas*. The next thing I knew I was slapped on my lips. Alyona Ivanovna grabbed my arm and was slapping me on the lips.

Scandal. Parents told their kids never to play with me again. Dima's parents took him to another daycare. After a while, my grandma stopped bringing me there. Her home became my daycare. Sometimes, she'd leave me with a neighbor. Our neighbor was Auntie Zina. She had a dog, Toshka. We would often play together.

Sometimes she took me with her to work. At some point, my dearest grandma was ready to retire. I was about six years old at the time. We were planning a trip to the sea. She signed me up for a dance class, junior group, at the local art school. Again, Erika was in a place where everyone loved her.

Pause.

In November, my grandma retired. There was a farewell party at the factory, a big one, with drinks and a banquet. Once in a while, she would bring me over to my parents. November snowstorm. I missed my grandma so much, my tummy started to hurt. An ambulance took me to the hospital. On Friday night, my grandma passed away. My parents left. I thought everyone had forgotten about me.

It was windy. Twigs were scraping across the window. The whirlwind of snowflakes hid the streetlights. It was cold and scary. About ten days later, my parents came to take me home. Never again did they bring me to my grandma's place.

A military, cold apartment. A commanding voice. It commanded me. My father kept repeating that you aren't worth anything if you haven't served.

A tough eight years at school. A grueling test. Every morning brought hard labor. It was only during the winter holidays that I got a taste of freedom. I finally had an excuse to ransack my mother's closet and turn myself into a gypsy girl, a princess, or a little mermaid. Whomever I wanted. I stopped braiding ribbons into my hair. They kept cutting it short. But I could still tie a scarf on my head.

My friends. My only friends. Books . . .

At school, there were dozens of Alyona Ivanovnas. The majority of my classmates. And older kids, too. They all had this desire to correct the mistake. To slap, to kick, to push. Whatever they could think of. Naturally, I was at the hospital quite often. With bruises. With the liver that wouldn't stop hurting. With a concussion.

When I was in the seventh grade, my parents signed me up for ballet again. I guess they were tired of fighting me. Hard work. Stretch. Warm-up. First position. Battement. There are no boundaries in ballet. It's a realm of masks. You can be whoever you want to be. The Little Mermaid from *The Song of Love and Sorrow*, or Autumn from *Hades and Persephone*.

When I finished school, I had to wait a year before I could apply to the Choreography School. Everyone was against it. It was not a real job. Everyone fought me on it.

Winter, the season that took my grandma away from me gave me a gift many years later. A mature young man was offered the part of the Prince in *The Little Mermaid*. He was dazzling, insanely handsome. He was twenty-two or twenty-four at the time. A fantastic dancer.

Of course, he didn't even notice me. I was no one next to him. Any beautiful girl in the company could be his. Or any beautiful guy. He charmed girls and guys alike. It was stupid to dream of him. He was a star from another planet. The planet of perfection. What could he possibly see in this ugly duckling? Unwanted. Forgotten. Forlorn.

We were assigned a duet. For the company's Valentine's Day party. It was unbelievable. The lifts, the warmth of his hands. The features, the lines of his body. Every time he lifted me up in the air, my heart would skip a beat.

We were alone in the practice room. Our rehearsal had gone long. We were practicing a lift; I had to jump into his hands, he would hold me, and I would float above him. Like on a rainbow. A jump. Another. Suddenly, he caught me. A bit higher. He raised my face. Kissed me. The heat of the kiss burned me. It was different from the kiss little Dima had given me years before. It was a real, adult kiss. I felt hot, like from a hearth fire. Outside, a February wind was blowing, and in the rehearsal room, my Prince put me down on the floor. And he kissed me over and over again. I wanted to commit the warmth of his lips to memory. The smell of his body. It felt scary to be kissing him. None of it seemed real. I wanted to pinch myself to make sure it wasn't a dream. But even if it was, I didn't want it to end. I wanted it to last forever. But all dreams end. In the morning, my Prince was as cold and distant as before. Nothing changed.

March. April. Soon we heard rumors that he was getting married. To the daughter of one of our sponsors. A very rich man. At first it seemed like just a rumor. But then everyone received an invitation to their wedding. May 4th.

It was more than I could bear. More than my desire to live. I'm neither a boy, nor a girl. My parents don't love me. Rather, they resent me. The ray of light was gone. It took the air out of my chest. I fell to my knees. Erika did not exist anymore. Nobody would ever love me. The way my grandma loved me. That's why it had to be today. I realized I couldn't stay alive anymore. May 4th.

Cold water. It pierced me with hundreds of tiny needles. I saw myself, my ashy-gray hair braided, I was wearing a pink lace dress. A sudden sharp pain at the roots of my hair. A fisherman who happened to be nearby spotted a failed drowner and pulled me out of the water by my hair.

Scene Two: Acknowledgement. Acceptance. Medical Board

Hospital room. **Erika** *in a green hospital robe. Her hair is messy. She is tired. She recollects how she got there.*

—A failed suicide. A failed college application. I had no choice but move to another city. Krasnogorsk.

Soon I joined a private ballet group. An independent company. Our artistic director was very demanding, but also fair. It took Mark a while to get to know me before he became my friend and mentor. We had several shows in our repertoire. Now I dance contemporary. Mark tried to set me free, like a bird. To give me wings. To give me hope.

We would rehearse for seventeen hours in a row. He couldn't make me open up on stage. So, he decided to talk to me. He wanted to hear my story. What was in my head. What was eating me. I resisted letting him in. It was my universe. My pain.

I couldn't see how he could possibly help me. In my nightmare. No one can wake me from it. Nobody can warm me. At least, not the way people who loved me could.

Finally. One night. Everything. About the dolls. The dresses. Little Dima. New Year's dress ups. The Prince. The Fairytale. My Fairytale.

"Listen, Erik. There are lots of people like you. It's not a mistake. It's not a screwup of your parents or somebody's influence. Whatever others may say." He was taking the time to find proper words.

"You shouldn't torment yourself. You have to live. To love. There's a way. It's hard. It's painful. With lots of challenges. It exists. I did it. Eleven years ago. In some way, I'm still doing it. Be patient. Be resilient. It won't be easy. I want you to know that. Nobody will help you. Nobody will get you. But you have to go through it. That's the only way to Freedom. To Happiness. To Harmony."

He introduced me to Leia. She was one of the first special girls I met. He also introduced me to an endocrinologist who specialized in andrology and to a sexologist. I saw hope. A direction.

To get hormone therapy approved, I needed a diagnosis from a psychologist and a psychiatrist. I went to see them for a year. Every two weeks. We discussed my childhood. My motivation. Why I needed this change. What the reason for my depression was. Whether I had had a sexual experience. If I'd had it with a woman. Every visit to a doctor was a test. After that, I was examined by the chief of psychiatry.

"Why do you need it? To wear dresses? It won't make you a woman anyway. You won't be able to give birth. Ever. So why then would you do it? What is this fantasy? People will say things to you. Beat you. No one will hire you. Think twice before it's too late. You're a handsome guy. Go serve your country. Have sex with a girl. That will help you get rid of all this nonsense."

I wanted to disappear from the face of the Earth. Dissipate. Go deaf. Anything—just to not hear this, to not see the expression on his face. Finally, he approved my admittance to the hospital.

Nobody promised it was going to be easy. Nobody promised any help or support. I wasn't surprised. It hurt, but I had to keep going. I had to survive nurses with their everyday "Are you sure you want this?" I had to survive all the patients who shared the hospital room with me.

This fellow, a soldier. He wished he'd been killed in action. He screamed in his sleep every night. He dreamt about shelling.

Marie. A girl with a Bible. She prayed every day and asked God to take her from this cruel, unjust world.

Lyonya who had been bullied at school to the point that he didn't see any reason to live. Kind but unhappy people. The room was filled with death and despair. With disillusionment. It was impossible to survive forty days in that place.

As I was there only for a medical evaluation, I had my nooks of freedom. I could go outside when we went to the dining hall for meals. At night, when all these soldiers, these criers, these jumpers, Auntie Ira who was sure she was being bitten by bugs, were asleep, I would sneak out to the bathroom and sit there alone. That's where I met Kai. I mean, that's what I called him. His real name was Misha. He had a girlfriend, Alisa. She told him he wasn't mature enough. That he hadn't yet found himself. That he didn't have a college diploma. Or a promising career. She, on the other hand, was very strong. That's why she'd made a decision for both of them. An abortion. An act that killed not only their baby but also Kai.

The two of us would sit in the bathroom together. We talked about *The Little Prince* by Antoine de Saint-Exupéry. We debated. Was he happy? Did he get what he wanted? Did he find what he was looking for? The Little Prince. Boredom. Infinity. Would we ever be happy? What did the end of our challenges look like? Would somebody ever love us? We talked about how all this time, after my act of despair, I managed to keep living. Go to college. Graduate with honors. Become an assistant to the CEO of a big company. Keep dancing.

Life is not black and white. We are not defined by our differences alone. They are not 100 percent of our life. While they *are* part of our life, they are also only a *part* of our life. Sooner or later, life balances out. It puts everything in its place.

The inner and the outer. What experience we have. What knowledge we've gained. This will be our perfect, real life. Which is too short to wait for an appropriate moment. For a miracle. For everything to just change. Just change by itself. We can waste our whole life waiting. But for what? To hold nothing but regret when we're forty-five, fifty years old? To pretend it's still possible to turn things around? When it's all gone. And we can't change anything. Any attempts will be painful and futile. And there's no real life ahead.

We have to live here and now. We have to fight and succeed. And do so with dignity, without losing respect for our own lives. And ignore the people saying that this path will only lead to prostitution, Thailand, and HIV. We have to live; we have to strive toward the light. Then instead of regret, life will fill you with a comforting exhaustion. Tomorrow will come. The light of sunrise will make any darkness dissipate. Even the darkness that seemed so dark no light could breach it. When the Judge looks into your eyes, what will you feel, what will you remember?

Scene Three: Survive No Matter What

Erika *is sitting on the floor. Bracing her legs, wearing jeans, a black cardigan. She raises her head. You can see a big bruise around her left eye. Tears in her eyes. No fear. She's tired. It's clear it's not the first time this has happened.*

I'll have to spray tan for a month now. Bruises take a long time to heal. At least, the concussion is not that bad. A couple of days, and everything will be ok. It's hard to feel safe. Anywhere. High school, dorm, college. Work. Street. They're sure they're right. They have the politicians, the media to back them up. They have the lawmakers who create the laws that are easy to read between the lines—laws that violate human rights. Laws that provoke beatings, bullying, attacks . . . murders.

It's as dangerous to live now as it was under the Third Reich. When the Nazis not only sent people to concentration camps but burned them alive. In today's civilized and enlightened world, in Russia— a self-proclaimed law-abiding state—life's not that much safer.

When you go outside, you face a violence that eludes punishment. Powerlessness before your aggressors. Whoever tells you that the system of justice protects everyone in the same way is a hypocrite. It doesn't matter if they try to hide their hypocrisy or not.

We have put reality on a pause. We no longer look around. No longer follow the lives of other people. Their joys, their sorrows, their griefs. We no longer show compassion or sympathize with them. But we really need to do that. Does anyone see how important it is? When a hand rises against another human being, is there any thought of them as a person? If there were, our mothers wouldn't be calling us "propaganda." Or branding us as an American conspiracy. Or the result of society's Westernization.

You can't just use a template to determine who lives with whom, who is happy with whom. A person lives, creates, loves. It's different now. The West is further ahead in terms of acceptance.

The first time I got beaten was in the college dorm. I had just started school. Had been there for a month, maybe six weeks or so. At night, two guys from the Caucasus broke into my room. They were seniors.

"There, the queeny one. Take that!" He kicked me hard. It was so sudden that I landed between the beds. A dead end. Nowhere to go, nowhere to hide. There was no way back. I just had to stay strong. Until they got tired. They had a lot of strength though. They were kicking me as if I were not a human being but a chance to get revenge for all those soccer goals and basketball shots that they hadn't scored.

I never went to the police. My roommates told me that if I did, they'd come back and kill me. I just had to go on living. Without fear. Of leaving the room and walking down the corridor; of leaving the dorm to walk down the street. Of getting in a taxi. That was quite a challenge—most taxi drivers are from the Caucasus. But I had to keep living.

When I was little, my grandma taught me what to do if, for example, a dog attacked me. You can't show it you're afraid. You must stare right back at it and hide any signs of fear or defenselessness. Even if you feel that your life is at stake. It's the same in real life.

I read a post by a blogger who said he identified people like us on the metro because of our fear. That's just wrong. That shouldn't be happening. We are all humans. You may be "traditional," but it doesn't make you better or more correct. More honest, more reliable. Quite possibly, it's the other way around.

A lot of people don't have a college degree or ever even went to any sort of college. They do not necessarily have a great career. Or healthy relationships. Alcoholism and promiscuity are not rare among them. But whom else would they blame for the demographic crisis?

Or for the mass emigration to the West? Take any rural area—who is guilty that people are drinking their lives away there? Is it our fault, too? What about the babies of drug addicts, who grow up in foster care? Are we to blame, too, that their life turned this way?

It hurts. It hurts. I am not afraid. My parents turned away from me. They saw disgrace when they looked at their child and couldn't think of me in any other way. It gets in your face. It doesn't let you breathe. It stands in your way of loving your family. No.

It hurts because I know I don't live only for myself. There are people around me who love me. They give me their affection, care, warmth. They are around. Even if we don't feel them right now. We think we're alone. That there's no one but the void around us.

These thoughts had made me first jump to the river, then poison myself. Finally, I realized that I had been wrong. I had been wrong. I acknowledge that. It's wonderful that I realized it before it was too late.

That's how I found strength to live. Even if my way of life gets in somebody's face. Even if people around me think that me or people like me are sick, perverts. That there's no place for us in a "normal" society. That we are STD carriers, nothing more. That we get the money to pay for the transition by prostituting ourselves. That we're unhappy. That we'll die unhappy and alone. No, no, no. It's not true. I've said it a hundred times before and I'll keep saying it.

Indeed, to be born different is a great test. It's hard to pass it. It's hard to do it with dignity. One way or another. To stay clean, morally as well as physically. Every human life is a beautiful creation. It's a gift. It's like a City Flower. It should be impossible for it to survive in the limitations that the city imposes on it. To grow through asphalt, through cement. To not be able to see the sun. Or get fresh air. But to keep growing, nevertheless. Keep striving upwards. It's a miracle. Just as every human life is a miracle. A perfection.

I was walking my friend back home today. It was early, we were returning from the hospital. From a doctor's appointment, early in the morning. We were walking along the park. Suddenly, three big muscular guys. Keith tried to protect me. I tried to stop the fight. The last thing I heard was "Don't you hit a woman!" It was one of the passers-by. "She's not a woman," and then a blow to my head.

What will make people change? What will make them kinder? What will make them respect others? I only have questions. It is up to society to find answers to them.

The lights fade.

Scene Four

Darkness—rays of light pierce it.

To survive a suicide attempt. The loss of your loved ones. Never to be understood by people around you. Disappointment. There's still hope—hope that life can change. That these changes will lead to a happy ending.

After all my struggles with medical boards, with experts and tests, they finally confirmed there were no contraindications. Finally—the certificate I've been waiting for. I've walked a long road to get it. A victory I deserved.

Once I brought the certificate, the endocrinologist prescribed me hormone therapy. It took a year for the changes to start setting in. But the body has started to change. Very slowly. Gradually. It fought. It resisted the change. The side effects lasted four, maybe six months. Every meal made me nauseous, dizzy; smells repulsed me. I could only take in milk and green tea. My whole body hurt. Ached. There was a sharp pain in my chest. It was yet another difficult test. Every day I woke up and realized I had to pass it. It was the price I had to pay. Surely, I thought, another body would have an easier time with all this. Maybe not. There's no answer to that question. There's no point in looking for an answer.

The only thing that matters is to get ready, to be prepared. A scalpel, not a magic wand. It won't make a new human being. But at the same time, the person that comes out from under the scalpel will be a new one, with a new life. A life free of social expectations. That are impossible to live up to.

The life every person lives is unique; some have more difficulties, some fewer. I found strength. Even before the transition, I graduated from college, I laid a foundation for my career. Now the only thing left is to adapt. To build lasting, healthy relationships. A person is not defined by just one event in their life, but by their whole life. By their way of saying who they are and living it.

A choreographic interlude.

P.S.

Erika*, in a gown. She stands in the spotlight.*

—Every life is a challenge. Every story deserves a beautiful happy ending. An ending which marks not the end of life, but the beginning of a new, wonderful, long-awaited life.

The most important thing. I am not alone anymore. On my birthday. It's a present I've earned. Like a blessing, a talented, smart, and loving man entered my life. It is in his hands that a City Flower will blossom.

2017